The I Hate Dick Cheney, John Ashcroft, Donald Rumsfeld, Condi Rice . . . READER

The I Hate Dick Cheney, John Ashcroft, Donald Rumsfeld, Condi Rice . . . Reader

BEHIND THE BUSH CABAL'S WAR ON AMERICA

EDITED BY CLINT WILLIS

THUNDER'S MOUTH PRESS
NEW YORK

THE I HATE DICK CHENEY, JOHN ASHCROFT, DONALD RUMSFELD, CONDI RICE . . . READER:
Behind the Bush Cabal's War on America

Published by
Thunder's Mouth Press
An Imprint of Avalon Publishing Group Incorporated
245 West 17th St., 11th floor
New York, NY 10011-5300

AVALON
publishing group incorporated

Library of Congress Cataloging-in-Publication Data is available.

ISBN 1-56025-620-6

Interior design by Paul Paddock

Printed in the United States of America
Distributed by Publishers Group West

For Nate Hardcastle

A good writer, a good friend . . . and a good liberal

CONTENTS

INTRODUCTION

My father-in-law—a life-long Democrat and the best advance man Hubert H. Humphrey ever had—owns a sweet little cabin near Moose, Wyoming. The cabin is a brief stroll from perhaps the most beautiful sight I have ever seen: a view across the Snake River to the snow-veined peaks of the Tetons—the Middle and the Grand, Owen and Teewinot, Moran and the rest. The peaks are laid out south to north like some gifted child's notion of mountains; they rise up behind the river and hang against the sky like a map of the Divine.

You get to the cabin by turning off a two-lane highway onto a long gravel road. You drive past a small hill adorned with sagebrush, where deer and antelope once played. I used to spot the creatures there during Wyoming's long summer evenings, when the sun sank behind the mountains and the hill was cool in the shadow of the range.

The deer and the antelope departed this little hill for the last time several years ago; they left to make way for some sort of security station, complete with camouflage and a dish that sometimes revolves. Locals tell me that this dish tracks aircraft when Dick Cheney visits his vacation home in Jackson Hole. They say the military keeps a couple of jets on hand during those visits; the jets are assigned to destroy planes that seem to threaten Cheney's security. Some of the locals complain that Cheney's visits to the region cost taxpayers huge sums. Some of the locals think the vice president should spend more time back East, in the vice-president's mansion.

I drive by the little hill on the way to and from my father-in-law's cabin about 20 or 30 times every summer. I see the camouflage and the dish, and I think of the deer and the antelope that once visited this spot and have now retreated to the flats and hollows that surround it, and I get sad and angry. It occurs to me that even as we spend large sums and disrupt the local wildlife to safeguard Cheney and other members of the Bush administration, the politicians we protect pursue greed- and fear-driven policies that endanger us all and make the world uglier.

I get sad and angry, but I don't really hate Cheney or Rumsfeld or Ashcroft or Rice or the other major players in the Bush administration. On my best days, I feel compassion for them; after all, they live in fear. They are frightened of everyone: not only Muslims, Communists, poor people, criminals, lesbians, liberals, union members and ethnic minorities but (this is supposed to be a secret) students, retirees, veterans, soldiers, truck-drivers, teachers, journalists, realtors, sales clerks, lawyers and other ordinary Americans.

We scare Dick Cheney and his colleagues in the Bush administration because we threaten their delusional notion that they—and their rich and powerful constituents—have certain rights: the right to consume most of the world's resources, to destroy the environment and to ignore or crush the aspirations of the rest of humanity. We scare them because we want peace, freedom and justice—not just here in America, but around the world—goals they see as inimical to their interests and the interests of their corporate masters.

They're wrong about that. A peaceful, more just world is essential for prosperity of any sort: financial, emotional, spiritual. We are all connected; all of us suffer when we harm other beings. This is true whether the victims live in Baghdad or Jerusalem or Tokyo or Beijing or Madrid or New York or, for that matter, Wyoming. We should demand that our leaders act from an understanding of this interconnectedness—the most fundamental and necessary wisdom. If they cannot or will not do so, we should replace them.

George W. Bush after his contested election to the presidency built an administration of men and women who lack the courage to see the world as it is. They refuse to acknowledge the vast web of connections that we cannot escape—a web that nourishes us all.

Their fear makes them shallow; it forces them to lie. They move quickly to punish or vilify colleagues who speak out against ruinous and deceptive and murderous policies: whistleblowers such as Ambassador Joseph Wilson IV or former Treasury Secretary Paul O'Neill or former counter-terrorism czar Richard Clarke or former Air Force lieutenant colonel Karen Kwiatkowski.

The careerists, the opportunists, the cynics and the cowards in the Bush government respond to the truth with lies and violence. They do so in hopes of renewing their grip on what they perceive to be power—in the fierce but forlorn hope that power can protect them from the way things are.

Let us renew our grip on the truth. The truth is that the Bush administration's power comes from us; that Dick

Cheney and his colleagues and advisers are meant to exercise that power for our good and for the good of every creature; that there are no important differences between the two.

—Clint Willis

DICK CHENEY

with quotes by Newt Gingrich and Dick Cheney;
cartoons by Pat Oliphant, Gary Trudeau, Ruben Bolling, and Aaron McGruder;
and anagrams

Dick Cheney is a high-paid servant of privilege. He has spent his career amassing personal power, which he exercises at the expense of the rest of us. In Congress, Cheney fought tirelessly against the welfare of ordinary Americans, in particular women, children and . . . police officers. (He was one of only twenty-one members of Congress to oppose the ban on sales of armor-piercing bullets, so handy for killing . . . police officers.) He made huge sums of money as CEO of Halliburton, where he exploited his government contacts for profit (and initiated a disastrous merger). He has been the most influential vice president in history; he has used that influence to push for the invasion of Iraq, which has infuriated our allies, inflamed a new generation of potential terrorists and enriched his old friends at Halliburton. His constituency comes down to himself, his masters in the Bush family and his corporate sponsors.

He Said It . . .

"Cheney's voting record was slightly more conservative than mine . . ."

—Newt Gingrich, *Washington Times*, 7/25/2000

Cheney's specialties include the art of exercising power without accountability.

Dick Cheney, Commander in Chief

from AlterNet (10/27/03)

Jim Lobe

"Like with a horse, [Colin] Powell is always able to lead Bush to water. But just as [Bush] is about to put his head down, Cheney up in the saddle says, 'Un-uh,' and yanks up the reins before Bush can drink the water. That's my image of how it goes," said Sen. Joseph Biden, the ranking member of the Senate Foreign Relations Committee, describing the power relationship between George Bush and Dick Cheney in a recent interview with the *National Journal*.

The image of the president of the United States as a tame horse, saddled up and ridden by his own vice president, may seem overblown, but Biden is not alone in his assessment of this White House's internal dynamics. When it comes to foreign policy, Cheney is increasingly seen as holding the reins in the power circles within Washington.

While the mainstream media mostly continue to cast Bush as the captain of his ship, hints that Cheney is the dominant figure shaping Washington's diplomatic policy have become too numerous to ignore. A recent *Washington Post* article assessing Condoleezza Rice's performance as national security adviser revealed a most stunning example of this lopsided state of affairs. According to the *Post*, Bush had ordered Cabinet officials not to give any preferential treatment to Ahmed Chalabi's Iraqi National Congress (INC) when U.S. forces moved into Iraq last spring. But soon after, in flagrant violation of his directive, the Pentagon flew Chalabi and 600 of his armed followers into southern Iraq in early April, "with the approval of the vice president."

It would not be the first or last time that Cheney simply ignored his commander-in-chief. The extent of Cheney's power is not surprising given the degree to which Bush relied on him during his presidential campaign and in the administration's early days. And the fact that Cheney, who was asked by Bush to recommend his running mate in 2000, picked himself for the job reveals that he expected to wield extraordinary power if Bush won the election.

Cheney's dominance has been the decisive factor in the ongoing battle between the Pentagon and the State Department over U.S. foreign policy. Secretary of State Colin Powell, according to Biden's account, has sometimes talked Bush into pursuing a more conciliatory foreign-policy line, as he has done with North Korea or the United Nations from time to time. But thus far Cheney's views have always won out in the long run.

Enforcing policy discipline, especially in a divided administration, is ordinarily the task of the national security adviser. But Rice, an academic whose substantive knowledge of foreign policy is largely confined to the Soviet Union and Russia, has not been equal to the job. Her failure combined with Bush's own passivity and inexperience has enabled Cheney to dominate the policy process, particularly with respect to the Middle East where Cheney's views are almost entirely consistent with those of Israeli prime minister Ariel Sharon.

A Republican right-winger, Cheney is surrounded by neo-conservatives, many with close ties to Israel's Likud Party. Even before Sept. 11, Cheney had endorsed Israel's selective assassination policy—even as the State Department was busy denouncing it. One year later, Cheney told Israel's defense minister, albeit privately, that he thought Palestinian President Yasser Arafat "should be hanged." Biden told reporters in October, "If you look at Afghanistan, if you look at the (Israeli-Palestinian peace) road map, if you look at Iraq, if you look at bilateral and multilateral dealings with the Europeans, just as Powell looks like he will stitch the garment back together again, Cheney goes to the Heritage Foundation and re-enunciates the policy of preemption."

Cheney has played a much more important role than Rice since the early days of the administration, despite her closer personal relationship with the president. It was Cheney's choices that prevailed in the appointment of both cabinet and sub-cabinet national-security officials, beginning with that of Donald Rumsfeld as Defense Secretary. Not only did Cheney personally intervene to ensure that Powell's best friend, Richard Armitage, was denied the deputy defense secretary position, but he also secured the post for his own protégé, Paul Wolfowitz. Moreover, it was Cheney who insisted that the ultra-unilateralist John Bolton be placed in a top State Department arms job—a position from which Bolton has consistently pursued policies that run counter to Powell's own views.

Moreover, Cheney's own national-security staff is the largest ever employed by a vice president. Its members have largely been chosen for both their ideological affinity with their boss and proven Washington experience. "They play to win," said one State Department official. Cheney's chief of staff and national security adviser, I. Lewis "Scooter" Libby, a Washington lawyer and Wolfowitz protégé, is considered a far more skilled and experienced bureaucratic and political operator than Rice. With several of his political allies on Rice's own staff—including deputy national security adviser Stephen Hadley and Middle East director Elliott Abrams—Libby "is able to run circles around Condi," noted a former NSC official.

Cheney's muscle is most apparent in shaping the White House's Iraq policy. He played a key role in assigning responsibility for post-war reconstruction to the Pentagon, a major departure from the long-standing tradition to giving the State Department the lead in such areas. Similarly, Cheney backed the Pentagon's decision to entirely exclude the State Department from the planning process. The State Department's mammoth "Future of Iraq Project," which pulled together hundreds of Iraqi expatriates and other experts to come up with a detailed plan for the post-war reconstruction of Iraq, was simply ignored and so was Tom Warrick, a highly regarded Iraq specialist who oversaw the project.

According to retired intelligence officers, Cheney and Libby played the decisive role in distorting the intelligence used to make Bush's case for war. Libby made frequent trips to the Central Intelligence Agency (CIA) in the run-up to the Iraq war, pressuring analysts to include questionable evidence supplied by the INC and Rumsfeld-led hawks.

More recently, it was Cheney who led the effort to deny Powell the authority to negotiate a new UN Security Council resolution that would have reduced the Pentagon's control over the political transition in Iraq, even though the president initially approved such a deal.

The vice president is currently working within the White House to resist congressional pressure to reduce Pentagon's control over Iraq policy and to oust several senior hawks in the DoD. Beginning with Undersecretary of Defense for Policy Douglas Feith, the neoconservatives in the Pentagon are under fire for misleading Congress on both the evidence used to justify the war and the post-war situation.

Cheney's clout has even elicited rebukes from the Hill. Senate Foreign Relations Committee chairman Richard Lugar and Joe Biden, the Committee's ranking Democrat, explicitly mentioned the vice president as part of their bipartisan appeal to Bush, asking him to take control over his foreign policy.

"I would say, Mr. President, take charge. Take charge . . . Let your secretary of defense, state, and your vice president know 'This is my policy, any one of you that divert from the policy is off the team,'" said Biden on NBC's "Meet the Press" in early October. Lugar, a staunch, albeit moderate Republican, appearing on the same show echoed the sentiment, adding, "The president has to be president. That means the president over the vice president and over these secretaries."

Recent announcements that Rice has hired Robert Blackwill, Bush's former ambassador to India and reputedly a skilled bureaucratic and Republican infighter himself, as her top deputy and that she is heading up a new, inter-agency Iraq Stabilization Group, are designed to create the appearance that she is at last taking charge of the country's foreign policy. So far, however, there is little evidence that Cheney is prepared to turn over control of his favorite hobbyhorse.

ANAGRAM

George Bush with Dick Cheney
Heck, be cheesy, right wing duo!

I Hate Dick Cheney...

Dick Cheney exudes an air of unsentimental competence, which many Americans find reassuring. What if he's incompetent as well as evil?

Vice Grip

from *The Washington Monthly* (January/February 2003)

Joshua Micah Marshall

Early last December, Vice President Dick Cheney was dispatched to inform his old friend, Treasury Secretary Paul O'Neill, that he was being let go. O'Neill, the president's advisers felt, had made too many missteps, given too much bad advice, uttered too many gaffes. He had become a liability to the administration. As Cheney himself once said in a different context, it was time for him to go. It couldn't have been a fun conversation—especially since it was Cheney who had picked O'Neill two years earlier.

O'Neill stormed off to Pittsburgh and within days the White House had announced his replacement. Yet the new treasury secretary nominee turned out not to be much of an improvement. Like O'Neill, John Snow was a veteran of the Ford administration who ran an old-economy titan (the railroad firm CSX) and seemed to lack the global market financial experience demanded of modern day treasury secretaries. Like other Bush appointees, Snow came from a business that traded heavily on the Washington influence game. And—again typical of the president and his men—the size of Snow's compensation package seemed inversely proportional to the returns he made for his shareholders. Of the three new members of the president's economic team nominated in early December, Snow was the only one to get almost universally poor reviews. He was also Dick Cheney's pick.

Week after week, one need only read the front page of *The Washington Post* to find similar Cheney lapses. Indeed, just a few days after Cheney hand-picked Snow, *Newsweek* magazine featured a glowing profile of National Security Adviser Condoleezza Rice that began with an anecdote detailing her deft efforts to clean up another Cheney mess. In a July speech, the vice president had argued that weapons inspections in Iraq were useless and shouldn't even be tried. That speech nearly upended the administration's careful late-summer repositioning in favor of a new United Nations-backed inspections program. As the article explained, Rice—the relatively junior member of the president's inner circle of foreign policy advisers—had to take the vice president aside and walk him through how to repair the damage he'd done, with a new statement implicitly retracting his earlier gaffe. Such mistakes—on energy policy, homeland security, corporate reform—abound. Indeed, on almost any issue, it's usually a sure bet that if Cheney has lined up on one side, the opposite course will turn out to be the wiser.

Yet somehow, in Washington's collective mind, Cheney's numerous stumbles and missteps have not displaced the reputation he enjoys as a sober, reliable, skilled inside player. Even the *Newsweek* article, so eager to convey Rice's competence, seemed never to explicitly note the obvious subtext: Cheney's evident incompetence. If there were any justice or logic in this administration as to who should or shouldn't keep their job, there'd be another high-ranking official in line for one of those awkward conversations: Dick Cheney.

Overruling Dick

Consider the evidence. Last year, Cheney's White House energy task force produced an all-drilling-and-no-conservation plan that failed not just on policy grounds but as a political matter as well, saddling the administration with a year-long public relations headache after Cheney insisted on running his outfit with a near-Nixonian level of secrecy. (To this day, Cheney and his aides have refused to provide the names of most of those industry executives who "advised" him on the task force's recommendations. A federal judge has now rejected the Government Accounting Office's effort to make them do so.) During the spring of 2001, rather than back congressional efforts to implement the findings of the Hart-Rudman commission that called for forceful action to combat terrorism (including the creation of a department of homeland security), Cheney opted to spearhead his own group—not because he disagreed with the commission's proposals, but to put the administration's stamp on whatever anti-terrorism reforms did get adopted. Cheney's security task force did nothing for four months, lurching into action only *after* terrorists actually attacked America on September 11. In the months that followed, Cheney was one of several key advisers arguing that the White House should keep Tom Ridge's Office of Homeland Security within the White House rather than upgrade it to a cabinet department and thus open it to congressional scrutiny. Cheney's obstinacy ensured that the administration's efforts were stuck in neutral for nearly eight months.

Cheney has not fared much better in the diplomatic arena. Last March, he went on a tour of Middle Eastern capitals to line up America's allies for our war against Saddam. He returned a week later with the Arabs lining up behind Saddam and against us—a major embarrassment for the White House. Much of the success of the administration's Iraq policy came only after it abandoned the strategy of unilateral action against Saddam, the strategy Cheney championed, to one of supporting a U.N. inspections regime—a necessary and successful course correction that Cheney resisted and almost halted. Indeed, broadly speaking, the evolution of White House Iraq policy might be described fairly as a slow process of overruling Dick Cheney.

And there's more. Remember those corporate scandals that came close to crippling Bush? Last summer, White House advisers were pondering whether to back the sort of tough corporate accountability measures that Democrats and the press were demanding. The president was scheduled to deliver a big speech on Wall Street in early July. His advisers were divided. Some argued that strong reforms were at the least a political necessity. But Cheney, along with National Economic Council chair Larry Lindsey, opposed the idea, arguing that new restrictions on corporations would further weaken the economy. The president took Cheney's advice, and gave a speech on Wall Street that recommended only mild and unspecific reforms. "He mentioned a lot of things in the speech that the Securities and Exchange Commission already does," one nonplussed Wall Streeter told *The Washington Post* with a yawn. The day after the president's speech, the Dow shed 282 points, the biggest single-day drop since the post-terrorist tailspin of Sept. 20. Within days the president was backpedaling and supporting what Cheney had said he shouldn't. Lindsey got the boot later in the year. Cheney is still in the West Wing shaping economic policy.

Cartel Capitalists

Much of the reason Cheney so often calls things wrong—even on those business issues that would seem his area of expertise—can be traced to the culture in which he's spent most of his professional life. Despite his CEO credentials and government experience, Dick Cheney has been surprisingly insulated from the political and financial marketplace. He began his career as a Nixon-administration functionary under Donald Rumsfeld. Later, he joined the Ford administration as a deputy assistant to the president before becoming White House chief of staff. From there he moved into elective office, but to the ultra-safe House seat from Wyoming, a post only slightly less shielded from the tides of American politics than were his posts in the Ford administration.

Cheney resigned his House seat in 1989 and moved back to the executive branch where he belonged, serving—with distinction—as defense secretary under the first President Bush. From there he moved to the corporate suite at Halliburton, where he eventually earned tens of millions of dollars. But Halliburton is a peculiar kind of enterprise. It doesn't market shoes or design software. Rather, its business—providing various products and services to the oil industry and the military—is based on securing lucrative contracts and concessions from a handful of big customers, primarily energy companies and the U.S. and foreign governments. Success in that business comes not by understanding and meeting the demands of millions of finicky customers, but by cementing relationships with and winning the support of a handful of powerful decision-makers.

Indeed, that's why Halliburton came to Cheney in the first place. His ties with the Bush family, his post-Gulf War friendships with Arab emirs, and the Rolodex he'd compiled from a quarter century in Washington made him a perfect rainmaker. And though he did rather poorly on the management side—he shepherded Halliburton's disastrous merger with Dresser Industries, which saddled the new company with massive asbestos liabilities—he handled the schmoozing part of the enterprise well.

Cheney is conservative, of course, but beneath his conservatism is something more important: a mindset rooted in his peculiar corporate-Washington-insider class. It is a world of men—very few women—who have been at the apex of both business and government, and who feel that they are unique in their mastery of both. Consequently, they have an extreme assurance in their own judgment about what is best for the country and how to achieve it. They see themselves as men of action. But their style of action is shaped by the government bureaucracies and cartel-like industries in which they have operated. In these institutions, a handful of top officials make the plans, and then the plans are carried out. Ba-da-bing. Ba-da-boom.

In such a framework all information is controlled tightly by the principals, who have "maximum flexibility" to carry out the plan. Because success is measured by securing the deal rather than by, say, pleasing millions of customers, there's no need to open up the decision-making process. To do so, in fact, is seen as governing by committee. If there are other groups (shareholders, voters, congressional committees) who agree with you, fine, you use them. But anyone who doesn't agree gets ignored or, if need be, crushed. *Muscle it through and when the results are in, people will realize we were right* is the underlying attitude.

The danger of this mindset is obvious. No single group of people has a monopoly on the truth. Whether it be plumbers, homemakers, or lobbyist bureaucrats, any group will inevitably see the world through its own narrow, mostly self-interested, prism. But few groups are so accustomed to self-dealing and self-aggrandizement as the cartel-capitalist class. And few are more used to equating their own self-interest with the interests of the country as a whole.

Not since the Whiz Kids of the Kennedy-Johnson years has Washington been led by men of such insular self-assurance. Their hierarchical, old economy style of management couldn't be more different from the loose, non-hierarchical style of, say, high-tech corporations or the Clinton White House, with all their open debate, concern with the interests of "stake-holders," manic focus on pleasing customers (or voters), and constant reassessment of plans and principles. The latter style, while often sloppy and seemingly juvenile, tends to produce pretty smart policy. The former style, while appearing so adult and competent, often produces stupid policy.

Over time, people in the White House have certainly had to deal with enough examples of Cheney's poor judgment. It's fallen to the White House's political arm, led by the poll-conscious Karl Rove, to rein in or overrule him. Yet the vice president has apparently lost little stature within the White House. That may be because his get-it-done-and-ignore-the-nay-sayers attitude is one that others in the administration share. Cheney stands up for the cartel-capitalist principles they admire. He is right, in a sense, even when he's wrong.

Why, though, has the press failed to grasp Cheney's ineptitude? The answer seems to lie in the power of political assumptions. The historian of science Thomas Kuhn famously observed that scientific theories or "paradigms"—Newtonian physics, for instance—could accommodate vast amounts of contradictory evidence while still maintaining a grip on intelligent people's minds. Such theories tend to give way not incrementally, as new and conflicting data slowly accumulates, but in sudden crashes, when a better theory comes along that explains the anomalous facts. Washington conventional wisdom works in a similar way. It doesn't take long for a given politician to get pegged with his or her own brief story line. And those facts and stories that get attention tend to be those that conform to the established narrative. In much the same way, Cheney's reputation as the steady hand at the helm of the Bush administration—the CEO to Bush's chairman—is so potent as to blind Beltway commentators to the examples of vice presidential incompetence accumulating, literally, under their noses. Though far less egregious, Cheney's bad judgment is akin to Trent Lott's ugly history on race: Everyone sort of knew it was there, only no one ever really took notice until it was pointed out in a way that was difficult to ignore. Cheney is lucky; as vice president, he can't be fired. But his terrible judgment will, at some point, become impossible even for the Beltway crowd not to see.

ANAGRAM

Bush Administration
Duh . . . I ain't bin so smart

The Bush Administration's appetite for empire owes a lot to Dick Cheney's ideas.

Dick Cheney's Song of America

from *Harper's Magazine* (October 2002)

David Armstrong

Few writers are more ambitious than the writers of government policy papers, and few policy papers are more ambitious than Dick Cheney's masterwork. It has taken several forms over the last decade and is in fact the product of several ghostwriters (notably Paul Wolfowitz and Colin Powell), but Cheney has been consistent in his dedication to the ideas in the documents that bear his name, and he has maintained a close association with the ideologues behind them. Let us, therefore, call Cheney the author, and this series of documents the Plan.

The Plan was published in unclassified form most recently under the title of Defense Strategy for the 1990s, as Cheney ended his term as secretary of defense under the elder George Bush in early 1993, but it is, like "Leaves of Grass," a perpetually evolving work. It was the controversial Defense Planning Guidance draft of 1992—from which Cheney, unconvincingly, tried to distance himself—and it was the somewhat less aggressive revised draft of that same year. This June it was a presidential lecture in the form of a commencement address at West Point, and in July it was leaked to the press as yet another Defense Planning Guidance (this time under the pen name of Defense Secretary Donald Rumsfeld). It will take its ultimate form, though, as America's new national security strategy—and Cheney et al. will experience what few writers have even dared dream: their words will become our reality.

The Plan is for the United States to rule the world. The overt theme is unilateralism, but it is ultimately a story of domination. It calls for the United States to maintain its overwhelming military superiority and prevent new rivals from rising up to challenge it on the world stage. It calls for dominion over friends and enemies alike. It says not that the United States must be more powerful, or most powerful, but that it must be absolutely powerful.

The Plan is disturbing in many ways, and ultimately unworkable. Yet it is being sold now as an answer to the "new realities" of the post–September 11 world, even as it was sold previously as the answer to the new realities of the post–Cold War world. For Cheney, the Plan has always been the right answer, no matter how different the questions.

Cheney's unwavering adherence to the Plan would be amusing, and maybe a little sad, except that it is now our plan. In its pages are the ideas that we now act upon every day with the full might of the United States military. Strangely, few critics have noted that Cheney's work has a long history, or that it was once quite unpopular, or that it was created in reaction to circumstances that are far removed from the ones we now face. But Cheney is a well-known action man. One has to admire, in a way, the Babe Ruth-like sureness of his political work. He pointed to center field ten years ago, and now the ball is sailing over the fence.

Before the Plan was about domination it was about money. It took shape in late 1989, when the Soviet threat was clearly on the decline, and, with it, public support for a large military establishment. Cheney seemed unable to come to terms with either new reality. He remained deeply suspicious of the Soviets and strongly resisted all efforts to reduce military spending. Democrats in Congress jeered his lack of strategic vision, and a few within the Bush Administration were whispering that Cheney had become an irrelevant factor in structuring a response to the revolutionary changes taking place in the world.

More adaptable was the up-and-coming General Colin Powell, the newly appointed chairman of the Joint Chiefs of Staff. As Ronald Reagan's national security adviser, Powell had seen the changes taking place in the Soviet Union firsthand and was convinced that the ongoing transformation was irreversible. Like Cheney, he wanted to avoid military cuts, but he knew they were inevitable. The best he could do was minimize them, and the best way to do that would be to offer a new security structure that would preserve American military capabilities despite reduced resources.

Powell and his staff believed that a weakened Soviet Union would result in shifting alliances and regional conflict. The United States was the only nation capable of managing the forces at play in the world; it would have to remain the preeminent military power in order to ensure the peace and shape the emerging order in accordance with American interests. U.S. military strategy, therefore, would have to shift from global containment to managing less-well-defined regional struggles and unforeseen contingencies. To do this, the United States would have to project a military "forward presence" around the world; there would be fewer troops but in more places. This plan still would not be cheap, but through careful restructuring and superior technology, the job could be done with 25 percent fewer troops. Powell insisted that maintaining superpower status must be the first priority of the U.S. military. "We have to put a shingle outside our door saying, 'Superpower Lives Here,' no matter what the Soviets do," he said at the time. He also insisted that the troop levels he proposed were the bare minimum necessary to do so. This concept would come to be known as the "Base Force."

Powell's work on the subject proved timely. The Berlin Wall fell on November 9, 1989, and five days later Powell had his new strategy ready to present to Cheney. Even as decades of repression were ending in Eastern Europe, however, Cheney still could not abide even the force and budget reductions Powell proposed. Yet he knew that cuts were unavoidable. Having no alternative of his own to offer, therefore, he reluctantly encouraged Powell to present his ideas to the president. Powell did so the next day; Bush made no promises but encouraged him to keep at it.

Less encouraging was the reaction of Paul Wolfowitz, the undersecretary of defense for policy. A lifelong proponent of the unilateralist, maximum-force approach, he shared Cheney's skepticism about the Eastern Bloc and so put his own staff to work on a competing plan that would somehow accommodate the possibility of Soviet backsliding.

As Powell and Wolfowitz worked out their strategies, Congress was losing patience. New calls went up for large cuts in defense spending in light of the new global environment. The harshest critique of Pentagon planning came from a usually dependable ally of the military establishment, Georgia Democrat Sam Nunn, chairman of the Senate Armed Services committee. Nunn told fellow senators in March 1990 that there was a "threat blank" in the administration's proposed $295 billion defense budget and that the Pentagon's "basic assessment of the overall threat to our national security" was "rooted in the past." The world had changed and yet the "development of a new military strategy that responds to the changes in the threat has not yet occurred." Without that response, no dollars would be forthcoming.

Nunn's message was clear. Powell and Wolfowitz began filling in the blanks. Powell started promoting a Zen-like new rationale for his Base Force approach. With the Soviets rapidly becoming irrelevant, Powell argued, the United

States could no longer assess its military needs on the basis of known threats. Instead, the Pentagon should focus on maintaining the ability to address a wide variety of new and unknown challenges. This shift from a "threat based" assessment of military requirements to a "capability based" assessment would become a key theme of the Plan. The United States would move from countering Soviet attempts at dominance to ensuring its own dominance. Again, this project would not be cheap.

Powell's argument, circular though it may have been, proved sufficient to hold off Congress. Winning support among his own colleagues, however, proved more difficult. Cheney remained deeply skeptical about the Soviets, and Wolfowitz was only slowly coming around. To account for future uncertainties, Wolfowitz recommended drawing down U.S. forces to roughly the levels proposed by Powell, but doing so at a much slower pace; seven years as opposed to the four Powell suggested. He also built in a "crisis response/reconstitution" clause that would allow for reversing the process if events in the Soviet Union, or elsewhere, turned ugly.

With these new elements in place, Cheney saw something that might work. By combining Powell's concepts with those of Wolfowitz, he could counter congressional criticism that his proposed defense budget was out of line with the new strategic reality, while leaving the door open for future force increases. In late June, Wolfowitz, Powell, and Cheney presented their plan to the president, and within as few weeks Bush was unveiling the new strategy.

Bush laid out the rationale for the Plan in a speech in Aspen, Colorado, on August 2, 1990. He explained that since the danger of global war had substantially receded, the principal threats to American security would emerge in unexpected quarters. To counter those threats, he said, the United States would increasingly base the size and structure of its forces on the need to respond to "regional contingencies" and maintain a peacetime military presence overseas. Meeting that need would require maintaining the capability to quickly deliver American forces to any "corner of the globe," and that would mean retaining many major weapons systems then under attack in Congress as overly costly and unnecessary, including the "Star Wars" missile-defense program. Despite those massive outlays, Bush insisted that the proposed restructuring would allow the United States to draw down its active forces by 25 percent in the years ahead, the same figure Powell had projected ten months earlier.

The Plan's debut was well timed. By a remarkable coincidence, Bush revealed it the very day Saddam Hussein's Iraqi forces invaded Kuwait.

The Gulf War temporarily reduced the pressure to cut military spending. It also diverted attention from some of the Plan's less appealing aspects. In addition, it inspired what would become one of the Plan's key features: the use of "overwhelming force" to quickly defeat enemies, a concept since dubbed the Powell Doctrine.

Once the Iraqi threat was "contained," Wolfowitz returned to his obsession with the Soviets, planning various scenarios involving possible Soviet intervention in regional conflicts. The failure of the hard-liner coup against Gorbachev in August 1991, however, made it apparent that such planning might be unnecessary. Then, in late December, just as the Pentagon was preparing to put the Plan in place, the Soviet Union collapsed.

With the Soviet Union gone, the United States had a choice. It could capitalize on the euphoria of the moment by nurturing cooperative relations and developing multilateral structures to help guide the global realignment then taking place; or it could consolidate its power and pursue a strategy of unilateralism and global dominance. It chose the latter course.

In early 1992, as Powell and Cheney campaigned to win congressional support for their augmented Base Force plan, a new logic entered into their appeals. The United States, Powell told members of the House Armed Services Committee, required "sufficient power" to "deter any challenger from ever dreaming of challenging us on the world stage." To emphasize the point, he cast the United States in the role of street thug. "I want to be the bully on the block," he said, implanting in the mind of potential opponents that "there is no future in trying to challenge the armed forces of the United States."

As Powell and Cheney were making this new argument in their congressional rounds, Wolfowitz was busy expanding the concept and working to have it incorporated into U.S. policy. During the early months of 1992, Wolfowitz supervised the preparation of an internal Pentagon policy statement used to guide military officials in the preparation of their forces, budgets, and strategies. The classified document, known as the Defense Planning Guidance, depicted a world dominated by the United States, which would maintain its superpower status through a combination of positive guidance and overwhelming military might. The image was one of a heavily armed City on a Hill.

The DPG stated that the "first objective" of U.S. defense strategy was "to prevent the re-emergence of a new rival."

Achieving this objective required that the United States "prevent any hostile power from dominating a region" of strategic significance. America's new mission would be to convince allies and enemies alike "that they need not aspire to a greater role or pursue a more aggressive posture to protect their legitimate interests."

Another new theme was the use of preemptive military force. The options, the DPG noted, ranged from taking preemptive military action to head off a nuclear, chemical, or biological attack to "punishing" or "threatening punishment of" aggressors "through a variety of means," including strikes against weapons-manufacturing facilities.

The DPG also envisioned maintaining a substantial U.S. nuclear arsenal while discouraging the development of nuclear programs in other countries. It depicted a "U.S.-led system of collective security" that implicitly precluded the need for rearmament of any king by countries such as Germany and Japan. And it called for the "early introduction" of a global missile-defense system that would presumably render all missile-launched weapons, including those of the United States, obsolete. (The United States would, of course, remain the world's dominant military power on the strength of its other weapons systems.)

The story, in short, was dominance by way of unilateral action and military superiority. While coalitions—such as the one formed during the Gulf War—held "considerable promise for promoting collective action," the draft DPG stated, the United States should expect future alliances to be "ad hoc assemblies, often not lasting beyond the crisis being confronted, and in many cases carrying only general agreement over the objectives to be accomplished." It was essential to create "the sense that the world order is ultimately backed by the U.S." and essential that America position itself "to act independently when collective action cannot be orchestrated" or in crisis situation requiring immediate action. "While the U.S. cannot become the world's policeman," the document said, "we will retain the preeminent responsibility for addressing selectively those wrongs which threaten not only our interests, but those of our allies or friends." Among the interests the draft indicated the United States would defend in this manner were "access to vital raw materials, primarily Persian Gulf oil, proliferation of weapons of mass destruction and ballistic missiles, [and] threats to U.S. citizens from terrorism."

The DPG was leaked to the *New York Times* in March 1992. Critics on both the left and the right attacked it immediately. Then–presidential candidate Pat Buchanan portrayed it as a "blank check" to America's allies by suggesting the United States would "go to war to defend their interests." Bill Clinton's deputy campaign manager, George Stephanopoulos, characterized it as an attempt by Pentagon officials to "find an excuse for big defense budgets instead of downsizing." Delaware Senator Joseph Biden criticized the Plan's vision of a "Pax Americana, a global security system where threats to stability are suppressed or destroyed by U.S. military power." Even those who found the document's stated goals commendable feared that its chauvinistic tone could alienate many allies. Cheney responded by attempting to distance himself from the Plan. The Pentagon's spokesman dismissed the leaked document as a "low-level draft" and claimed that Cheney had not seen it. Yet a fifteen-page section opened by proclaiming that it constituted "definitive guidance from the Secretary of Defense."

Powell took a more forthright approach to dealing with the flap: he publicly embraced the DPG's core concept. In a TV interview, he said he believed it was "just fine" that the United States reign as the world's dominant military power. "I don't think we should apologize for that," he said. Despite bad reviews in the foreign press, Powell insisted that America's European allies were "not afraid" of U.S. military might because it was "power that could be trusted" and "will not be misused."

Mindful that the draft DPG's overt expression of U.S. dominance might not fly, Powell in the same interview also trotted out a new rationale for the original Base Force plan. He argued that in a post-Soviet world, filled with new dangers, the United States needed the ability to fight on more than one front at a time. "One of the most destabilizing things we could do," he said, "is to cut our forces so much that if we're tied up in one area of the world . . . and we are not seen to have the ability to influence another area of the world, we might invite just the sort of crisis we're trying to deter." This two-war strategy provided a possible answer to Nunn's "threat blank." One unknown enemy wasn't enough to justify lavish defense budgets, but two unknown enemies might do the trick.

Within a few weeks the Pentagon had come up with a more comprehensive response to the DPG furor. A revised version was leaked to the press that was significantly less strident in tone, though only slightly less strident in fact. While calling for the United States to prevent "any hostile power from dominating a region critical to our interests," the new draft stressed that America would act in concert with its allies—when possible. It also suggested the United Nations might take an expanded role in future political, economic, and security matters, a concept conspicuously absent from the original draft.

The controversy died down, and, with a presidential campaign under way, the Pentagon did nothing to stir it up again. Following Bush's defeat, however, the Plan reemerged. In January 1993, in his very last days in office. Cheney released a final version. The newly titled Defense Strategy for the 1990s retained the soft touch of the revised draft DPG as well as its darker themes. The goal remained to preclude "hostile competitors from challenging our critical interests" and preventing the rise of a new super-power. Although it expressed a "preference" for collective responses in meeting such challenges, it made clear that the United States would play the lead role in any alliance. Moreover, it noted that collective action would "not always be timely." Therefore, the United States needed to retain the ability to "act independently, if necessary." To do so would require that the United States maintain its massive military superiority. Others were not encouraged to follow suit. It was kinder, gentler dominance, but it was dominance all the same. And it was this thesis that Cheney and company nailed to the door on their way out.

The new administration tacitly rejected the heavy-handed, unilateral approach to U.S. primacy favored by Powell, Cheney, and Wolfowitz. Taking office in the relative calm of the early post-Cold War era, Clinton sought to maximize America's existing position of strength and promote its interests through economic diplomacy, multilateral institutions (dominated by the United States), greater international free trade, and the development of allied coalitions, including American-led collective military action. American policy, in short, shifted from global dominance to globalism.

Clinton also failed to prosecute military campaigns with sufficient vigor to satisfy the defense strategists of the previous administration. Wolfowitz found Clinton's Iraq policy especially infuriating. During the Gulf War, Wolfowitz harshly criticized the decision—endorsed by Powell and Cheney—to end the war once the U.N. mandate of driving Saddam's forces from Kuwait had been fulfilled, leaving the Iraqi dictator in office. He called on the Clinton Administration to finish the job by arming Iraqi opposition forces and sending U.S. ground troops to defense a base of operation for them in the southern region of the country. In a 1996 editorial, Wolfowitz raised the prospect of launching a preemptive attack against Iraq. "Should we sit idly by," he wrote, "with our passive containment policy and our inept cover operations, and wait until a tyrant possessing large quantities of weapons of mass destruction and sophisticated delivery systems strikes out at us?" Wolfowitz suggested it was "necessary" to "go beyond the containment strategy."

Wolfowitz's objections to Clinton's military tactics were not limited to Iraq. Wolfowitz had endorsed President Bush's decision in late 1992 to intervene in Somalia on a limited humanitarian basis. Clinton later expanded the mission into a broader peacekeeping effort, a move that ended in disaster. With perfect twenty-twenty hindsight, Wolfowitz decried Clinton's decision to send U.S. troops into combat "where there is no significant U.S. national interest." He took a similar stance on Clinton's ill-fated democracy-building effort in Haiti, chastising the president for engaging "American military prestige" on an issue "of the little or no importance" to U.S. interests. Bosnia presented a more complicated mix of posturing and ideologics. While running for president, Clinton had scolded the Bush Administration for failing to take action to stem the flow of blood in the Balkans. Once in office, however, and chastened by their early misadventures in Somalia and Haiti, Clinton and his advisers struggled to articulate a coherent Bosnia policy. Wolfowitz complained in 1994 of the administration's failure to "develop an effective course of action." He personally advocated arming the Bosnian Muslims in their fight against the Serbs. Powell, on the other hand, publicly cautioned against intervention. In 1995 a U.S.-led NATO bombing campaign, combined with a Croat-Muslim ground offensive, forced the Serbs into negotiations, leading to the Dayton Peace Accords. In 1999, as Clinton rounded up support for joint U.S.-NATO action in Kosovo, Wolfowitz hectored the president for failing to act quickly enough.

After eight years of what Cheney et al. regarded as wrong-headed military adventures and pinprick retaliatory strikes, the Clinton Administration—mercifully, in their view—came to an end. With the ascension of George W. Bush to the presidency, the authors of the Plan returned to government, ready to pick up where they had left off. Cheney of course, became vice president, Powell became secretary of state, and Wolfowitz moved into the number two slot at the Pentagon, as Donald Rumsfeld's deputy. Other contributors also returned: Two prominent members of the Wolfowitz team that crafted the original DPG took up posts on Cheney's staff. I. Lewis "Scooter" Libby, who served as Wolfowitz's deputy during Bush I, became the vice president's chief of staff and national security adviser. And Eric Edelman, an assistant deputy undersecretary of defense in the first Bush Administration, became a top foreign policy adviser to Cheney.

Cheney and company had not changed their minds during the Clinton interlude about the correct course for U.S. policy, but they did not initially appear bent on resurrecting the Plan. Rather than present a unified vision of foreign policy to the world, in the early going the administration focused on promoting a series of seemingly unrelated initiatives. Notable among these were missile defense and space-based weaponry, long-standing conservative causes. In addition, a distinct tone of unilateralism emerged as the new administration announced its intent to abandon the Anti-Ballistic Missile Treaty with Russia in order to pursue missile defense; its opposition to U.S. ratification of an international nuclear-test-ban pact; and its refusal to become a party to an International Criminal Court. It also raised the prospect of ending the self-imposed U.S. moratorium on nuclear testing initiated by the President's father during the 1992 presidential campaign. Moreover, the administration adopted a much tougher diplomatic posture, as evidenced, most notably, by a distinct hardening of relations with both China and North Korea. While none of this was inconsistent with the concept of U.S. dominance, these early actions did not, at the time, seem to add up to a coherent strategy.

It was only after September 11 that the Plan emerged in full. Within days of the attacks, Wolfowitz and Libby began calling for unilateral military action against Iraq, on the shaky premise that Osama bin Laden's Al Qaeda network could not have pulled off the assaults without Saddam

Hussein's assistance. At the time, Bush rejected such appeals, but Wolfowitz kept pushing and the President soon came around. In his State of the Union address in January, Bush labeled Iraq, Iran, and North Korea an "axis of evil," and warned that he would "not wait on events" to prevent them from using weapons of mass destruction against the United States. He reiterated his commitment to preemption in his West Point speech in June. "If we wait for threats to fully materialize we will have waited too long," he said. "We must take the battle to the enemy, disrupt his plans and confront the worst threats before they emerge." Although it was less noted, Bush in that same speech also reintroduced the Plan's central theme. He declared that the United States would prevent the emergence of a rival power by maintaining "military strengths beyond the challenge." With that, the President effectively adopted a strategy his father's administration had developed ten years earlier to ensure that the United States would remain the world's preeminent power. While the headlines screamed "preemption," no one noticed the declaration of the dominance strategy.

In case there was any doubt about the administration's intentions, the Pentagon's new DPG lays them out. Signed by Wolfowitz's new boss, Donald Rumsfeld, in May and leaked to the *Los Angeles Times* in July, it contains all the key elements of the original Plan and adds several complementary features. The preemptive strikes envisioned in the original draft DPG are now "unwarned attacks." The old Powell-Cheney notion of military "forward presence" is now "forwarded deterrence." The use of overwhelming force to defeat an enemy called for in the Powell Doctrine is now labeled an "effects based" approach.

Some of the names have stayed the same. Missile defense is back, stronger than ever, and the call goes up again for a shift from a "threat based" structure to a "capabilities based" approach. The new DPG also emphasizes the need to replace the so-called Cold War strategy of preparing to fight two major conflicts simultaneously with what the *Los Angeles Times* refers to as "a more complex approach aimed at dominating air and space on several fronts." This, despite the fact that Powell had originally conceived—and the first Bush Administration had adopted—the two-war strategy as a means of filling the "threat blank" left by the end of the Cold War.

Rumsfeld's version adds a few new ideas, most impressively the concept of preemptive strikes with nuclear weapons. These would be earth-penetrating nuclear weapons used for attacking "hardened and deeply buried targets," such as command-and-control bunkers, missile silos, and heavily fortified underground facilities used to build and store weapons of mass destruction. The concept emerged earlier this year when the administration's Nuclear Posture Review leaked out. At the time, arms-control experts warned that adopting the NPR's recommendations would undercut existing arms-control treaties, do serious harm to nonproliferation efforts, set off new rounds of testing, and dramatically increase the prospects of nuclear weapons being used in combat. Despite these concerns, the administration appears intent on developing the weapons. In a final flourish, the DPG also directs the military to develop cyber-, laser-, and electronic-warfare capabilities to ensure U.S. dominion over the heavens.

Rumsfeld spelled out these strategies in Foreign Affairs earlier this year, and it is there that he articulated the remaining elements of the Plan; unilateralism and global dominance. Like the revised DPG of 1992, Rumsfeld feigns interest in collective action but ultimately rejects it as impractical. "Wars can benefit from coalitions," he writes, "but they should not be fought by committee." And coalitions, he adds, "must not determine the mission." The implication is the United States will determine the missions and lead the fights. Finally, Rumsfeld expresses the key concept of the Plan: preventing the emergence of rival powers. Like the original draft DPG of 1992, he states that America's goal is to develop and maintain the military strength necessary to "dissuade" rivals or adversaries from "competing." With no challengers, and a proposed defense budget of $379 billion for next year, the United States would reign over all it surveys.

Reaction to the latest edition of the Plan has, thus far, focused on preemption. Commentators parrot the administration's line, portraying the concept of preemptory strikes as a "new" strategy aimed at combating terrorism. In an op-ed piece for the *Washington Post* following Bush's West Point address, former Clinton adviser William Galston described preemption as part of a "brand-new security doctrine," and warned of possible negative diplomatic consequences. Others found the concept more appealing. Loren Thompson of the conservative Lexington Institute hailed the "Bush Doctrine" as "a necessary response to the new dangers that America faces" and declared it "the biggest shift in strategic thinking in two generations." *Wall Street Journal* editor Robert Bartley echoed that sentiment, writing that "no talk of this ilk has been heard from American leaders since John Foster Dulles talked of rolling back the Iron Curtain."

Preemption, of course, is just part of the Plan, and the Plan is hardly new. It is a warmed-over version of the strategy Cheney and his coauthors rolled out in 1992 as the answer to the end of the Cold War. Then the goal was global dominance, and it met with bad reviews. Now it is the answer to terrorism. The emphasis is on preemption, and the reviews are generally enthusiastic. Through all of this, the dominance motif remains, though largely undetected.

This country once rejected "unwarned" attacks such as Pearl Harbor as barbarous and unworthy of a civilized nation. Today many cheer the prospect of conducting sneak attacks—potentially with nuclear weapons—on piddling powers run by tin-pot despots.

We also once denounced those who tried to rule the world. Our primary objection (at least officially) to the Soviet Union was its quest for global domination. Through the successful employment of the tools of containment, deterrence, collective security, and diplomacy—the very methods we now reject—we rid ourselves and the world of the Evil Empire. Having done so, we now pursue the very thing for which we opposed it. And now that the Soviet Union is gone, there appears to be no one left to stop us.

Perhaps, however, there is. The Bush Administration and its loyal opposition seem not to grasp that the quests for dominance generate backlash. Those threatened with preemption may themselves launch preemptory strikes. And even those who are successfully "preempted" or dominated may object and find means to strike back. Pursuing such strategies may, paradoxically, result in greater factionalism and rivalry, precisely the things we seek to end.

Not all Americans share Colin Powell's desire to be "the bully on the block." In fact, some believe that by following a different path the United States has an opportunity to establish a more lasting security environment. As Dartmouth professors Stephen Brooks and William Woblforth wrote recently in *Foreign Affairs*, "Unipolarity makes it possible to be the global bully—but it also offers the United States the luxury of being able to look beyond its immediate needs to its own, and the world's, long-term interests. . . . Magnanimity and restraint in the face of temptation are tenets of successful statecraft that have proved their worth." Perhaps, in short, we can achieve our desired ends by means other than global domination.

Dick Cheney: The Droner Speaks

from *The Nation* (11/17/03)

Calvin Trillin

Though even Bush no longer's buying
The nine-eleven link (implying
Iraq's involvement in that dying),
From Dick this tale gets amplifying.
It seems he got so used to lying
He just can't stop. But is he trying?

He Said It . . .

"I felt there was a real danger here that you would get bogged down in a long, drawn-out conflict, that this was a dangerous, difficult part of the world; if you recall we were all worried about the possibility of Iraq coming apart . . . Now you can say, well, you should have gone to Baghdad and gotten Saddam. I don't think so. I think if we had done that we would have been bogged down there for a very long period of time with the real possibility we might not have succeeded . . . If Saddam wasn't there, his successor probably wouldn't be notably friendlier to the United States than he is. . . . Maybe it's part of our national character, you know,

we like to have these problems nice and neatly wrapped up, put a ribbon around it. You deploy a force, you win the war, and the problem goes away, and it doesn't work that way in the Middle East; it never has and isn't likely to in my lifetime."

—Dick Cheney, 1996, explaining why in 1991 he supported the decision not to oust Saddam.

"I really do believe we will be greeted [in Iraq] as liberators."

–Dick Cheney, 3/16/03

Cheney and Supreme Court Justice Antonin Scalia like to kill ducks—and democracy is also on their hit list.

Old McCheney had a Judge

from Salon.com (2/17/04)

Robert Scheer

Quack, quack. So much for the constitutionally mandated separation of powers.

Quack, quack. Say goodbye to judicial integrity. Quack, quack. Forget about holding the nation's vice president accountable for his dealings. Quack, quack. Trash the right of citizens to transparent government. Quack, quack.

Bizarre as it sounds, Supreme Court Justice Antonin Scalia quacked like a duck last week during his defensive denial that a duck-hunting trip with Vice President Dick Cheney was improper. According to Scalia, the visit of the two men to the private game reserve of a top oil executive was merely a pleasant social engagement.

But Scalia's glib response was disingenuous, coming shortly before the Supremes will rule on a White House appeal in a case involving private meetings of Cheney's energy task force. It's outrageous that he does not intend to recuse himself.

"It did not involve a lawsuit against Dick Cheney as a private individual," Scalia said of the appeal while speaking at Amherst College last Tuesday. "This was a government issue. It's acceptable practice to socialize with executive branch officials when there are not personal claims against them. That's all I'm going to say for now. Quack, quack."

The case in question is not a legalistic quibble, and Scalia seems determined to vote in what may be a hotly contested decision with enormous political effect. His Louisiana outing with Cheney came three weeks after the Supreme Court agreed to hear Cheney's appeal of a lower court order that he turn over records of the closed task force meetings he held with executives of the oil, coal, gas and nuclear companies in 2001. Those meetings became the basis for the president's national energy policy, which is chockablock with tax breaks and subsidies for these same industries. This all has particular resonance for Californians, who, during the manufactured "energy crisis," saw our state and household budgets go up in flames. Many of the same companies represented at Cheney's meetings, such as Kenneth Lay's Enron, had "gamed," or manipulated, electricity prices using federal loopholes created by previous GOP administrations under the broad banner of "deregulation."

Unfortunately for us, the Constitution has a glaring loophole: If a Supreme Court justice doesn't have the moral fiber or humility to do the right thing in a case like this—federal rules instruct a judge to disqualify himself "in any proceeding in which his impartiality might be questioned"—there is no check or balance whereby that decision can be reviewed or rebuked.

According to an Amherst official, Scalia—with his waterfowl impression—may have been trying to preempt protesters he thought were going to perform their own impromptu noises. Nevertheless, by arrogantly trying to make a joke out of his unethical behavior, Scalia has again made a mockery of the enormous responsibility the Constitution places on our highest court. After all, it was Scalia who led the Supreme Court with flimsy legal logic to validate the dubious 2000 Florida election results that were the difference in placing the current president in power. This time he may have gone too far in shredding the Supreme Court's vaunted reputation of impartiality.

"I'm surprised he's sticking by his guns. I would hope he does see the light," Georgetown University law professor Paul Rothstein said of Scalia's stubbornness to acknowledge what is simple common sense: If you are a longtime friend of the vice president and are accepting free junket flights from him, you'd best remove yourself from the fray when it comes time to rule on a decision that may damage his career.

Finally, we should remember what the legal case in question is about: transparency in government, which is one of the taproots of democracy. While Scalia twists and turns to avoid the obvious appearance of a conflict of interest, the case's co-plaintiffs—the liberal Sierra Club and the conservative Judicial Watch—have joined forces to demand accountability in government, so that we might see how corporate interests wield disproportionate power in the halls of government. The Scalia-Cheney hunting tryst shows that the old-boy network is still scamming the public.

TOM the DANCING BUG
BY RUBEN BOLLING
JUDGE SCALIA
in "the LONE WOLF OF LAW"
OUR STORY THUS FAR: CRUELLY BETRAYED BY HIS JUDICIAL BRETHREN, JUDGE SCALIA HAS OPTED TO TAKE HIS BRAND OF TOUGH, TRADITIONAL JUSTICE UNDERGROUND!
AH, THIS IS A THRILL THOSE PANTYWAIST JUSTICES, SITTING ON THEIR CUSHY BENCH IN WASHINGTON, WILL NEVER KNOW!
SUDDENLY, HIS NOSTRILS DETECT A HUMAN PRESENCE!
PERSPIRATION...
IRISH SPRING...
FLANNEL!
WITH PANTHER-LIKE STEALTH, HE INVESTIGATES!
WHAT A PLEASANT HIKE!
I THINK THE CABIN IS A MILE UP THIS PATH!
MUSCLES COILED, HE TRACKS HIS QUARRY UNTIL...
I FIND YOU GUILTY OF ATTEMPTED SODOMY!
?
WHAM
THERE'S NO SUCH THING!
OH, YES THERE IS... UNLESS YOU'VE GOT SOME RADICAL HOMOSEXUAL AGENDA!
PARK RANGER, MA'AM! EVERY-THING OKAY HERE?
SIR...?
SHRIEK!
THE FEDS!
H-HE WAS LIKE SOME KIND OF PRIMITIVE THROWBACK!
IF ONLY THOSE GIRLS WOULD COME BACK TO MAIN-STREAM AMERICAN SOCIETY!
WELL, I'D BETTER OPEN UP THAT DEER CARCASS--IT'S GONNA BE A COLD NIGHT!
END
DIST. BY UNIVERSAL PRESS SYNDICATE ©2003 R. BOLLING 657 www.tomthedancingbug.com

Dick Cheney's corporate connection may be the mother of all conflicts of interest.

Contract Sport

from *The New Yorker* (2/9/04)

Jane Mayer

Vice-President Dick Cheney is well known for his discretion, but his official White House biography, as posted on his Web site, may exceed even his own stringent standards. It traces the sixty-three years from his birth, in Lincoln, Nebraska, in 1941, through college and graduate school, and describes his increasingly powerful jobs in

Washington. Yet one chapter of Cheney's life is missing. The record notes that he has been a "businessman" but fails to mention the five extraordinarily lucrative years that he spent, immediately before becoming Vice-President, as chief executive of Halliburton, the world's largest oil-and-gas-services company. The conglomerate, which is based in Houston, is now the biggest private contractor for American forces in Iraq; it has received contracts worth some eleven billion dollars for its work there.

Cheney earned forty-four million dollars during his tenure at Halliburton. Although he has said that he "severed all my ties with the company," he continues to collect deferred compensation worth approximately a hundred and fifty thousand dollars a year, and he retains stock options worth more than eighteen million dollars. He has announced that he will donate proceeds from the stock options to charity.

Such actions have not quelled criticism. Halliburton has become a favorite target for Democrats, who use it as shorthand for a host of doubts about conflicts of interest, undue corporate influence, and hidden motives behind Bush Administration policy—in particular, its reasons for going to war in Iraq. Like Dow Chemical during the Vietnam War, or Enron three years ago, Halliburton has evolved into a symbol useful in rallying the opposition. On the night that John Kerry won the Iowa caucuses, he took a ritual swipe at the Administration's "open hand" for Halliburton.

For months, Cheney and Halliburton have insisted that he had no part in the government's decision about the Iraq contracts. Cheney has stuck by a statement he made last September on "Meet the Press": "I have absolutely no influence of, involvement of, knowledge of in any way, shape, or form of contracts led by the Corps of Engineers or anybody else in the federal government." He has declined to discuss Halliburton in depth, and, despite a number of recent media appearances meant to soften his public image, he turned down several requests for an interview on the subject. Cheney's spokesman, Kevin Kellems, responded to questions by e-mail.

Representative Henry Waxman, a liberal Democrat from California and the ranking minority member of the House Committee on Government Reform, has argued aggressively that the Bush Administration has left many questions about Halliburton unanswered. Last year, for example, a secret task force in the Bush Administration picked Halliburton to receive a noncompetitive contract for up to seven billion dollars to rebuild Iraq's oil operations. According to the *Times,* the decision was authorized at the "highest levels of the Administration." In an interview, Waxman asked, "Whose decision was it? Was it made outside the regular channels of the procurement process? We know that Halliburton got very special treatment. What we don't know is why."

Halliburton has been accused of exploiting its privileged status. Last year, a division of the company overcharged the government by as much as sixty-one million dollars in the course of buying and transporting fuel from Kuwait into Iraq. Halliburton charged the United States as much as $2.38 per gallon, an amount that a Pentagon audit determined to be about a dollar per gallon too high. Although Halliburton has denied any criminal wrongdoing, the inspector general for the Department of Defense is considering an investigation.

Halliburton blamed the high costs on an obscure Kuwaiti firm, Altanmia Commercial Marketing, which it subcontracted to deliver the fuel. In Kuwait, the oil business is controlled by the state, and Halliburton has claimed that government officials there pressured it into hiring Altanmia, which had no experience in fuel transport. Yet a previously undisclosed letter, dated May 4, 2003, and sent from an American contracting officer to Kuwait's oil minister, plainly describes the decision to use Altanmia as Halliburton's own "recommendation." The letter also shows that the Army Corps of Engineers, the federal agency that oversees such transactions, supported Halliburton's decision to use the expensive subcontractor—which may explain why it has been reluctant to criticize the deal.

Scott Saunders, a spokesman for the Army Corps of Engineers, confirmed the authenticity of the letter, and acknowledged that Halliburton had picked Altanmia. "Halliburton told us that only Altanmia could meet our requirements," he said.

Experts in the Persian Gulf oil business say that the Altanmia deal looks suspicious. "There is not a reason on earth to sell gasoline at the price they did," Youssef Ibrahim, the managing director of the Strategic Energy Investment Group, a consulting firm in Dubai, said. "Halliburton and their Kuwaiti partners made out like bandits." A well-informed Kuwaiti source called the prices charged by Altanmia "absurd," and said that Halliburton's arrangement to buy Kuwaiti oil through a middleman, rather than directly from the government, was "highly irregular." He added, "There is no way that this could have transpired without the knowledge and direction" of

Kuwait's oil minister, Sheikh Ahmad Al-Fahad Al-Sabah. Two sources told me that the oil minister's brother, Talal Al-Fahad Al-Sabah, may have secret financial ties to Altanmia. (The brothers are also nephews of the Emir and the Prime Minister of Kuwait.) "There are calls in parliament to open an investigation," the Kuwaiti source said. "It could shake the government."

Halliburton, meanwhile, is contending with two new scandals. Last week, the *Wall Street Journal* reported that the company had overcharged the government by sixteen million dollars on a bill for the cost of feeding troops at a military base in Kuwait. And last month the company made an astonishing confession: two of its employees, it said, had taken kickbacks resulting in overcharges of $6.3 million, in return for hiring a different Kuwaiti subcontractor in Iraq. Halliburton said that the employees, whose names it declined to reveal, had been fired and the funds returned. The day after this disclosure, the Pentagon awarded yet another contract to Halliburton, worth $1.2 billion, to rebuild the oil industry in southern Iraq.

Defenders of Halliburton deny that it has been politically favored, arguing that very few other companies could have handled these complex jobs. As Cheney said last September on "Meet the Press,""Halliburton is a unique kind of company. There are very few companies out there that have the combination of very large engineering construction capability and significant oil-field services." Dan Guttman, a fellow at Johns Hopkins University, agrees with Cheney's assessment, but sees Halliburton's dominance as part of a wider problem—one that has reached a crisis point in Iraq. After years of cutting government jobs in favor of hiring private firms, he said, "contractors have become so big and entrenched that it's a fiction that the government maintains any control." He wasn't surprised that Halliburton's admission of wrongdoing in Kuwait had failed to harm its position in Washington. "What can the government say—'Stop right there'?" Guttman said of Halliburton. "They're half done rebuilding Iraq."

The Vice-President has not been connected directly to any of Halliburton's current legal problems. Cheney's spokesman said that the Vice-President "does not have knowledge of the contracting disputes beyond what has appeared in newspapers." Yet, in a broader sense, Cheney does bear some responsibility. He has been both an architect and a beneficiary of the increasingly close relationship between the Department of Defense and an élite group of private military contractors—a relationship that has allowed companies such as Halliburton to profit enormously. As a government official and as Halliburton's C.E.O., he has long argued that the commercial marketplace can provide better and cheaper services than a government bureaucracy. He has also been an advocate of limiting government regulation of the private sector. His vision has been fully realized: in 2002, more than a hundred and fifty billion dollars of public money was transferred from the Pentagon to private contractors.

According to Peter W. Singer, a fellow at the Brookings Institution and the author of "Corporate Warriors," published last year, "We're turning the lifeblood of our defense over to the marketplace." Advocates of privatization, who have included fiscally minded Democrats as well as Republicans, have argued that competition in the marketplace is the best way to control costs. But Steven

Kelman, a professor of public management at Harvard, notes that the competition for Iraq contracts is unusually low. "On battlefield support, there are only a few companies that are willing and able to do the work," he said. Moreover, critics such as Waxman point out that public accountability is being sacrificed. "We can't even find out how much Halliburton charges to do the laundry," Waxman said. "It's inexcusable that they should keep this information from the Congress, and the people."

Unlike government agencies, private contractors can resist Freedom of Information Act requests and are insulated from direct congressional oversight. Jan Schakowsky, a Democratic representative from Illinois, told me, "It's almost as if these private military contractors are involved in a secret war." Private companies, she noted, can conceal details of their missions from public scrutiny in the name of protecting trade secrets. They are also largely exempt from salary caps and government ethics rules designed to protect policy from being polluted by politics. The Hatch Act, for example, forbids most government employees from giving money to political campaigns.

Halliburton has no such constraints. The company made political contributions of more than seven hundred thousand dollars between 1999 and 2002, almost always to Republican candidates or causes. In 2000, it donated $17,677 to the Bush-Cheney campaign. Indeed, the seventy or so companies that have Iraq contracts have contributed more money to President Bush than they did to any other candidate during the past twelve years.

Sam Gardiner, a retired Air Force colonel who has taught at the National War College, told me that so many of the contracts in Iraq are going to companies with personal connections with the Bush Administration that the procurement process has essentially become a "patronage system." Major Joseph Yoswa, a Department of Defense spokesman, denied this. He told me that multiple safeguards exist to insure that the department's procurement process for Iraq contracts is free of favoritism. Most important, he said, career civil servants, not political appointees, make final decisions on contracts.

Gardiner remains unconvinced. "The system is sick," he told me. Cheney, he added, can't see the problem. "He doesn't see the difference between public and private interest," he said.

George Sigalos, a Halliburton executive, recently gave a speech at a conference in Washington for businesspeople who hoped to obtain government contracts in Iraq. Many in the crowd had paid nearly four hundred dollars to attend, drawn by descriptions of Iraq as "the next Klondike," as James Clad, an official with the U.S. Overseas Private Investment Corporation, a federal agency, put it. Sigalos began by pointing out that private contractors supplied the bullets that the Continental Army used in the American Revolution. "This didn't begin with Halliburton," he said.

Halliburton's construction-and-engineering subsidiary, Brown & Root Services, started working with the U.S. military decades before Cheney joined the firm. Founded in Texas, in 1919, by two brothers, George and Herman Brown, and their brother-in-law, Dan Root, the firm grew from supervising small road-paving projects to building enormously complex oil platforms, dams, and Navy warships. The company's engineering feats were nearly matched by its talent for political patronage. As Robert A. Caro noted in his biography of Lyndon Johnson, Brown & Root had a symbiotic relationship with L.B.J.: the company served as a munificent sponsor of his political campaigns, and in return was rewarded with big government contracts. In 1962, Brown & Root sold out to Halliburton, a booming oil-well construction-and-services firm, and in the following years the conglomerate grew spectacularly. According to Dan Briody, who has written a book on the subject, Brown & Root was part of a consortium of four companies that built about eighty-five per cent of the infrastructure needed by the Army during the Vietnam War. At the height of the resistance to the war, Brown & Root became a target of protesters, and soldiers in Vietnam derided it as Burn & Loot.

Around this time, in 1968, Dick Cheney arrived in Washington. He was a political-science graduate student who had won a congressional fellowship with Bill Steiger, a Republican from his home state of Wyoming. One of Cheney's first assignments was to visit college campuses where antiwar protests were disrupting classes, and quietly assess the scene. Steiger was part of a group of congressmen who were considering ways to cut off federal funding to campuses where violent protests had broken out. It was an early lesson in the strategic use of government cutbacks.

Instead of returning to graduate school, Cheney got a job as the deputy for a brash congressional colleague of Steiger's, Donald Rumsfeld, whom Richard Nixon had appointed to head the Office of Economic Opportunity. The O.E.O., which had played a prominent role in Johnson's War on Poverty, was not favored by Nixon.

According to Dan Guttman, who co-wrote "The Shadow Government" (1976), Rumsfeld and Cheney diminished the power of the office by outsourcing many of its jobs. Their tactics were not subtle. At nine o'clock on the morning of September 17, 1969, Rumsfeld distributed a new agency phone directory; without explanation, a hundred and eight employee names had been dropped. The vast majority were senior career civil servants who had been appointed by Democrats.

The purging of the office was a mixed success. Bureaucratic resistance stymied Cheney and Rumsfeld on several fronts. But by the time Ronald Reagan became President the overriding principle that had guided their actions at the O.E.O.—privatization—had become a central precept of the conservative movement.

For most of the eighties, Cheney served in the House of Representatives. In 1988, after the election of George H. W. Bush, he was named Secretary of Defense. The end of the Cold War brought with it expectations of a "peace dividend," and Cheney's mandate was to reduce forces, cut weapons systems, and close military bases. Predictably, this plan met with opposition from every member of Congress whose district had a base in peril.

Cheney was widely admired for his judicious handling of the matter. By the time he was done, the armed forces were at their lowest level since the Korean War. However, a Democratic aide on the House Armed Services Committee during those years told me that "contrary to his public image, which was as a reasonable, quiet, soft-spoken, and inclusive personality, Cheney was a rank partisan." The aide said that Cheney practiced downsizing as political jujitsu. He once compiled a list of military bases to be closed; all were in Democratic districts. Cheney's approach to cutting weapons systems was similar: he proposed breathtaking cuts in the districts of Thomas Downey, David Bonior, and Jim Wright, all high-profile Democrats. The aide told me that Congress, which was then dominated by the Democrats, beat back most of Cheney's plans, because many of the cuts made no strategic sense. "This was about getting even," he said of Cheney. Cheney's spokesman disputed this account, saying that the armed services had specified which bases should be cut, and "Congress approved it without changes."

As Defense Secretary, Cheney developed a contempt for Congress, which, a friend said, he came to regard as "a bunch of annoying gnats." Meanwhile, his affinity for business deepened. "The meetings with businessmen were the ones that really got him pumped," a former aide said. One company that did exceedingly well was Halliburton. Toward the end of Cheney's tenure, the Pentagon decided to turn over to a single company the bulk of the business of planning and providing support for military operations abroad—tasks such as preparing food, doing the laundry, and cleaning the latrines. As Singer writes in "Corporate Warriors," the Pentagon commissioned Halliburton to do a classified study of how this might work. In effect, the company was being asked to create its own market.

Halliburton was paid $3.9 million to write its initial report, which offered a strategy for providing support to twenty thousand troops. The Pentagon then paid Halliburton five million dollars more to do a follow-up study. In August, 1992, Halliburton was selected by the U.S. Army Corps of Engineers to do all the work needed to support the military during the next five years, in accordance with the plan it had itself drawn up. The Pentagon had never relied so heavily on a single company before. Although the profit margins for this omnibus government contract were narrower than they were for private-sector jobs, there was a guaranteed profit of one per cent, with the possibility of as much as nine per cent—making it a rare bit of business with no risk.

In December, 1992, working under its new contract, Halliburton began providing assistance to the United States troops overseeing the humanitarian crisis in Somalia. Few other companies in the world could have mobilized as fast or as well. Halliburton employees were on the ground within twenty-four hours of the first U.S. landing in Mogadishu. By the time Halliburton left, in 1995, it had become the largest employer in the country, having subcontracted out most of the menial work, while importing experts for more specialized needs. (A mortician was hired, for example, to clean up the bodies of the slain soldiers.) For its services in Somalia, Halliburton was paid a hundred and nine million dollars. Over the next five years, the company billed the government $2.2 billion for similar work in the Balkans.

Halliburton's efforts in the field were considered highly effective. Yet Sam Gardiner, the retired Air Force colonel, told me that the success of private contractors in the battlefield has had an unforeseen consequence at the Pentagon. "It makes it too easy to go to war," he said. "When you can hire people to go to war, there's none of the grumbling and the political friction." He noted that much of the scut work now being contracted out to firms like Halliburton was traditionally performed by reserve soldiers, who often complain the loudest.

There are some hundred and thirty-five thousand American troops in Iraq, but Gardiner estimated that there would be as many as three hundred thousand if not for private contractors. He said, "Think how much harder it would have been to get Congress, or the American public, to support those numbers."

After Cheney's tenure at the Pentagon ended, in 1993, with the arrival of the Clinton Administration, he spent much of the next two years deciding whether to run for President. He formed a political-action committee, and crossed the country making speeches and raising money. He also became affiliated with the American Enterprise Institute, the conservative think tank. Records from the Federal Election Commission show that Cheney's pac contributors included executives at several of the companies that have since won the largest government contracts in Iraq. Among them were Thomas Cruikshank, Halliburton's C.E.O. at the time; Stephen Bechtel, whose family's construction-and-engineering firm now has a contract in Iraq worth as much as $2.8 billion; and Duane Andrews, then senior vice-president of Science Applications International Corporation, which has won seven contracts in Iraq.

When Newt Gingrich helped bring the House of Representatives into Republican hands, in 1994, Cheney felt reassured that the country was back on the right track, alleviating his need to run. His pac hadn't raised enough money, in any case. Equally important, colleagues said, Cheney had found that he didn't enjoy being the center of attention. He preferred to work behind the scenes.

Cheney was hired by Halliburton in 1995, not long after he went on a fly-fishing trip in New Brunswick,

Canada, with several corporate moguls. After Cheney had said good night, the others began talking about Halliburton's need for a new C.E.O. Why not Dick? He had virtually no business experience, but he had valuable relationships with very powerful people. Lawrence Eagleburger, the Secretary of State in the first Bush Administration, became a Halliburton board member after Cheney joined the company. He told me that Cheney was the firm's "outside man," the person who could best help the company expand its business around the globe. Cheney was close to many world leaders, particularly in the Persian Gulf, a region central to Halliburton's oil-services business. Cheney and his wife, Lynne, were so friendly with Prince Bandar, the Saudi Ambassador to the U.S., that the Prince had invited the Cheney family to his daughter's wedding. (Cheney did not attend.) "Dick was good at opening doors," Eagleburger said. "I don't mean that pejoratively. He had contacts from his former life, and he used them effectively."

Under Cheney's direction, Halliburton thrived. In 1998, the company acquired its main rival, Dresser Industries. Cheney negotiated the $7.7-billion deal, reportedly during a weekend of quail-hunting. The combined conglomerate, which retained the Halliburton name, instantly became the largest company of its kind in the world. But, in its eagerness to merge, Halliburton had failed to detect the size of the legal liability that Dresser faced from long-dormant lawsuits dealing with asbestos poisoning. The claims proved so ruinous that several Halliburton divisions later filed for bankruptcy protection. The asbestos settlements devastated the company's stock price, which fell by eighty per cent in just over a year.

Cheney's defenders have argued that no one could have anticipated the extent of the asbestos problem. Yet the incident presaged a current criticism of Cheney: that he can be blindsided by insular decision-making. Eagleburger, who was on Dresser's board of directors before it merged with Halliburton, told me, "I can't fault Cheney as such on asbestos, but somebody slipped up somewhere in the due diligence. Somebody should have caught it."

The Dresser merger also raised ethical questions. The United States had concluded that Iraq, Libya, and Iran supported terrorism and had imposed strict sanctions on them. Yet during Cheney's tenure at Halliburton the company did business in all three countries. In the case of Iraq, Halliburton legally evaded U.S. sanctions by conducting its oil-service business through foreign subsidiaries that had once been owned by Dresser. With Iran and Libya, Halliburton used its own subsidiaries. The use of foreign subsidiaries may have helped the company to avoid paying U.S. taxes.

In some ways, the Libya and Iran transactions were consistent with Cheney's views. He had long opposed economic sanctions as a political tool, even against South Africa's apartheid regime. During the 2000 campaign, however, Cheney said he viewed Iraq differently. "I had a firm policy that we wouldn't do anything in Iraq, even arrangements that were supposedly legal," he told ABC News. But, under Cheney's watch, two foreign subsidiaries of Dresser sold millions of dollars' worth of oil services and parts to Saddam's regime. The transactions were not illegal, but they were politically suspect. The deals occurred under the United Nations Oil-for-Food program, at a time when Saddam Hussein chose which companies his government would work with. Corruption was rampant. It may be that it was simply Halliburton's expertise that attracted Saddam's regime, but a United Nations diplomat with the Oil-for-Food program has doubts. "Most American companies were blacklisted," he said. "It's rather surprising to find Halliburton doing business with Saddam. It would have been very much a senior-level decision, made by the regime at the top." Cheney has said that he personally directed the company to stop doing business with Saddam. Halliburton's presence in Iraq ended in February, 2000.

During the 2000 Vice-Presidential debate, Senator Joseph Lieberman teased Cheney about the fortune he had amassed at Halliburton. "I'm pleased to see, Dick, that *you're* better off than you were eight years ago," he said.

"I can tell you that the government had absolutely nothing to do with it," Cheney shot back. In fact, despite having spent years championing the private sector and disparaging big government, Cheney devoted himself at Halliburton to securing government funds. In the five years before Cheney joined Halliburton, the company received a hundred million dollars in government credit guarantees. During Cheney's tenure, this amount jumped to $1.5 billion. One alliance that Cheney worked hard to make was with the Export-Import Bank, in Washington; he won the support of James Harmon, a Clinton appointee and the bank's chairman. Harmon agreed to make a four-hundred-and-ninety-million-dollar loan guarantee to a Russian company that was drilling a huge oil field in Siberia. It was the largest loan guarantee to a

Russian company in the bank's history, and a big chunk of it would facilitate the Russian company's purchase of Halliburton's services. There was a hitch, however: the Russian company, Tyumen Oil, was caught in a messy dispute with several competitors, all of whom accused the others of being corrupt.

Cheney was undeterred by these charges. But he almost lost the Export-Import loan when the State Department attempted to block it, on the ground that Tyumen was involved in illegal activity. According to a source who worked at the State Department at the time, Cheney personally lobbied the government in an effort to keep the deal alive. He was particularly incensed by the involvement of the Central Intelligence Agency, which sided with the State Department. According to a friend of Cheney's, he was convinced that the C.I.A. had been duped by opposition research spread by Tyumen's rivals. Eventually, the deal went through. By then, though, Cheney's frustration with government had become profound. As he said in a speech in 1998, "The average Halliburton hand knows more about the world than the average member of Congress."

In the spring of 2000, Cheney's two worlds—commerce and politics—merged. Halliburton allowed its C.E.O. to serve simultaneously as the head of George W. Bush's Vice-Presidential search committee. At the time, Bush said that his main criterion for a running mate was "somebody who's not going to hurt you." Cheney demanded reams of documents from the candidates he considered. In the end, he picked himself—a move that his longtime friend Stuart Spencer recently described, with admiration, as "the most Machiavellian fucking thing I've ever seen."

One man who was especially pleased by Cheney's candidacy was Ahmed Chalabi, the Iraqi dissident who was the leading proponent of overthrowing Saddam Hussein. Cheney had come to know Chalabi through conservative circles in Washington. "I think he is good for us," Chalabi told a U.P.I. reporter in June, 2000.

For months there has been a debate in Washington about when the Bush Administration decided to go to war against Saddam. In Ron Suskind's recent book "The Price of Loyalty," former Treasury Secretary Paul O'Neill charges that Cheney agitated for U.S. intervention well before the terrorist attacks of September 11, 2001. Additional evidence that Cheney played an early planning role is contained in a previously undisclosed National Security Council document, dated February 3, 2001. The top-secret document, written by a high-level N.S.C. official, concerned Cheney's newly formed Energy Task Force. It directed the N.S.C. staff to cooperate fully with the Energy Task Force as it considered the "melding" of two seemingly unrelated areas of policy: "the review of operational policies towards rogue states," such as Iraq, and "actions regarding the capture of new and existing oil and gas fields."

A source who worked at the N.S.C. at the time doubted that there were links between Cheney's Energy Task Force and the overthrow of Saddam. But Mark Medish, who served as senior director for Russian, Ukrainian, and Eurasian affairs at the N.S.C. during the Clinton Administration, told me that he regards the document as potentially "huge." He said, "People think Cheney's Energy Task Force has been secretive about domestic issues," referring to the fact that the Vice-President has been unwilling to reveal information about private task-force meetings that took place in 2001, when information was being gathered to help develop President Bush's energy policy. "But if this little group was discussing geostrategic plans for oil, it puts the issue of war in the context of the captains of the oil industry sitting down with Cheney and laying grand, global plans."

The Bush Administration's war on terror has became a source of substantial profit for Halliburton. The company's commercial ties to terrorist states did not prevent it from assuming a prominent role. The Navy, for instance, paid Halliburton thirty-seven million dollars to build prison camps in Cuba's Guantánamo Bay for suspected terrorists. The State Department gave the company a hundred-million-dollar contract to construct a new embassy in Kabul. And in December, 2001, a few years after having lost its omnibus military-support contract to a lower bidder, Halliburton won it back; before long, the company was supporting U.S. troops in Afghanistan, Kuwait, Jordan, Uzbekistan, Djibouti, the Republic of Georgia, and Iraq. Halliburton's 2002 annual report describes counterterrorism as offering "growth opportunities."

The Department of Defense's decision to award Halliburton the seven-billion-dollar contract to restore Iraq's oil industry was made under "emergency" conditions. The company was secretly hired to draw up plans for how it would deal with putting out oil-well fires, should they occur during the war. This planning began in the fall of 2002, around the time that Congress was debating whether to grant President Bush the authority to use force, and before the United Nations had fully debated the issue.

In early March, 2003, the Army quietly awarded Halliburton a contract to execute those plans.

As it turned out, oil-well fires were not a problem. An Army War College study shows that of the fifteen hundred oil wells in Iraq's two major oil fields, only nine were damaged during the war. Colonel Gardiner said he was puzzled by the Pentagon's inability to predict this outcome. "Our intelligence before the war was good enough to know that," he said.

After months spent trying to obtain more information about the classified Halliburton deals, Representative Waxman's staff discovered that the original oil-well-fire contract entrusted Halliburton with a full restoration of the Iraqi oil industry. "We thought it was supposed to be a short-term, small contract, but now it turns out Halliburton is restoring the entire oil infrastructure in Iraq," Waxman said. The Defense Department's only public acknowledgments of this wide-ranging deal had been two press releases announcing that it had asked Halliburton to prepare to help put out oil-well fires.

The most recent budget request provided by the Coalition Provisional Authority in Iraq mentions the building of a new oil refinery and the drilling of new wells. "They said originally they were just going to bring it up to prewar levels. Now they're getting money to dramatically *improve* it," Waxman complained. Who is going to own these upgrades, after the United States government has finished paying Halliburton to build them? "Who knows?" Waxman said. "Nobody is saying."

It is so complicated to secure an Iraq contract from the United States government that several big Washington law firms have gone into the business of shepherding applicants through the process. More than twenty billion dollars has been set aside for Iraqi relief and reconstruction projects, with work contracts being awarded by the Defense, State, and Commerce Departments, and by the U.S. Agency for International Development, in coordination with L. Paul Bremer, the head of the Coalition Provisional Authority. There's an additional five billion dollars sitting in the Development Fund for Iraq, also administered by the C.P.A. Officials at the C.P.A. say that contracts are awarded on the basis of competitive bidding, but rumors proliferate about political influence. When asked if connections helped, an executive whose firm has received several contracts replied, "Of course." One businessman with close ties to the Bush Administration told me, "Anything that has to do with Iraq policy, Cheney's the man to see. He's running it, the way that L.B.J. ran the space program."

Cheney's spokesman confirmed that the Vice-President speaks "on occasion" with officials at the C.P.A., and refers inquiries to the authority from third parties "expressing interest in getting involved in Iraq." The businessman offered an example of Cheney's backstage role. He said that Jack Kemp, the former Republican congressman and Secretary of Housing and Urban Development, got help from Cheney with a venture involving Iraq. Last summer, the businessman said, Kemp had Cheney over for dinner, along with two sons of the President of the United Arab Emirates. In an interview, Kemp confirmed the event, and his business plans, but denied receiving any special assistance from Cheney. "It was just social," Kemp said. "We're old friends. We didn't talk about business." He acknowledged, however, that Cesar Conda, who until last fall was Cheney's domestic-policy adviser, was helping him with a study on how to fashion a public-private partnership plan to develop the Iraqi economy.

Kemp said that he is working on two business ventures in Iraq. He described the first project, a company called Free Market Global, as "an international company that trades in gas, petroleum, and other resources." Although Kemp provided only vague details about the project, he said, "I can tell you that General Tommy Franks has joined the advisory board of Free Market Global." Last year, General Franks commanded the invasion of Iraq.

Franks's lawyer, Marty Edelman, confirmed his client's participation: "That is correct. But it is my understanding that he won't be dealing with Iraq or the military for a year" (to comply with government ethics rules). Asked how Kemp and Franks had joined forces, Edelman said, "It seems like everyone on that level knows each other." Edelman himself is now on the advisory board of Free Market Global.

Kemp's second project, in which he said he would play an advisory role, is something called al-Ruba'yia. He describes it as a two-hundred-million-dollar fund to be invested in various ventures in Iraq, from energy to education. He is trying to attract American investors. Kemp is well positioned for this task: his political organization, Empower America, counts among its supporters some of the current Bush Administration's top figures. Donald Rumsfeld, for example, is a former board member. "It's like Russia," the businessman said. "This is how corruption is done these days. It's not about bribes. You just help your friends to get access. Cheney doesn't call the Defense Department and tell them, 'Pick Halliburton.' It's just having dinner with the right people."

So far, other than the irregularities at Halliburton, there has been no evidence of large-scale corruption in the rebuilding of Iraq. But a number of friends of the Administration have landed important positions, and others have obtained large contracts. For instance, Peter McPherson, who took a leave from his job as president of Michigan State University to serve as Paul Bremer's economic deputy in Iraq, has been friends with Cheney since they both served in Gerald Ford's White House. The head of private-sector development at the C.P.A., one of the most powerful posts in Iraq, is Thomas Foley, a Connecticut-based business-school classmate of President Bush, who later became finance chairman for Bush's Presidential campaign in Connecticut. Foley was a "pioneer," meaning that he raised more than a hundred thousand dollars for Bush.

Last month, an inspector general was appointed for the C.P.A., as required by Congress when it approved the President's eighty-seven-billion-dollar supplemental budget for Iraq last year. Rather than choosing a nonpartisan outsider for this watchdog role, as most government agencies do, the Administration selected Stuart Bowen, Jr., who spent two years as White House counsel in the Bush Administration. According to *The Hill,* a Washington newspaper, L. Marc Zell, a former law partner of Douglas Feith, the Under-Secretary of Defense for Policy, is helping with international marketing for a concern called the Iraqi International Law Group. Billing itself as a group of lawyers and businessmen interested in helping investors in Iraq, the venture is run by Ahmed Chalabi's nephew Salem, who doubles as a legal adviser to Iraq's governing council, of which his uncle is a member.

Tom Korologos, a well-connected Republican lobbyist in Washington, recently took a temporary assignment as a senior counsellor to Bremer. Korologos acknowledged that Washington lobbyists are scrambling to solicit business in Iraq. "By definition, it's going to boom, because of the numbers," he said. "The question is who's going to get the contracts. There's a lot of money. Somebody's got to build the bridges and roads." He added that talk of political influence over the process was "bullshit."

Yet a look at one prominent defense contractor, Science Applications International Corporation, based in San Diego, suggests the importance of connections. One of its board members is Army General Wayne Downing, who commanded the Special Forces in the first Gulf War and ran counterterrorism in the Bush White House for the better part of a year after September 11th. During that time, he accompanied Cheney on visits to the C.I.A. to discuss U.S. intelligence on Iraq. For years, Downing has been an unpaid adviser to Ahmed Chalabi and the Iraqi National Congress, and he was an early advocate of armed insurrection against the old Iraqi regime. S.A.I.C.'s seven Iraq contracts are worth fifty million dollars.

It is unclear what special expertise S.A.I.C. brings to several of its contracts. One company executive, who asked not to be named, said that its chief credential for setting up what was supposed to be an independent media for Iraq, modelled on the BBC, was military work in "informational warfare"—signal jamming, "perception management," and the like. Some of S.A.I.C.'s government contracts require that specific individuals—referred to as "executive management consultants"—be paid more than two hundred dollars an hour. One contract cites a man named Owen Kirby as someone who will advise Iraqis on the process of building democracy. Kirby is a program director of the International Republican Institute, an organization devoted to promoting democracy abroad. In October, 2001, the group gave its Freedom Award to Dick Cheney. Before that, it gave the award to Lynne Cheney.

It is not surprising that Cheney, after five years of running Halliburton, a company that considers war as providing "growth opportunities," regards winning the peace in Iraq as a challenge for private enterprise as well as for government. Yet it is reasonable to ask if Cheney's faith in companies like Halliburton contributed to his conviction that the occupation of Iraq would be a tidy, easily managed affair. Now that Cheney's vision has been shown to be overly optimistic, and Iraqis and American soldiers are still getting killed ten months after Saddam's overthrow, critics are questioning the propriety of a reconstruction effort that is fuelled by the profit motive. "I'm appalled that the war is being used by people close to the Bush Administration to make money for themselves," Waxman said. "At a time when we're asking young men and women to make perhaps the ultimate sacrifice, it's just unseemly." Many of those involved, however, see themselves as part of a democratic vanguard. Jack Kemp's spokesman, P. J. Johnson, told me, "We're doing good by doing well." Joe Allbaugh, Bush's former campaign manager, who has established New Bridge

Strategies, a firm aimed specifically at setting up for-profit ventures in Iraq, makes no apologies. "We are proud of the leadership the American private sector is taking in the reconstruction of Iraq," he said.

Another top Republican lobbyist in Washington, Charlie Black, told me that his firm, BKSH & Associates, has plans to help Iraqis set up their own affiliated public-relations and government-relations firm; the company would become perhaps the first lobbying shop in Baghdad. Black is excited by the opportunities in Iraq, but he, too, has complaints. "The problem in Iraq so far is it's slow, and very confusing for people to figure out how to do business there," he said. "One week you go to Baghdad, and they say the decisions are being made at the Pentagon. Then you go to the Pentagon, and they say the decisions are being made in Baghdad. Only Halliburton is making money now!" He laughed. "Is there too much cronyism? I just wish I could find the cronies."

ANAGRAMS

Halliburton Corporation
I'll not abhor a corruption.

Bush Administration
This bandit is our man!

TOM the DANCING BUG
by RUBEN BOLLING
PRESIDENT BUSH LAID IT OUT VERY CLEARLY--
ONLY THOSE WHO SACRIFICED AND RISKED THEIR LIVES WILL BE ELIGIBLE FOR IRAQ RECONSTRUCTION CONTRACTS. AND SO, I AWARD THE FOLLOWING CONTRACTS:
$1.3 billion "Program Management Services - Public Works / Water Resources Sector" to U.S. ARMY SGT. 1st CLASS ED REICH
WOW, I GET IN ON SOME OF THAT WAR PROFITEERING SCRATCH?
SUH-WEET! PARTY AT MY PLACE!
$2.1 billion "Program Management Services - Oil Sector" to U.S. ARMY SPC. JEREMY REYES
IT'S BEEN A HELLUVA YEAR. I'M LUCKY TO BE ALIVE. SO AN OPPORTUNITY TO PRICE GOUGE AND FRAUDULENTLY INFLATE COSTS WILL BE A WELCOME CHANGE OF PACE.
$1.4 billion "Design - Build IDIQ Construction Services for Transportation Projects" to U.S. ARMY PFC. BENJAMIN SUTTER
HOW WILL I DO IT? SIMPLE. SUBCONTRACT TO THE IRAQIS -- THEY'RE THE EXPERTS, AND THEY'RE CHEAP.
I'M BUYING A MANSION ON HILTON HEAD AND TAKING UP GOLF.
$1.9 billion "Restore Iraq Oil Services (Southern region)" to MARINE GUNNERY SGT. JED HENSEN
FINALLY, SOMEONE DESERVING WILL GET TO LAP AT THE GOLDEN NECTAR OF U.S. TAXPAYER MONEY CONVERTED INTO ILLICIT PROFIT!
UM.. GEORGE...
psstpsst
OH. THANKS, DICK.
ACTUALLY, WHEN I SAID, "SACRIFICED AND RISKED THEIR LIVES," I WAS REFERRING TO U.S. DEFENSE CONTRACTING CORPORATIONS. SORRY, FELLAS.
DIST BY UNIVERSAL PRESS SYNDICATE ©2003 R. BOLLING 679 www.tomthedancingbug.com

AXIS OF WAR

with quotes by Richard Perle;
a cartoon by Gary Trudeau;
a quiz by Paul Slansky;
and anagrams

The attacks of 9/11 provided the Bush administration with the excuse they needed to invade Iraq. But why did they want to invade Iraq in the first place? Was it GWB's personal vendetta against Saddam Hussein? Was it a grab for Iraq's oil, and a signal to other Arab countries that they'd best fall in line? Was it the start of some imagined march toward empire, or an attempt to make money for the administration's friends and colleagues at Halliburton and other corporations? Whatever it was, the invasion of Iraq had little to do with the Bush administration's stated motivations: concerns about weapons of mass destruction or the desire to free Iraqis from oppression.

The people in Ted Kennedy's office said they'd rather we did not run this speech; they're not comfortable with this book's title. We're running the speech anyway, with apologies to Kennedy—whose tireless and courageous work during the past several decades has made him a towering figure in the annals of the Senate.

The Axis of War: Cheney, Rumsfeld and Wolfowitz

Speech to the Center for American Progress (1/14/04)

Senator Edward M. Kennedy

The enduring accomplishments of our nation's leaders are those that are grounded in the fundamental values that gave birth to this great country. As our founders so eloquently stated in the preamble to our Constitution, this nation was founded by "We the People . . . in Order to form a more perfect Union, establish Justice, insure domestic Tranquility, provide for the common defence, promote the general Welfare, and secure the Blessings of Liberty to ourselves and our Posterity." Over the course of two centuries, these ideals inspired and enabled 13 tiny quarreling colonies to transform themselves—not just into the most powerful nation on earth, but also into the "last, best hope of earth." These ideals have been uniquely honored by history and advanced by each new generation of Americans, often through great sacrifice.

In these uncertain times, it is imperative that our leaders hold true to those founding ideals and protect the fundamental trust between the government and the people. Nowhere is this trust more important than between the people and the president of the United States. As the leader of our country and the voice of America to the world, our president has the obligation to lead and speak with truth and integrity if this nation is to continue to reap the blessings of liberty for ourselves and our posterity.

The citizens of our democracy have a fundamental right to debate and even doubt the wisdom of a president's policies. And the citizens of our democracy have a sacred obligation to sound the alarm and shed light on the policies of an administration that is leading this country to a perilous place.

I believe that this administration is indeed leading this country to a perilous place. It has broken faith with the American people, aided and abetted by a congressional majority willing to pursue ideology at any price, even the price of distorting the truth. On issue after issue, they have moved brazenly to impose their agenda on America and on the world. They have pursued their goals at the expense of urgent national and human needs and at the expense of the truth. America deserves better.

The administration and the majority in Congress have put the state of our union at risk, and they do not deserve another term in the White House or in control of Congress.

I do not make these statements lightly. I make them as an American deeply concerned about the future of the republic if the extremist policies of this administration continue.

By far the most extreme and most dire example of this administration's reckless pursuit of its single-minded ideology is in foreign policy. In its arrogant disrespect for the United Nations and for other peoples in other lands, this administration and this Congress have squandered the immense goodwill that other nations extended to our country after the terrorist attacks of 9/11. And in the process, they made America a lesser and a less respected land.

Nowhere is the danger to our country and to our founding ideals more evident than in the decision to go to war in Iraq. Former Treasury Secretary Paul O'Neill has now revealed what many of us have long suspected. Despite protestations to the contrary, the president and his senior aides began the march to war in Iraq in the earliest days of the administration, long before the terrorists struck this nation on 9/11.

The examination of the public record and of the statements of President Bush and his aides reveals that the debate about overthrowing Saddam began long before the beginning of this administration. Its roots began 13 years ago, during the first Gulf War, when the first President Bush decided not to push on to Baghdad and oust Saddam.

President Bush and his national security advisor, Brent Scowcroft, explained the reason for that decision in their 1997 book, "A World Transformed." They wrote the following: "Trying to eliminate Saddam, extending the ground war into an occupation of Iraq, would have violated our guideline about not changing objectives in midstream . . . and would have incurred incalculable human and political costs . . . We would have been forced to occupy Baghdad and, in effect, rule Iraq. The coalition would instantly have collapsed, the Arabs deserting it in anger and other allies pulling out as well. Under those circumstances, there was no viable exit strategy we could see, violating another of our principles . . . Had we gone the invasion route, the United States could conceivably still be an occupying power in a bitterly hostile land." Those words are eerily descriptive of our current situation in Iraq.

During the first Gulf War, Paul Wolfowitz was a top advisor to then Secretary of Defense Dick Cheney, and he disagreed strongly with the decision by the first President Bush to stop the war after driving Saddam out of Kuwait.

After that war ended, Wolfowitz convened a Pentagon working group to make the case that regime change in Iraq could easily be achieved by military force. The Wolfowitz group concluded that "U.S. forces could win unilaterally or with the aid of a small group of a coalition of forces within 54 days of mid to very high intensity combat."

Saddam's attempted assassination of President Bush during a visit to Kuwait in 1993 added fuel to the debate.

After his tenure at the Pentagon, Wolfowitz became dean of the Johns Hopkins School of Advanced International Studies and continued to criticize the decision not to end the reign of Saddam. In 1994 he wrote: "With hindsight, it does seem like a mistake to have announced, even before the war was over, that we would not go to Baghdad. . . "

Wolfowitz's resolve to oust Saddam was unwavering. In 1997, he wrote, "We will have to confront him sooner or later—and sooner would be better . . . Unfortunately, at this point, only the substantial use of military force could prove that the U.S. is serious and reverse the slow collapse of the international coalition."

The following year, Wolfowitz, Donald Rumsfeld and 16 others—10 of whom are now serving in or officially advising the current Bush administration—wrote President Clinton, urging him to use military force to remove Saddam. They said, "The only acceptable strategy is one that eliminates the possibility that Iraq will be able to use or threaten to use weapons of mass destruction. In the near term, this means a willingness to undertake military action, as diplomacy is clearly failing. In the long term, it means removing Saddam Hussein and his regime from power. That now needs to become the aim of American foreign policy."

That was 1998. President Clinton was in office, and regime change in Iraq did become the policy of the Clinton administration—but not by war.

As soon as the current President Bush took office in 2001, he brought a group of conservatives with him, including Wolfowitz, Rumsfeld and others, who had been outspoken advocates for most of the previous decade for the forcible removal of Saddam Hussein.

At first, President Bush was publicly silent on the issue. But as Paul O'Neill has told us, the debate was alive and well.

I happen to know Paul O'Neill, and I have great respect for him. I worked with him on key issues of job safety and healthcare when he was at Alcoa in the 1990s. He's a person of great integrity, intelligence and vision, and he had impressive ideas for improving the quality of healthcare in the Pittsburgh area. It is easy to understand why he was so concerned by what he heard about Iraq in the Bush administration.

In his "60 Minutes" interview last Sunday, O'Neill said that overthrowing Saddam was on the agenda from Day One of the new administration. O'Neill said, "From the very beginning there was a conviction that Saddam Hussein was a bad person and that he needed to go . . . It was all about finding a way to do it. That was the tone of it. The president was saying, Go find me a way to do this."

The agenda was clear: Find a rationale to end Saddam's regime.

But there was resistance to military intervention by those who felt that the existing sanctions on Iraq should be strengthened. Saddam had been contained and his military capabilities had been degraded by the Gulf War and years of U.N. sanctions and inspections. At a press conference a month after the inauguration, Secretary of State Colin Powell said: "We have kept him contained, kept him in his box." The next day, Secretary Powell very clearly stated that Saddam "has not developed any significant capability with respect to weapons of mass destruction. . ."

Then, on Sept. 11, 2001, terrorists attacked us and everything changed. Secretary of Defense Rumsfeld immediately began to link Saddam Hussein to al-Qaida and the attacks. According to notes taken by an aide to Rumsfeld on 9/11, the very day of the attacks, the secretary ordered the military to prepare a response to the attacks. The notes quote Rumsfeld as saying that he wanted the best information fast, to judge whether the information was good enough to hit Saddam and not just Osama bin Laden. "Go massive," the notes quote him as saying. "Sweep it all up. Things related and not."

The advocates of war in Iraq desperately sought to make the case that Saddam was linked to 9/11 and al-Qaida, and that he was on the verge of acquiring a nuclear capability. They created an Office of Special Projects in the Pentagon to analyze the intelligence for war. They bypassed the traditional screening process and put pressure on intelligence officers to produce the desired intelligence and analysis.

As the world now knows, Saddam's connection to 9/11 was false. Saddam was an evil dictator. But he was never close to having a nuclear capability. The administration has found no arsenals of chemical or biological weapons. It has found no persuasive connection to al-Qaida. All this should have been clear. The administration should not have looked at the facts with ideological blinders and with a mindless dedication to the results they wanted.

A recent report by the Carnegie Endowment concluded that administration officials systematically misrepresented the threat from Iraq's nuclear, chemical and biological weapons programs. They also concluded that the intelligence community was unduly influenced by the policy-makers' views and intimidating actions, such as Vice President Cheney's repeated visits to CIA headquarters and demands by officials for access to the raw intelligence from which the analysts were working. The report also noted the unusual speed with which the National Intelligence Estimate was written and the high number of dissents in what is designed to be a consensus document.

In the immediate aftermath of 9/11, President Bush himself made clear that his highest priority was finding Osama bin Laden. At a press conference on Sept. 17, 2001, he said that he wanted bin Laden "dead or alive." Three days later, in an address to a Joint Session of Congress, President Bush demanded of the Taliban: "Deliver to the United States authorities all the leaders of al-Qaida who hide in your land." And Congress cheered. On Nov. 8, the president told the country, "I have called our military into action to hunt down the members of the al-Qaida organization who murdered innocent Americans." In doing that, he had the full support of Congress and the nation—and rightly so.

Soon after the war began in Afghanistan, however, the president started laying the groundwork in public to shift attention to Iraq. In the Rose Garden on Nov. 26, he said: "Afghanistan is still just the beginning."

Three days later, even before Hamid Karzai had been approved as interim Afghan president, Vice President Cheney publicly began to send signals about attacking Iraq. On Nov. 29, he said, "I don't think it takes a genius to figure out that this guy [Saddam Hussein] is clearly . . . a significant potential problem for the region, for the United States, for everybody with interests in the area."

On Dec. 12, the vice president elaborated further: "If I were Saddam Hussein, I'd be thinking very carefully about the future, and I'd be looking very closely to see what happened to the Taliban in Afghanistan."

Prior to the terrorist attacks on 9/11, President Bush's approval rating was only 50 percent. But with his necessary and swift action in Afghanistan against the Taliban for harboring bin Laden and al-Qaida, his approval soared to 86 percent.

Soon, Karl Rove joined the public debate, and war with Iraq became all but certain. At a meeting of the Republican National Committee in Los Angeles on January 19, 2002, Rove made clear that the war on terrorism could be used politically, and that Republicans, as he put it, could "go to the country on this issue."

Ten days later, the deal was all but sealed. In his State of the Union Address, President Bush broadened his policy on Afghanistan to other terrorist regimes. He unveiled the "Axis of Evil"—Iraq, Iran and North Korea. Those three words forged the lock-step linkage between the Bush administration's top political advisers and the Big Three of Cheney, Rumsfeld and Wolfowitz. We lost our previous clear focus on the most imminent threat to our national security—Osama bin Laden and the al-Qaida terrorist network.

What did President Bush say about bin Laden in the State of the Union Address that day? Nothing.

What did the President say about al-Qaida? One fleeting mention.

What did he say about the Taliban? Nothing.

Nothing about bin Laden. One fleeting mention of al-Qaida. Nothing about the Taliban in that State of the Union Address.

Barely four months had passed since the worst terrorist atrocity in American history. Five bin Laden videotapes had been broadcast since 9/11, including one that was aired after bin Laden escaped at the battle of Tora Bora. President Bush devoted 12 paragraphs in his State of the Union Address to Afghanistan, and 29 paragraphs to the global war on terrorism. But he had nothing to say about bin Laden and only one single fleeting mention of al-Qaida.

Why not more? Because of an extraordinary policy coup. Cheney, Rumsfeld, and Wolfowitz—the Axis of War—had prevailed. The president was changing the subject to Iraq.

In the months that followed, administration officials began to draw up the war plan and develop a plausible rationale for the war. Richard Haass, director of policy planning at the State Department during this period, said recently that "the agenda was not whether Iraq, but how." Haass said the actual decision to go to war had been made in July 2002. He had questioned the wisdom of war with Iraq at that time, but National Security Advisor Condoleezza Rice told him, "Essentially . . . that decision's been made. Don't waste your breath."

It was Vice President Cheney who outlined to the country the case against Iraq that he had undoubtedly been making to President Bush all along. On Aug. 26, 2002, in an address to the Veterans of Foreign Wars, the vice president argued against U.N. inspections in Iraq and announced that Saddam had weapons of mass destruction, meaning chemical and biological weapons. He also said: "We now know that Saddam has resumed his efforts to acquire nuclear weapons. Among other sources, we've gotten this from the firsthand testimony of defectors, including Saddam's own son-in-law, who was subsequently murdered at Saddam's direction. Many of us are convinced that Saddam will acquire nuclear weapons fairly soon." Those were Cheney's words.

It is now plain what was happening: The drumbeat for war was sounding, and it drowned out those who believed that Iraq posed no imminent threat. On Aug. 29, just two days after Cheney's speech, President Bush signed off on the war plan.

On Sept. 12, the president addressed the United Nations and said: "Iraq likely maintains stockpiles of VX, mustard and other chemical agents and has made several attempts to buy high-strength aluminum tubes used to enrich uranium for a nuclear weapon." He told the United Nations that Iraq would be able to build a nuclear weapon "within a year," if Saddam acquired nuclear material.

President Bush was focusing on Iraq and Saddam, even though one year after the attack on our country, bin Laden was still nowhere to be found. A sixth bin Laden tape had been aired, and news reports of the time revealed new military threats in Afghanistan. U.S. and Afghan military and intelligence officials were quoted as saying that al-Qaida had established two main bases inside Pakistan. An Afghan military intelligence chief said: "al-Qaida has regrouped, together with the Taliban, Kashmiri militants, and other radical Islamic parties, and they are just waiting for the command to start operations."

Despite the obvious al-Qaida threat in Afghanistan, the White House had now made Iraq our highest national security priority. The steamroller of war was moving into high gear. The politics of the timing is obvious. September 2002. The hotly contested 2002 election campaigns were entering the home stretch. Control of Congress was clearly at stake. Republicans were still furious over the conversion of Sen. Jim Jeffords that had cost them control of the Senate in 2001. Election politics prevailed, but they should not have prevailed over foreign policy and national security.

The decision on Iraq could have been announced earlier. Why time it for September? As White House Chief of Staff Andrew Card explained on Sept. 7, "From a marketing point of view, you don't introduce new products in August."

That was the bottom line. War in Iraq was a war of choice, not a war of necessity. It was a product they were methodically rolling out. There was no imminent threat, no immediate national security imperative, and no compelling reason for war.

In public, the administration continued to deny that the president had made the decision to actually go to war. But the election timetable was clearly driving the marketing of the product. The administration insisted that Congress vote to authorize the war before it adjourned for the November elections. Why? Because the debate in Congress would distract attention from the troubled economy and the troubled effort to capture bin Laden. The strategy was to focus on Iraq, and do so in a way that would divide the Congress. And it worked.

To keep the pressure on, President Bush spoke in Cincinnati on Iraq's nuclear weapons program, just three days before the congressional vote. He emphasized the ties between Iraq and al-Qaida. He emphasized Saddam's access to weapons of mass destruction, especially nuclear weapons. He said, "If the Iraqi regime is able to produce or steal an amount of highly enriched uranium a little larger than a single softball, it could have a nuclear weapon in less than a year. And if we allow that to happen, a terrible line would be crossed . . . Saddam Hussein would be in a position to pass nuclear technology to terrorists."

The scare tactics worked. Congress voted to authorize the use of force in October 2002. Republicans voted almost unanimously for war and kept control of the House in the election in November. Democrats were deeply divided and lost their majority in the Senate. The Iraq card had been played successfully. The White House now had control of both houses of Congress as well.

As 2003 began, many in the military and foreign policy communities urged against a rush to war. United Nations weapons inspectors were in Iraq, searching for weapons of mass destruction. Saddam appeared to be contained. There was no evidence that Iraq had been involved in the attacks on 9/11. Many insisted that bin Laden and al-Qaida and North Korea were greater threats, but their concerns were dismissed out of hand.

Cheney, Rumsfeld and Wolfowitz insisted that Iraq was

the issue and that war against Iraq was the only option, with or without international support. They convinced the president that the war would be brief, that American forces would be welcomed as liberators, not occupiers, and that ample intelligence was available to justify going to war.

The gross abuse of intelligence was on full display in the president's State of Union Address last January, when he spoke the now infamous 16 words—"The British government has learned that Saddam Hussein recently sought significant quantities of uranium from Africa." The president did not say that U.S. intelligence agencies agreed with this assessment. He simply and deviously said, "the British government has learned."

As we all now know, that allegation was false. It had already been debunked a year earlier by the U.S. intelligence community. Yet it was included in the president's State of the Union Address. Has any other State of the Union Address ever been so disgraced by such blatant falsehood?

In March 2003, on the basis of a grossly exaggerated threat and grossly inadequate postwar planning, and with little international support, the United States invaded Iraq when we clearly should not have done so.

Major combat operations ended five weeks later. Dressed in a flight suit, the president flew out to an aircraft carrier and proclaimed "Mission Accomplished." It was a nice image for the 2004 campaign, until the facts intruded. The mission was far from accomplished. As the war dragged on and casualties mounted, the image on the aircraft carrier was ridiculed. The administration replaced it with a new image—the president in Baghdad with cheering troops on Thanksgiving Day. Again, the image-makers stumbled. This time, the image was of the president holding his policy on Iraq—a turkey.

On a recent visit to Iraq, the writer Lucian Truscott, a 1969 graduate of West Point, spoke with an Army colonel in Baghdad. In an Op-Ed article in the *New York Times* last month, he wrote that Army officers spoke of feeling that "every order they receive is delivered with next November's election in mind, so there is little doubt at and near the top about who is really being used for what over here."

There is little doubt as well that the administration's plan to transfer sovereignty to the Iraqi people by this summer—and the pressure to hold elections in Afghanistan at that time—are intended to build momentum for the November elections in this country as well.

Our troubles in foreign policy today are as clear as they are self-made. America cannot force its vision of democracy on the Iraqi people on our terms and on our election timetable.

We cannot simply walk away from the wreckage of a war we never should have fought so that President Bush can wage a political campaign based on dubious boasts of success. Our overarching interest now is in the creation of a new Iraqi government that has legitimacy in the eyes of its own citizens, so that in the years ahead, the process of constructing democratic institutions and creating a stable peace can be completed. The date of Iraq's transition must not be determined by the date of U.S. elections.

We all agree that the Iraqi people are safer with Saddam behind bars. They no longer fear that he will ever return to power. But the war in Iraq itself has not made America safer.

Saddam's evil regime was not an adequate justification

for war, and the administration did not seriously try to make it one until long after the war began and all the other plausible justifications had proven false. The threat he posed was not imminent. The war has made America more hated in the world, especially in the Islamic world. And it has made our people more vulnerable to attacks both here and overseas.

By far the most serious consequence of the unjustified and unnecessary war in Iraq is that it made the war on terrorism harder to win. We knocked al-Qaida down in the war in Afghanistan, but we let it regroup by going to war in Iraq.

For nearly three weeks, our nation was recently on higher terrorist alert again. And certain places will continue to be on high alert for the foreseeable future. As Homeland Security Secretary Tom Ridge said so ominously in announcing the recent alert: "Al-Qaida's continued desire to carry out attacks against our homeland are perhaps greater now than at any point since 9/11."

Eleven times in the two years since 9/11, al-Qaida attacked Americans in other parts of the world and other innocent civilians. War with Iraq has given al-Qaida a new recruiting program for terrorists. For each new group of terrorist recruits, the pool is growing of others ready to support them and encourage them.

As another dangerous consequence of the war, our Army is overstretched, overstressed and overextended. Nearly 3,500 of our servicemen and women have been killed or wounded. By the end of 2004, eight of our 10 active Army divisions will have been deployed for at least a year in the Middle East in support of Afghanistan or Iraq. The Army is offering reenlistment bonuses of $10,000 to soldiers in

Iraq, but many are turning the money down and turning a new tour of duty down. Members of the National Guard and Reserve are being kept on active duty and away from their families, jobs and communities for over a year.

Al-Qaida and the Taliban fighters who support them are stepping up their terrorist campaign in Afghanistan, launching more and more attacks against military personnel and civilians alike. The warlords are jeopardizing the stability of the country. They make their money from the drug trade, which is now booming again. International humanitarian assistance workers, once considered immune from violence, are now targets of a new Afghan insurgency.

In all these ways, we are reaping the poison fruit of our misguided and arrogant foreign policy. The administration capitalized on the fear created by 9/11 and put a spin on the intelligence and a spin on the truth to justify a war that could well become one of the worst blunders in more than two centuries of American foreign policy. We did not have to go to war. Alternatives were working. War must be a last resort. And this war never should have happened.

We all care deeply about national security. We all care deeply about national defense. We take immense pride in the ability and dedication of the men and women in our armed forces and in the Reserves and the National Guard. The president should never have sent them in harm's way in Iraq for ideological reasons and on a timetable based on the marketing of a political product.

We know the high price we have also had to pay—in our credibility with the international community—in the loss of life—in the individual tragedies of loved ones left behind in communities here at home—in the billions of dollars that should have been spent on jobs and housing and healthcare and education and civil rights and the environment and a dozen other clear priorities and should not have been spent on a misguided war in Iraq.

The administration is breathtakingly arrogant. Its leaders are convinced they know what is in America's interest, but they refuse to debate it honestly. After repeatedly linking Saddam Hussein to al-Qaida and Osama bin Laden in his justification for war, the president now admits there was no such link. Paul Wolfowitz admitted in an interview that the administration settled for "bureaucratic reasons" on weapons of mass destruction because it was "the one reason everyone could agree on."

The administration is vindictive and mean-spirited. When Ambassador Joseph Wilson publicly challenged the administration for wrongly claiming that Iraq had purchased uranium from Niger for its nuclear weapons program, the administration retaliated against his wife, potentially endangering her life and her career.

President Bush and his advisors should have presented their case honestly, so that Congress and the American people could have engaged in the debate our democracy is owed, above all, on the issue of war and peace.

That is what democracy means, and it is the great strength of the checks and balances under the Constitution that has served us so well for so long.

President Bush said it all when a television reporter asked him whether Saddam actually had weapons of mass destruction, or whether there was only the possibility that he might acquire them. President Bush answered, "So what's the difference?" The difference, Mr. President, is whether you go to war or not.

No president of the United States should employ misguided ideology and distortion of the truth to take the nation to war. In doing so, the president broke the basic bond of trust between government and the people. If Congress and the American people had known the whole truth, America would never have gone to war.

To remain silent when we feel so strongly would be irresponsible. It would betray the fundamental ideals for which our troops are sacrificing their lives on battlefields half a world away. No president who does that to this land we love deserves to be reelected.

At our best, America is a great and generous country, ever looking forward, ever seeking a better nation for our people and a better world for peoples everywhere. I'm optimistic that these high ideals will be respected and reaffirmed by the American people in November. The election cannot come too soon.

ANAGRAMS

Bush Administration
Must do in Arabs in hit

Republicans
A sniper club

The intelligence community in the wake of 9/11 became a political tool for Cheney and other hawks in the Bush administration.

The First Casualty

from *The New Republic* (6/30/03)

John B. Judis & Spencer Ackerman

Foreign policy is always difficult in a democracy. Democracy requires openness. Yet foreign policy requires a level of secrecy that frees it from oversight and exposes it to abuse. As a result, Republicans and Democrats have long held that the intelligence agencies—the most clandestine of foreign policy institutions—should be insulated from political interference in much the same way as the higher reaches of the judiciary. As the Tower Commission, established to investigate the Iran-Contra scandal, warned in November 1987, "The democratic processes . . . are subverted when intelligence is manipulated to affect decisions by elected officials and the public."

If anything, this principle has grown even more important since September 11, 2001. The Iraq war presented the United States with a new defense paradigm: preemptive war, waged in response to a prediction of a forthcoming attack against the United States or its allies. This kind of security policy requires the public to base its support or opposition on expert intelligence to which it has no direct access. It is up to the president and his administration—with a deep interest in a given policy outcome—nonetheless to portray the intelligence community's findings honestly. If an administration represents the intelligence unfairly, it effectively forecloses an informed choice about the most important question a nation faces: whether or not to go to war. That is exactly what the Bush administration did when it sought to convince the public and Congress that the United States should go to war with Iraq.

From late August 2002 to mid-March of this year, the Bush administration made its case for war by focusing on the threat posed to the United States by Saddam Hussein's nuclear, chemical, and biological weapons and by his purported links to the Al Qaeda terrorist network. Officials conjured up images of Iraqi mushroom clouds over U.S. cities and of Saddam transferring to Osama bin Laden chemical and biological weapons that could be used to create new and more lethal September elevenths. In Nashville on August 26, 2002, Vice President Dick Cheney warned of a Saddam "armed with an arsenal of these weapons of terror" who could "directly threaten America's friends throughout the region and subject the United States or any other nation to nuclear blackmail." In Washington on September 26, Secretary of Defense Donald Rumsfeld claimed he had "bulletproof" evidence of ties between Saddam and Al Qaeda. And, in Cincinnati on October 7, President George W. Bush warned, "The Iraqi dictator must not be permitted to threaten America and the world with horrible poisons and diseases and gases and atomic weapons." Citing Saddam's association with Al Qaeda, the president added that this "alliance with terrorists could allow the Iraqi regime to attack America without leaving any fingerprints."

Yet there was no consensus within the American intelligence community that Saddam represented such a grave and imminent threat. Rather, interviews with current and former intelligence officials and other experts reveal that the Bush administration culled from U.S. intelligence those assessments that supported its position and omitted those that did not. The administration ignored, and even suppressed, disagreement within the intelligence agencies and pressured the CIA to reaffirm its preferred version of the Iraqi threat. Similarly, it stonewalled, and sought to discredit, international weapons inspectors when their findings threatened to undermine the case for war.

Three months after the invasion, the United States may yet discover the chemical and biological weapons that various governments and the United Nations have long believed Iraq possessed. But it is unlikely to find, as the Bush administration had repeatedly predicted, a reconstituted nuclear weapons program or evidence of joint exercises with Al Qaeda—the two most compelling security arguments for war. Whatever is found, what matters as far as American democracy is concerned is whether the administration gave Americans an honest and accurate account of what it knew. The evidence to date is that it did not, and the cost to U.S. democracy could be felt for years to come.

The Battle Over Intelligence
Fall 2001–Fall 2002

The Bush administration decided to go to war with Iraq in the late fall of 2001. At Camp David on the weekend after the September 11 attacks, Deputy Defense Secretary Paul Wolfowitz floated the idea that Iraq, with more than 20 years of inclusion on the State Department's terror-sponsor list, be held immediately accountable. In his memoir, speechwriter David Frum recounts that, in December, after the Afghanistan campaign against bin Laden and his Taliban sponsors, he was told to come up with a justification for war with Iraq to include in Bush's State of the Union address in January 2002. But, in selling the war to the American public during the next year, the Bush administration faced significant obstacles.

In the wake of September 11, 2001, many Americans had automatically associated Saddam's regime with Al Qaeda and enthusiastically backed an invasion. But, as the immediate horror of September 11 faded and the war in Afghanistan concluded successfully (and the economy turned downward), American enthusiasm diminished. By midAugust 2002, a Gallup poll showed support for war with Saddam at a post-September 11 low, with 53 percent in favor and 41 percent opposed—down from 61 percent to 31 percent just two months before. Elite opinion was also turning against war, not only among liberal Democrats but among former Republican officials, such as Brent Scowcroft and Lawrence Eagleburger. In Congress, even conservative Republicans such as Senate Majority Leader Trent Lott and House Majority Leader Dick Armey began to express doubts that war was justified. Armey declared on August 8, 2002, "If we try to act against Saddam Hussein, as obnoxious as he is, without proper provocation, we will not have the support of other nation-states who might do so."

Unbeknownst to the public, the administration faced equally serious opposition within its own intelligence agencies. At the CIA, many analysts and officials were skeptical that Iraq posed an imminent threat. In particular, they rejected a connection between Saddam and Al Qaeda. According to a *New York Times* report in February 2002, the CIA found "no evidence that Iraq has engaged in terrorist operations against the United States in nearly a decade, and the agency is also convinced that President Saddam Hussein has not provided chemical or biological weapons to Al Qaeda or related terrorist groups."

CIA analysts also generally endorsed the findings of the International Atomic Energy Agency (IAEA), which concluded that, while serious questions remained about Iraq's nuclear program—many having to do with discrepancies in documentation—its present capabilities were virtually nil. The IAEA possessed no evidence that Iraq was reconstituting its nuclear program and, it seems, neither did U.S. intelligence. In CIA Director George Tenet's January 2002 review of global weapons-technology proliferation, he did not even mention a nuclear threat from Iraq, though he did warn of one from North Korea. The review said only, "We believe that Iraq has probably continued at least low-level theoretical R&D [research and development] associated with its nuclear program." This vague determination didn't reflect any new evidence but merely the intelligence community's assumption that the Iraqi dictator remained interested in building nuclear weapons. Greg Thielmann, the former director for strategic proliferation and military affairs at the State Department's Bureau of Intelligence and Research (INR), tells *The New Republic,* "During the time that I was office director, 2000 to 2002, we never assessed that there was good evidence that Iraq was reconstituting or getting really serious about its nuclear weapons program."

The CIA and other intelligence agencies believed Iraq still possessed substantial stocks of chemical and biological weapons, but they were divided about whether Iraq was rebuilding its facilities and producing new weapons.

The intelligence community's uncertainty was articulated in a classified report from the Defense Intelligence Agency (DIA) in September 2002. "A substantial amount of Iraq's chemical warfare agents, precursors, munitions, and production equipment were destroyed between 1991 and 1998 as a result of Operation Desert Storm and UNSCOM [United Nations Special Commission] actions," the agency reported. "There is no reliable information on whether Iraq is producing and stockpiling chemical weapons, or where Iraq has—or will—establish its chemical warfare agent production facilities."

Had the administration accurately depicted the consensus within the intelligence community in 2002—that Iraq's ties with Al Qaeda were inconsequential; that its nuclear weapons program was minimal at best; and that its chemical and biological weapons programs, which had yielded significant stocks of dangerous weapons in the past, may or may not have been ongoing—it would have had a very difficult time convincing Congress and the American public to support a war to disarm Saddam. But the Bush administration painted a very different, and far more frightening, picture. Representative Rush Holt, a New Jersey Democrat who ultimately voted against the war, says of his discussions with constituents, "When someone spoke of the need to invade, [they] invariably brought up the example of what would happen if one of our cities was struck. They clearly were convinced by the administration that Saddam Hussein—either directly or through terrorist connections—could unleash massive destruction on an American city. And I presume that most of my colleagues heard the same thing back in their districts." One way the administration convinced the public was by badgering CIA

Director Tenet into endorsing key elements of its case for war even when it required ignoring the classified findings of his and other intelligence agencies.

As a result of its failure to anticipate the September 11 attacks, the CIA, and Tenet in particular, were under almost continual attack in the fall of 2001. Congressional leaders, including Richard Shelby, the ranking Republican on the Senate Intelligence Committee, wanted Tenet to resign. But Bush kept Tenet in his job, and, within the administration, Tenet and the CIA came under an entirely different kind of pressure: Iraq hawks in the Pentagon and in the vice president's office, reinforced by members of the Pentagon's semiofficial Defense Policy Board, mounted a year-long attempt to pressure the CIA to take a harder line against Iraq—whether on its ties with Al Qaeda or on the status of its nuclear program.

A particular bone of contention was the CIA's analysis of the ties between Saddam and Al Qaeda. In the immediate aftermath of September 11, former CIA Director James Woolsey, a member of the Defense Policy Board who backed an invasion of Iraq, put forth the theory—in this magazine and elsewhere—that Saddam was connected to the World Trade Center attacks. In September 2001, the Bush administration flew Woolsey to London to gather evidence to back up his theory, which had the support of Wolfowitz and Richard Perle, then the Defense Policy Board chairman. While Wolfowitz and Perle had their own long-standing and complex reasons for wanting to go to war with Iraq, they and other administration officials believed that, if they could tie Saddam to Al Qaeda, they could justify the war to the American people. As a veteran aide to the Senate Intelligence Committee observes, "They knew that, if they could really show a link between Saddam Hussein and Al Qaeda, then their objective, . . . which was go in and get rid of Hussein, would have been a foregone conclusion."

But this theory immediately encountered resistance from the CIA and other intelligence agencies. Woolsey's main piece of evidence for a link between Saddam and Al Qaeda was a meeting that was supposed to have taken place in Prague in April 2001 between lead September 11 hijacker Mohamed Atta and an Iraqi intelligence official. But none of the intelligence agencies could place Atta in Prague on that date. (Indeed, receipts and other travel documents placed him in the United States.) An investigation by Czech officials dismissed the claim, which was based on a single unreliable witness. The CIA was also receiving other information that rebutted a link between Iraq and Al Qaeda. After top Al Qaeda leader Abu Zubaydah was captured in March 2002, he was debriefed by the CIA, and the results were widely circulated in the intelligence community. As *The New York Times* reported, Zubaydah told his captors that bin Laden himself rejected any alliance with Saddam. "I remember reading the Abu Zubaydah debriefing last year, while the administration was talking about all of these other reports [of a Saddam-Al Qaeda link], and thinking that they were only putting out what they wanted," a CIA official told the paper. Zubaydah's story, which intelligence analysts generally consider credible, has since been corroborated by additional high-ranking Al Qaeda terrorists now in U.S. custody, including Ramzi bin Al Shibh and September 11 architect Khalid Shaikh Mohammed.

Facing resistance from the CIA, administration officials began a campaign to pressure the agency to toe the line. Perle and other members of the Defense Policy Board, who acted as quasi-independent surrogates for Wolfowitz, Cheney, and other administration advocates for war in Iraq, harshly criticized the CIA in the press. The CIA's analysis of Iraq, Perle said, "isn't worth the paper it is written on." In the summer of 2002, Vice President Cheney made several visits to the CIA's Langley headquarters, which were understood within the agency as an attempt to pressure the low-level specialists interpreting the raw intelligence. "That would freak people out," says one former CIA official. "It is supposed to be an ivory tower. And that kind of pressure would be enormous on these young guys."

But the Pentagon found an even more effective way to pressure the agency. In October 2001, Wolfowitz, Rumsfeld, and Undersecretary of Defense for Policy Douglas Feith set up a special intelligence operation in the Pentagon to "think through how the various terrorist organizations relate to each other and . . . state sponsors," in Feith's description. Their approach echoed the "Team B" strategy that conservatives had used in the past: establishing a separate entity to offer alternative intelligence analyses to the CIA. Conservatives had done this in 1976, criticizing and intimidating the agency over its estimates of Soviet military strength, and again in 1998, arguing for the necessity of missile defense. (Wolfowitz had participated in both projects; the latter was run by Rumsfeld.) This time, the new entity—headed by Perle protege Abram Shulsky—reassessed intelligence already collected by the CIA along with information from Iraqi defectors and, as Feith remarked coyly at a press conference earlier this month, "came up with some interesting observations about the linkages between Iraq and Al Qaeda." In August 2002, Feith brought the unit to Langley to brief the CIA about its findings. If the separate intelligence unit wasn't enough to challenge the CIA, Rumsfeld also began publicly discussing the creation of a new Pentagon position, an undersecretary for intelligence, who would rival the CIA director and diminish the authority of the agency.

In its classified reports, the CIA didn't diverge from its initial skepticism about the ties between Al Qaeda and Saddam. But, under pressure from his critics, Tenet began to make subtle concessions. In March 2002, Tenet told the Senate Armed Services Committee that the Iraqi regime "had contacts with Al Qaeda" but declined to elaborate. He would make similar ambiguous statements during the congressional debate over war with Iraq.

The intelligence community was also pressured to exaggerate Iraq's nuclear program. As Tenet's early 2002 threat assessments had indicated, U.S. intelligence showed precious little evidence to indicate a resumption of Iraq's nuclear program. And, while the absence of U.N. inspections had introduced greater uncertainty into intelligence collection on Iraq, according to one analyst, "We still knew enough, [and] we could watch pretty closely what was happening."

These judgments were tested in the spring of 2002, when intelligence reports began to indicate that Iraq was trying to procure a kind of high-strength aluminum tube. Some analysts from the CIA and DIA quickly came to the conclusion that the tubes were intended to enrich uranium for a nuclear weapon through the kind of gas-centrifuge project Iraq had built before the first Gulf war. This interpretation seemed plausible enough at first, but over time analysts at the State Department's INR and the Department of Energy (DOE) grew troubled. The tubes' thick walls and particular diameter made them a poor fit for uranium enrichment, even after modification. That determination, according to the INR's Thielmann, came from weeks of interviews with "the nation's experts on the subject, . . . they're the ones that have the labs, like Oak Ridge National Laboratory, where people really know the science and technology of enriching uranium." Such careful study led the INR and the DOE to an alternative analysis: that the specifications of the tubes made them far better suited for artillery rockets. British intelligence experts studying the issue concurred, as did some CIA analysts.

But top officials at the CIA and DIA did not. As the weeks dragged on, more and more high-level intelligence officials attended increasingly heated interagency bull sessions. And the CIA-DIA position became further and further entrenched. "They clung so tenaciously to this point of view about it being a nuclear weapons program when the evidence just became clearer and clearer over time that it wasn't the case," recalls a participant. David Albright of the Institute for Science and International Security, who had been asked to provide the administration with information on past Iraqi procurements, noticed an anomaly in how the intelligence community was handling the issue. "I was told that this dispute had not been mediated by a competent, impartial technical committee, as it should have been according to accepted practice," he wrote on his organization's website this March. By September 2002, when the intelligence agencies were preparing a joint National Intelligence Estimate (NIE) on Saddam's weapons of mass destruction, top CIA officials insisted their opinion prevail. Says Thielmann, "Because the CIA is also the head of the entire U.S. intelligence community, it becomes very hard not to have the ultimate judgment being the CIA's judgment, rather than who in the intelligence community is most expert on the issue."

By the fall of 2002, when public debate over the war really began, the administration had created consternation in the intelligence agencies. The press was filled for the next two months with quotes from CIA officials and analysts complaining of pressure from the administration to toe the line on Iraq. Says one former staff member of the Senate Intelligence Committee, "People [kept] telling you first that things weren't right, weird things going on, different people saying, 'There's so much pressure, you know, they keep telling us, go back and find the right answer,' things like that." For the most part, this pressure was not reflected in the CIA's classified reports, but it would become increasingly evident in the agency's declassified statements and in public statements by Tenet. The administration hadn't won an outright endorsement of its analysis of the Iraqi threat, but it had undermined and intimidated its potential critics in the intelligence community.

The Battle in Congress
Fall 2002

The administration used the anniversary of September 11, 2001, to launch its public campaign for a congressional resolution endorsing war, with or without U.N. support, against Saddam. The opening salvo came on the Sunday before the anniversary in the form of a leak to Judith Miller and Michael R. Gordon of *The New York Times* regarding the aluminum tubes. Miller and Gordon reported that, according to administration officials, Iraq had been trying to buy tubes specifically designed as "components of centrifuges to enrich uranium" for nuclear weapons. That same day, Cheney, Rumsfeld, and national security adviser Condoleezza Rice appeared on the political talk shows to trumpet the discovery of the tubes and the Iraqi nuclear threat. Explained Rice, "There will always be some uncertainty about how quickly [Saddam] can acquire nuclear weapons. But we don't want the smoking gun to be a mushroom cloud." Rumsfeld added, "Imagine a September eleventh with weapons of mass destruction. It's not three thousand—it's tens of thousands of innocent men, women, and children."

Many of the intelligence analysts who had participated in the aluminum-tubes debate were appalled. One described the feeling to *TNR*: "You had senior American officials like Condoleezza Rice saying the only use of this aluminum really is uranium centrifuges. She said that on television. And that's just a lie." Albright, of the Institute for Science and International Security, recalled, "I became dismayed when a knowledgeable government scientist told me that the administration could say anything it wanted about the tubes while government scientists who disagreed were expected to remain quiet." As Thielmann puts it, "There was a lot of evidence about the Iraqi chemical and biological weapons programs to be concerned about. Why couldn't we just be honest about that without hyping the nuclear account? Making the case for active pursuit of nuclear weapons makes it look like the administration was trying to scare the American people about how dangerous Iraq was and how it posed an imminent security threat to the United States."

In speeches and interviews, administration officials also warned of the connection between Saddam and Al Qaeda. On September 25, 2002, Rice insisted, "There clearly are contacts between Al Qaeda and Iraq. . . . There clearly is testimony that some of the contacts have been important contacts and that there's a relationship there." On the same day, President Bush warned of the danger that "Al Qaeda becomes an extension of Saddam's madness." Rice, like Rumsfeld—who the next day would call evidence of a Saddam-bin Laden link "bulletproof"—said she could not share the administration's evidence with the public without endangering intelligence sources. But Bob Graham, the Florida Democrat who chaired the Senate Intelligence Committee, disagreed. On September 27, Paul Anderson, a spokesman for Graham, told *USA Today* that the senator had seen nothing in the CIA's classified reports that established a link between Saddam and Al Qaeda.

The Senate Intelligence Committee, in fact, was the greatest congressional obstacle to the administration's push for war. Under the lead of Graham and Illinois Senator Richard Durbin, the committee enjoyed respect and deference in the Senate and the House, and its members could speak authoritatively, based on their access to classified information, about whether Iraq was developing nuclear weapons or had ties to Al Qaeda. And, in this case, the classified information available to the committee did not support the public pronouncements being made by the CIA.

In the late summer of 2002, Graham had requested from Tenet an analysis of the Iraqi threat. According to knowledgeable sources, he received a 25-page classified response reflecting the balanced view that had prevailed earlier among the intelligence agencies—noting, for example, that evidence of an Iraqi nuclear program or a link to Al Qaeda was inconclusive. Early that September, the committee also received the DIA's classified analysis, which reflected the same cautious assessments. But committee members became worried when, midway through the month, they received a new CIA analysis of the threat that highlighted the Bush administration's claims and consigned skepticism to footnotes. According to one congressional staffer who read the document, it highlighted "extensive Iraqi chem-bio programs and nuclear programs and links to terrorism" but then included a footnote that read, "This information comes from a source known to fabricate in the past." The staffer concluded that "they didn't do analysis. What they did was they just amassed everything they could that said anything bad about Iraq and put it into a document."

Graham and Durbin had been demanding for more than a month that the CIA produce an NIE on the Iraqi threat—a summary of the available intelligence, reflecting the judgment of the entire intelligence community—and toward the end of September, it was delivered. Like Tenet's earlier letter, the classified NIE was balanced in its assessments. Graham called on Tenet to produce a declassified version of the report that could guide members in voting on the resolution. Graham and Durbin both hoped the declassified report would rebut the kinds of overheated claims they were hearing from administration spokespeople. As

Durbin tells *TNR*, "The most frustrating thing I find is when you have credible evidence on the intelligence committee that is directly contradictory to statements made by the administration."

On October 1, 2002, Tenet produced a declassified NIE. But Graham and Durbin were outraged to find that it omitted the qualifications and countervailing evidence that had characterized the classified version and played up the claims that strengthened the administration's case for war. For instance, the intelligence report cited the much-disputed aluminum tubes as evidence that Saddam "remains intent on acquiring" nuclear weapons. And it claimed, "All intelligence experts agree that Iraq is seeking nuclear weapons and that these tubes could be used in a centrifuge enrichment program"—a blatant mischaracterization. Subsequently, the NIE allowed that "some" experts might disagree but insisted that "most" did not, never mentioning that the DOE's expert analysts had determined the tubes were not suitable for a nuclear weapons program. The NIE also said that Iraq had "begun renewed production of chemical warfare agents"—which the DIA report had left pointedly in doubt. Graham demanded that the CIA declassify dissenting portions.

In response, Tenet produced a single-page letter. It satisfied one of Graham's requests: It included a statement that there was a "low" likelihood of Iraq launching an unprovoked attack on the United States. But it also contained a sop to the administration, stating without qualification that the CIA had "solid reporting of senior-level contacts between Iraq and al-Qaeda going back a decade." Graham demanded that Tenet declassify more of the report, and Tenet promised to fax over additional material. But, later that evening, Graham received a call from the CIA, informing him that the White House had ordered Tenet not to release anything more.

That same evening, October 7, 2002, Bush gave a major speech in Cincinnati defending the resolution now before Congress and laying out the case for war. Bush's speech brought together all the misinformation and exaggeration that the White House had been disseminating that fall. "The evidence indicates that Iraq is reconstituting its nuclear weapons program," the president declared. "Iraq has attempted to purchase high-strength aluminum tubes and other equipment needed for gas centrifuges, which are used to enrich uranium for nuclear weapons." Bush also argued that, through its ties to Al Qaeda, Iraq would be able to use biological and chemical weapons against the United States. "Iraq could decide on any given day to provide a biological or chemical weapon to a terrorist group or individual terrorists," he warned. If Iraq had to deliver these weapons on its own, Bush said, Iraq could use the new unmanned aerial vehicles (UAVs) that it was developing. "We have also discovered through intelligence that Iraq has a growing fleet of manned and unmanned aerial vehicles that could be used to disperse chemical or biological weapons across broad areas," he said. "We are concerned that Iraq is exploring ways of using these UAVs for missions targeting the United States." This claim represented the height of absurdity. Iraq's UAVs had ranges of, at most, 300 miles. They could not make the flight from Baghdad to Tel Aviv, let alone to New York.

After the speech, when reporters pointed out that

Bush's warning of an imminent threat was contradicted by Tenet's statement the same day that there was little likelihood of an Iraqi attack, Tenet dutifully offered a clarification, explaining that there was "no inconsistency" between the president's statement and his own and that he had personally fact-checked the president's speech. He also issued a public statement that read, "There is no question that the likelihood of Saddam using weapons of mass destruction against the United States or our allies . . . grows as his arsenal continues to build."

Five of the nine Democrats on the Senate Intelligence Committee, including Graham and Durbin, ultimately voted against the resolution, but they were unable to convince other committee members or a majority in the Senate itself. This was at least in part because they were not allowed to divulge what they knew: While Graham and Durbin could complain that the administration's and Tenet's own statements contradicted the classified reports they had read, they could not say what was actually in those reports.

Bush, meanwhile, had no compunction about claiming that the "evidence indicates Iraq is reconstituting its nuclear weapons program." In the words of one former Intelligence Committee staffer, "He is the president of the United States. And, when the president of the United States says, `My advisers and I have sat down, and we've read the intelligence, and we believe there is a tie between Iraq and Al Qaeda,' . . . you take it seriously. It carries a huge amount of weight." Public opinion bears the former staffer out. By November 2002, a Gallup poll showed 59 percent in favor of an invasion and only 35 percent against. In a December *Los Angeles Times* poll, Americans thought, by a 90 percent to 7 percent margin, that Saddam was "currently developing weapons of mass destruction." And, in an ABC/*Washington Post* poll, 81 percent thought Iraq posed a threat to the United States. The Bush administration had won the domestic debate over Iraq—and it had done so by withholding from the public details that would have undermined its case for war.

The Battle With the Inspectors
Winter–Spring 2003

By January 2003, American troops were massing on Iraq's borders, and the U.N. Security Council had unanimously approved Resolution 1441, which afforded Saddam a "final opportunity" to disarm verifiably. The return of U.N. inspectors to Iraq after four years had raised hopes both in the United States and abroad that the conflict could be resolved peacefully. On January 20, French Foreign Minister Dominique de Villepin launched a surprise attack on the administration's war plans, declaring bluntly, "Nothing today justifies envisaging military action." Nor was this sentiment exclusively French: By mid-January, Gallup showed that American support for the impending war had narrowed to 52 percent in favor of war and 43 percent opposed. Equally important, most of the nations that had backed Resolution 1441 were warning the United States not to rush into war, and Germany, which opposed military action, was to assume the chair of the Security Council in February, on the eve of the planned invasion.

In his State of the Union address on January 28, 2003, Bush introduced a new piece of evidence to show that Iraq was developing a nuclear arms program: "The British government has learned that Saddam Hussein recently sought significant quantities of uranium from Africa. . . . Saddam Hussein has not credibly explained these activities. He clearly has much to hide."

One year earlier, Cheney's office had received from the British, via the Italians, documents purporting to show Iraq's purchase of uranium from Niger. Cheney had given the information to the CIA, which in turn asked a prominent diplomat, who had served as ambassador to three African countries, to investigate. He returned after a visit to Niger in February 2002 and reported to the State Department and the CIA that the documents were forgeries. The CIA circulated the ambassador's report to the vice president's office, the ambassador confirms to *TNR*. But, after a British dossier was released in September detailing the purported uranium purchase, administration officials began citing it anyway, culminating in its inclusion in the State of the Union. "They knew the Niger story was a flat-out lie," the former ambassador tells *TNR*. "They were unpersuasive about aluminum tubes and added this to make their case more persuasive."

On February 5, Secretary of State Colin Powell took the administration's case to the Security Council. Powell's presentation was by far the most impressive the administration would make—according to *U.S. News and World Report*, he junked much of what the CIA had given him to read, calling it "bullshit"—but it was still based on a hyped and incomplete view of U.S. intelligence on Iraq. Much of what was new in Powell's speech was raw data that had come into the CIA's possession but had not yet undergone serious analysis. In addition to rehashing the aluminum-tube claims, Powell charged, for instance, that Iraq was trying to obtain magnets for uranium enrichment. Powell also described a "potentially . . . sinister nexus between Iraq and the Al Qaeda terrorist network, a nexus that combines classic terrorist organizations and modern methods of murder." But Powell's evidence consisted of tenuous ties between Baghdad and an Al Qaeda leader, Abu Musab Al Zarqawi, who had allegedly received medical treatment in Baghdad and who, according to Powell, operated a training camp in Iraq specializing in poisons. Unfortunately for Powell's thesis, the camp was located in northern Iraq, an area controlled by the Kurds rather than Saddam and policed by U.S. and British warplanes. One Hill staffer familiar with the classified documents on Al Qaeda tells *TNR*, "So why would that be proof of some Iraqi government connection to Al Qaeda? [It] might as well be in Iran."

But, by the time Powell made his speech, the administration had stopped worrying about possible rebukes from U.S. intelligence agencies. On the contrary, Tenet sat directly behind Powell as he gave his presentation. And, with the GOP takeover of the Senate, the Intelligence Committee had passed into the hands of a docile Republican chairman, Pat Roberts of Kansas.

As Powell cited U.S. intelligence supporting his claim of a reconstituted nuclear weapons program in Iraq, Jacques Baute listened intently. Baute, the head of the IAEA's Iraq inspections unit, had been pestering the U.S. and British governments for months to share their intelligence with his office. Despite repeated assurances of cooperation, *TNR* has learned that Baute's office received nothing until the day before Powell's presentation, when the U.S. mission in Vienna provided the IAEA with an oral briefing while Baute was en route to New York, leaving no printed material with the nuclear inspectors. As IAEA officials recount, an astonished Baute told his aides, "That won't do. I want the actual documentary evidence." He had to register his complaints through a United Nations Monitoring, Verification, and Inspection Commission (UNMOVIC) channel before receiving the documents the day Powell spoke. It was an incident that would characterize America's intelligence-sharing with the IAEA.

After a few weeks of traveling back and forth between Baghdad and Vienna, Baute sat down with the dozen or so pages of U.S. intelligence on Saddam's supposed nuclear procurements—the aluminum tubes, the Niger uranium, and the magnets. In the course of a day, Baute determined, like the ambassador before him, that the Niger document was fraudulent. Though the "president" of Niger made reference to his powers under the constitution of 1965, Baute performed a quick Google search to learn that Niger's latest constitution was drafted in 1999. There were other obvious mistakes—improper letterhead, an obviously forged signature, a letter from a foreign minister who had not been in office for eleven years. Baute also made quick work of the aluminum tubes. He assembled a team of experts—two Americans, two Britons, and a German—with 120 years of collective experience with centrifuges. After reviewing tens of thousands of Iraqi transaction records and inspecting Iraqi front companies and military production facilities with the rest of the IAEA unit, they concluded, according to a senior IAEA official, that "all evidence points to that this is for the rockets"—the same conclusion reached by the State and Energy Departments. As for the magnets, the IAEA cross-referenced Iraq's declarations with intelligence from various member states and determined that nothing in Iraq's magnet procurements "pointed to centrifuge enrichment," in the words of an IAEA official with direct knowledge of the effort. Rather, the magnets were for projects as disparate as telephones and short-range missiles. Baute, who according to a senior IAEA official was in "almost daily" contact with the American diplomatic mission in Vienna, was surprised at the weakness of the U.S. evidence. In one instance, Baute contacted the mission after discovering the Niger document forgeries and asked, as this official described it, "Can your people help me understand if I'm wrong? I'm not ready to close the book on this file. If you've got any other evidence that might be authentic, I need to see it, and I'll follow up." Eventually, a response came: The Americans and the British were not disputing the IAEA's conclusions; no more evidence would be provided.

On March 7, IAEA Director-General Mohammed ElBaradei delivered Baute's conclusions to the Security Council. But, although the United States conceded most of the IAEA's inconvenient judgments behind closed doors, Vice President Cheney publicly assaulted the credibility of the organization and its director-general. "I think Mr. ElBaradei frankly is wrong," Cheney told Tim Russert on NBC's "Meet the Press" on March 16. "I think, if you look at the track record of the International Atomic Energy Agency and this kind of issue, especially where Iraq's concerned, they have consistently underestimated or missed what it was Saddam Hussein was doing. I don't have any reason to believe they're any more valid this time than they've been in the past." Incredibly, Cheney added, "We believe [Saddam] has, in fact, reconstituted nuclear weapons."

Cheney was correct that the IAEA had failed to uncover

Iraq's covert uranium-enrichment program prior to the Gulf war. But, before the war, the IAEA was not charged with playing the role of a nuclear Interpol. Rather, until the passage of Resolution 687 in 1991, the IAEA was merely supposed to review the disclosures of member states in the field of nuclear development to ensure compliance with the Nuclear Non-Proliferation Treaty. By contrast, in the '90s, the IAEA mounted more than 1,000 inspections in Iraq, mostly without advance warning; sealed, expropriated, or destroyed tons of nuclear material; and destroyed thousands of square feet of nuclear facilities. In fact, its activities formed the baseline for virtually every intelligence assessment regarding Iraq's nuclear weapons program.

UNMOVIC Chairman Hans Blix received similar treatment from American officials—even though he repeatedly told the Security Council that the Iraqis had yet to account for the chemical and biological weapons they had once possessed, a position that strengthened the U.S. case for war. According to *The Washington Post*, in early 2002 Wolfowitz ordered a CIA report on Blix. When the report didn't contain damning details, Wolfowitz reportedly "hit the ceiling." And, as the inspections were to begin, Perle said, "If it were up to me, on the strength of his previous record, I wouldn't have chosen Hans Blix." In his February presentation, Powell suggested that Blix had ignored evidence of Iraqi chemical and biological weapons production. After stalling for months, the United States finally shared some of its intelligence with UNMOVIC. But, according to unmovic officials, none of the intelligence it received yielded any incriminating discoveries.

Aftermath

"What we must not do in the face of a mortal threat," Cheney instructed a Nashville gathering of the Veterans of Foreign Wars in August 2002, "is give in to wishful thinking or willful blindness." Cheney's admonition is resonant, but not for the reasons he intended. The Bush administration displayed an acute case of willful blindness in making its case for war. Much of its evidence for a reconstituted nuclear program, a thriving chemical-biological development program, and an active Iraqi link with Al Qaeda was based on what intelligence analysts call "rumint." Says one former official with the National Security Council, "It was a classic case of rumint, rumor-intelligence plugged into various speeches and accepted as gospel."

In some cases, the administration may have deliberately lied. If Bush didn't know the purported uranium deal between Iraq and Niger was a hoax, plenty of people in his administration did—including, possibly, Vice President Cheney, who would have seen the president's State of the Union address before it was delivered. Rice and Rumsfeld also must have known that the aluminum tubes that they presented as proof of Iraq's nuclear ambitions were discounted by prominent intelligence experts. And, while a few administration officials may have genuinely believed that there was a strong connection between Al Qaeda and Saddam Hussein, most probably knew they were constructing castles out of sand.

The Bush administration took office pledging to restore "honor and dignity" to the White House. And it's true: Bush has not gotten caught having sex with an intern or lying about it under oath. But he has engaged in a pattern of deception concerning the most fundamental decisions a government must make. The United States may have been justified in going to war in Iraq—there were, after all, other rationales for doing so—but it was not justified in doing so on the national security grounds that President Bush put forth throughout last fall and winter. He deceived Americans about what was known of the threat from Iraq and deprived Congress of its ability to make an informed decision about whether or not to take the country to war.

The most serious institutional casualty of the administration's campaign may have been the intelligence agencies, particularly the CIA. Some of the CIA's intelligence simply appears to have been defective, perhaps innocently so. Durbin says the CIA's classified reports contained extensive maps where chemical or biological weapons could be found. Since the war, these sites have not yielded evidence of any such weapons. But the administration also turned the agency—and Tenet in particular—into an advocate for the war with Iraq at a time when the CIA's own classified analyses contradicted the public statements of the agency and its director. Did Tenet really fact-check Bush's warning that Iraq could threaten the United States with UAVs? Did he really endorse Powell's musings on the links between Al Qaeda and Saddam? Or had Tenet and his agency by then lost any claim to the intellectual honesty upon which U.S. foreign policy critically depends—particularly in an era of preemptive war?

Democrats such as Durbin, Graham, and Senator Jay Rockefeller, who has become the ranking member of the Intelligence Committee, are now pressing for a full investigation into intelligence estimates of the Iraqi threat. This would entail public hearings with full disclosure of documents and guarantees of protection for witnesses who come forward to testify. But it is not likely to happen. Senator John Warner, the chairman of the Armed Services Committee, initially called for public hearings but recanted after Cheney visited a GOP senators' lunch on June 4. Cheney, according to Capitol Hill staffers, told his fellow Republicans to block any investigation, and it looks likely they will comply. Under pressure from Democrats, Roberts, the new Intelligence Committee chairman, has finally agreed to a closed-door hearing but not to a public or private investigation. According to Durbin, the Republican plan is to stall in the hope that the United States finds sufficient weapons of mass destruction in Iraq to quiet the controversy.

The controversy might, indeed, go away. Democrats don't have the power to call hearings, and, apart from Graham and former Vermont Governor Howard Dean, the leading Democratic presidential candidates are treating the issue delicately given the public's overwhelming support for the war. But there are worse things than losing an election by going too far out on a political limb—namely, failing to defend the integrity of the country's foreign policy and its democratic institutions. It may well be that, in the not-too-distant future, preemptive military action will become necessary—perhaps against a North Korea genuinely bent on incinerating Seoul or a nuclear Pakistan that has fallen into the hands of radical Islamists. In such a case, we the people will look to our leaders for an honest assessment of the threat. But, next time, thanks to George W. Bush, we may not believe them until it is too late.

Paul Wolfowitz at the Al Rasheed Hotel

from *The Nation* (11/17/03)

Calvin Trillin

He's been this war's great glorifier.
With Vietnam, he seemed much shyer:
He didn't think that war'd require
Himself. No grunt, his goals were higher.
The situation's getting dire:
A Sissy Hawk's been under fire.

Think Bush's Iraq adventure is a disaster? Richard Perle and David Frum are hoping that it's just a start.

War's Preachers

from TomPaine.com (1/13/04)

Robert Dreyfuss

In *An End to Evil,* Richard Perle and David Frum present us with a long To-Do List. And they seem like they're in a hurry.

Iraq, of course—in their view at least—has already been checked off. Still to come: It's time for the United States to "overthrow the terrorist mullahs of Iran"; force regime change in Syria by "interdict[ing]" Syria's arms supply, cutting off its oil supply, and conducting "hot pursuit" raids into its territory; launch a "comprehensive air and naval blockade of North Korea" and plan a "preemptive strike against North Korea's nuclear facilities"; and promote the dismantling of Saudi Arabia by supporting a breakway Shi'ite minority state in that country's eastern province, which just happens to be where the oil is.

And they don't stop there. It's also time to treat France as an "enemy," to divide Europe, to "squeeze" China, to pull out of the United Nations, and, of course, on every neocon's favorite wish list, crush once and for all the national aspirations of the Palestinians.

Wait, there's more: They also want to end "evil" at home, and they don't mean domestic terrorists—they mean the evils of the CIA, the State Department, the FBI, the military, and the U.S. government at large. All of it, say Perle and Frum, is hopelessly mired in Old-Think, and badly wants a makeover. In a kind of Neocon Eye for the Government Guy, Perle and Frum tell us how. The FBI? Junk it, they say, and reassign its counterterrorism units to a "new domestic intelligence agency" reporting to the Department of Homeland Security, with broad new powers (the Patriot Act was just a start), including power to hold noncitizen terrorist "suspects" without charges, so that the new agency can "squeeze information out of them," not prosecute them. The CIA? Fire CIA Director George Tenet—that's a no-brainer for neoconservatives—strip the agency down to its analysts, and put all CIA and military covert operations teams into a "single paramilitary structure . . . answerable to the secretary of defense" for "wars . . . that must be waged in the shadows." The State Department? Abolish the regional bureaus, especially Near Eastern Affairs (home of the dreaded "Arabists"), and fill the department with political appointees as officials and ambassadors who "will forcefully and unapologetically champion American policy abroad."

Whew.

They don't give us a timetable for all this, but—since they consider the reelection of President Bush as the *sine qua non* of a neoconservative foreign policy—it's fair to say that it's a rough outline of what they'd like Bush's second term to look like.

Who Is This Fab Duo?

Before elaborating, it's necessary to say a few words about the authors and the book itself. Perle and Frum are a kind of odd couple: Perle, a veteran of decades of political trench warfare, is the chief heir to Albert Wohlstetter, the godfather of the neocon defense strategists (he's married to Wohlstetter's daughter), making him a sort of an in-law Uday to Wohlstetter's Saddam. He's seen it all, knows where the bodies are buried, and his bulky frame exudes the sort of grizzled-veteran experience that comes with being a long-time Washington insider. Frum, on the other hand, is a boyish, baby-faced beginner, best known for a brief stint inside the Bush White House, where, as a speechwriter, he coined the phrase "axis of evil," and he's since settled in as a writer for *National Review.* He's Stan to Perle's Ollie.

An End to Evil is less a book, really, than a 285-page screed, a kind of stream-of-consciousness rant, *sans* index and footnotes, filled with smirky bon mots, score-settling gotchas and ponderous denunciations of enemies at home and abroad. It's the policy-book analog to the current wave of popular political books written by Ann

Coulter et al. on the right and Al Franken on the left: barb-studded, loaded with red meat and looking like it was written over a long weekend from some researcher's notes. (In Perle and Frum's case, one of their researchers was one Daniel Feith, presumably a scion of Perle's intimate friend Douglas Feith, the undersecretary of defense for policy.) I actually read the whole thing—and my copy is filled with asterisks, heavy underlinings and exclamation points in the margins. If my reaction to the book was mildly apoplectic, it's precisely the reaction the book is intended to elicit among left-wingers; among those on the right, it's meant to engender a collective "Hoo-ah!"

The Neocons' Last Gasp

But underneath it all is this: Perle and Frum are running scared. Despite their bravado, the Iraqi adventure is turning out to be an utter failure. Everything that Perle and Frum told us before the war turned out to be wrong. They said that Iraq was stuffed with weapons of mass destruction, that Saddam maintained close ties to Al Qaeda, that U.S. forces would be welcomed in Baghdad with open arms, that Ahmed Chalabi of the Iraqi National Congress would be a popular leader—that the invasion of Iraq would transform the Middle East. None of that turned out to be true. And even Perle's claim that Iraq is now better off because of the U.S. invasion isn't so obvious; should Iraq plummet into civil war, pitting Kurdish warlords against Sunni sheikhs and fundamentalist Shi'ite mullahs, Iraq will be far worse off than it was under Saddam.

Having been responsible for the mess in Iraq, you'd think Perle, Frum & Co. would be a little gun shy. But no. On the theory, perhaps, that the best defense is a good offense, they propose their headlong prescription for Two, Three, Many Iraqs. It's hard to avoid the conclusion that Perle, Frum and Co. are worried that America's appetite for a bullying foreign policy—and America's ability to stomach neoconservatism—may be wearing off.

Consider this: Perle has been laboring for years to win support for his version of a "muscular" foreign policy, to little avail. It's not only the left that has resisted him and his friends, it's the establishment—including the Council on Foreign Relations, the mainstream foreign policy thinktanks and, above all, the foreign affairs veterans at the State Department, the CIA and among the U.S. military. Indeed, Perle and Frum's plan to "radically reorganize" the U.S. national security bureaucracy is explicitly aimed at defanging the critics of the neocons inside the establishment. Perle and Frum themselves admit, in the book, that they and their friends are a "tiny minority" against the "enormous majority in government who wish to continue to do things as they have always done." Because they are a noisy but influential minority, Perle, Frum et al. are often unfairly characterized as conspiratorial, they write. "It's no wonder that those few policy makers who have urged a strong policy against terror have been called a 'cabal.'"

In the book, Perle and Frum are at pains to dispel the "myth of the neoconservative cabal." Indeed, cabal may not be the right word. I prefer fraternity. There's no doubt that Perle and his allies inside and outside of government are a closely knit band who share a history, a worldview and a web of thinktanks, associations and journals that bind them together. For decades, they've almost reveled in their outsider status, seeing themselves (not entirely incorrectly) as a League of Extraordinary Gentlemen whose ideas never quite captured the public imagination. In my reporting on the Iraq policy, however, over the past 15 months, it's become clear to me that the neocons believe that 9/11 changed all that, and that the shock and trauma of the 2001 attacks caused America, and President Bush, to yearn for exactly the kind of muscle-bound foreign policy bullying that the neoconservatives have called for all these years.

It was, at last, their moment in the sun.

Now their fear is that the moment is wearing off. The impact of 9/11 is slowly dissipating. America may be coming to its senses. In a moment of utter shock, America pushed the panic button, and called for a foreign policy directed by Clint Eastwood and starring Arnold Schwarzenegger. Now, we are all collectively coming out of the matinee, rubbing our eyes in the sunlight, and realizing that this is not a movie. This is real life. And—what?—the neocons are running things! All of a sudden, it seems more and more likely that Perle's "tiny minority" could get the collective boot. That's infinitely more likely should Iraq's tottering accomplishment collapse into chaos, and if public concern that President Bush lied about Iraq's threat to the United States—it's mythical ties to terrorism and WMD—becomes a major political issue in 2004.

Playing The Anti-Semite Card

In desperate moments, people lash out. Perhaps the clearest sign of Perle and Frum's desperation is their shameless effort to preempt their opponents' attacks by claiming that anyone who criticizes them is an anti-Semite. In disparaging the "myth of the neoconservative cabal," Perle and Frum say that "the neoconservative myth offers Europeans and liberals a useful euphemism for expressing their hostility to Israel." It's a standard refrain for defenders of Israel's own excesses: if you dare to criticize Ariel Sharon's thuggish policy toward the occupied territories, the expansionist settler movement, the building of The Wall, etc., then you are *prima facie* anti-Semitic. In similar fashion, if you disagree with the Perle-Frum vision of an endless war on terror and preemptive regime-change wars, and if you excoriate the relatively small group of neocon partisans who advocate that policy, you hate Jews. (David Brooks, writing in *The New York Times* recently, went so far as to say that when critics use the word neocons, "neo" means Jewish!) Journalists around the world, Perle and Frum say, constantly ask them: "Is the war on terror a Zionist plot?" Well, no, it's not. But neither are Perle's critics anti-Semites.

Still, in gatherings at neocon thinktanks and in conversations with leading neoconservative strategists, it's common to hear it said, half-humorously, that not all neocons are Jewish, a fact that Newt Gingrich, Jim Woolsey and Jeanne Kirkpatrick can attest to. Why so many neoconservatives are Jewish, however, is a fascinating topic for another article. The answer involves history, culture, politics and religion in equal measure. But in any case, though it is obvious that there is no justification for Perle and Frum to try to tar their critics (the vast majority of them, anyway) as anti-Semites, they do it anyway. Perhaps their fear is that, as neoconservatives, they have no real political constituency in the population at large: not among liberals, not among conservatives (some of whom are, in fact, anti-Semitic), and not even among Jews, among whom they are a small minority. In fact, few Jews are neocons, and most Jews vote Democratic.

In the end, Perle and Frum make the breathtaking argument that they are fighting for civilization itself, even if civilization doesn't appreciate it. "We are fighting on behalf of the civilized world," they write. "We will never cease to hope for the civilized world's support." Well. The civilized world may not be listening to Perle and Frum. The problem is, President Bush is.

He Said It . . .

"If we let our vision of the world go forth and don't try to piece together clever diplomacy, but wage total war . . . our children will sing great songs about us."

—Richard Perle

ANAGRAM

The Republicans

Plan butcheries?

This piece, a recap of our Iraq policy during 2003, offers background for anyone who wonders what went wrong in Iraq in 2004.

The Imperial Gong Show Year

from Tomdispatch.com (1/2/04)

Tom Engelhardt

I haven't checked my Chinese calendar but if 2003 wasn't the Year of the Rat, I don't know what it was. We would normally heave a collective sigh of relief to have left it even a day or two behind us—if 2004 didn't lie ahead. Still, if the year was bad for the rest of us, it wasn't exactly dazzling for the Bush administration either and perhaps we should count a few modest post-New Year's blessings for that at least.

2002 should certainly have been dubbed the Year of the New Rome, the year neocon pundits (and a few liberal commentators as well) proudly urged us to shoulder our new imperial burden and emulate the Romans, or at least the 19th century Brits, forever and a day. If so, then 2003 was the year in which our homegrown imperialists fell silent on the subject of empire, while our legions, setting out to remake the Middle East and then the world, fell into the nearest nation-building ditch.

In the spring of 2003, after a series of global skirmishes with enemies of some significance—France, Germany, Russia, and that "other superpower," the protesting peoples of the world—the Bush administration launched its long-desired, long prepared for war against an enemy of no consequence. "Mission accomplished."

But when we sent our first proconsul out to rule the newest part of our Middle Eastern Imperium of Freedom, he came back quicker than you can say "Jay Garner." The second team was off the bench in no time and Coach Bush (having fronted for a second-rate baseball team earlier in his remarkably empty career) promptly rushed them onto the field, led by the well-appointed, well-booted L. Paul Bremer. Having left a cushy "risk management" company stateside to risk manage what was tagged as the future capital of Middle Eastern oil, he arrived in Baghdad speaking, like George himself, in the imperative. (Have we ever, by the way, had a president who told so many people in so many places so publicly what they "must" do?) Bursting with energy, Bremer dismissed the Iraqi army and the Baathist bureaucracy only to find—no Lawrence of Arabia he—that he couldn't even get a phone line to Sadr City, no less a government into Baghdad or an army of useful natives into the field.

The latest Baghdad joke, according to Herbert Docena, reporting from that city for the *Asia Times* on-line, is: How many American troops does it take to screw in a light bulb? "About 130,000 so far, but don't hold your breath." And sadly, that's not really a joke. Feeling his oats, Bremer promptly announced the dismemberment of the last thing at hand—what was left of the devastated Iraqi economy. Every strip-mining plan ever imagined by some right-wing Washington think-tank was promptly hauled out and dumped on a prostrate and largely unemployed Iraqi populace. And so Iraq was "opened" for business—without a government and with a foreign army in place—the way you might slit open a still breathing animal.

As it turned out, however, there were other "risk

managers" around ready to play quite a different, if no less chancy game—and they turned out to be brutally good at it. After all, eight months and a right turn past victory later, and Baghdad International Airport is still not open to commercial traffic, thanks to those pesky shoulder-fired missiles that seem to litter Iraq and the shoulders to hoist them on. So while, from London to Maine, corporate privatizers can hold conferences galore on the country's new economy, about all that will get them into deepest (and part of the time quite literally) darkest imperial Baghdad is a dangerous drive overland, some body armor, and private guards.

Recently, even our proconsul narrowly escaped a roadside ambush near the capital. (Hint: the new police force, the new military, and the new Iraqi intelligence service we seem to be reconstituting from retread Saddamites are obviously riddled with people feeding information to the armed opposition.) So L. Paul now finds himself ensconced behind concertina wire, inside Baghdad's ecologically unfriendly Green Zone, backing down on various proposals and swatting off obdurate Shiite clerics calling for democratic elections, while wondering what hit him and where in the world he'll ever find a "sovereign" government to which to turn over some shred of power next June. So it goes in our unexpected world.

THE EMPIRE STRIKES OUT

2002 was the year of the Nuclear Posture Review, the National Security Strategy, the Axis of Evil, and the Bush Doctrine. It was the year when, as the Greta Garbo of hyperpowers, we declared our desire to be alone at the top; practically shouted out our plans to dominate the planet militarily to the end of time; publicized our desire to conquer the heavens with previously forbidden weaponry straight out of Flash Gordon; swore our fealty to the nuclear option till the (mad) cows come home (as they just have); insisted in the name of national security on the rejection, ripping up, or even unsigning of every protective, multilateral treaty or measure devised by the human mind in recent decades to keep our proliferating, global warming world somewhere on this side of the law; and insisted that "regime change" was in order—and that we would carry it out everywhere but in the United States. 2003 then might be considered the year when the planet proved its bedrock, cranky, anti-imperial recalcitrance.

So, with a nod to the neocons, here, retooled from the 1960s, is my adage for the New Year and beyond (and I'm willing to loan it out to anyone in Washington who finds it useful): Beware of domino theories. They tend to rear up and bite you in the butt.

In the 1960s, if we didn't defend any small piece of global turf against nationalist and communist insurgencies, our leaders swore that its loss would be but the first toppling domino—as with South Vietnam—starting a cascade that would sweep the nations of the world into the communist camp. It's perhaps symbolic of our unipolar world that our new imperialists imagined a far more "proactive" set of dominoes—not ones they would have to defend from toppling, but ones they would shove over themselves.

Their war in Iraq was to be just the first push in a domino cascade that would reorder the planet into a Pax Americana. Hostile Syrian and Iranian regimes, sideswiped by a collapsing Iraqi domino, would go down; so would the supposedly friendly Saudi one; the Palestinians, helpless and alone, would be the next to follow, making a peace of the defeated with neocon darling Ariel Sharon; even Kim Jong-il, the "dear leader" of North Korea, halfway across the planet would be crushed beneath a pile of American dominoes, and while we were at it, the French, Germans, and Russians would go down too, though peaceably, leaving the superpower contender of the future, China, in a thoroughly exposed and indefensible position.

Of course, none of this happened. It seems years ago, though it was only months back that Syria, Iran and North Korea were in our gun sights (with Cuba, Libya and the Sudan not far behind). Only last June, the United States was threatening to become the national equivalent of a serial killer.

And yet, by year's end, the road to Damascus was closed; the President was welcoming Libyan strongman Qaddafi (the Saddam Hussein of the Age of Reagan) back into the comity of nations; U.S. aid was being readied for and sanctions temporarily lifted on an Iran suffering unparalleled devastation from a natural catastrophe (and American officials were even muttering about a new era in relations); something approaching actual negotiation with North Korea was being carried out through the Chinese government; and administration officials along with Bremer were searching madly for "withdrawal" formulas in Iraq (even if they were meant to leave our troops, Halliburton, and Bechtel there for an eternity). Meanwhile, in Washington, the neocons, jobs at risk, were threatening war and crying foul (or is it fowl?) as their global war-fighting plans were sent back to the think-tanks—at least for now—and the multilateralists of Father Bush's administration were slipping back into positions of authority.

In 2002, thanks largely to Osama bin Laden, the Bush administration was flying higher than a cruise missile. By year's end 2003, the only hawk still openly talking the talk of empire was the Vice-President, who included the following quotation from Benjamin Franklin in his Christmas card: "And if a sparrow cannot fall to the ground without His notice, is it probable that an empire can rise without His aid?" In short, by the end of 2003, despite a brief Alka-Seltzer moment of relief with the capture of Saddam Hussein (but not, of course, Osama bin Laden), something was wobbling in the House of Bush.

In instant retrospect, 2003 already looks like a Gong Show year for the American Empire. Put another way, when early in the year the administration reached into its mighty imperial arsenal, all it pulled out was brute force applied brutally in a three-week shock-and-awe campaign against Saddam Hussein's pathetic military (and then reapplied with counterproductive ineffectiveness ever since). No one can deny that empires work on a principle of brute force. It's a necessity if you plan to conquer others and rule them against their wishes, but it can't be the only arrow in your quiver. A little finesse is usually necessary, if you plan to stick around for a while. Some plums need to be offered, at least to some of the conquered and those from elsewhere who fight in your legions. There has to be some way to join the empire as a junior partner and benefit somehow. None of this was available in the Bush version of shouldering the imperial burden.

To the extent that we proved imperial in 2003, it was largely in the Pentagon's long-term planning for weapons systems, large and small, slated to dominate the planet for the next half-century or more. Can there be any doubt that we already have the weaponry of 40 Roman empires and 20 British ones with more to come? After all, we even have futuristic weapons on the drawing boards for 2050.

But here's a lesson for the year (also retooled from the 1960s): You can't rule this bedeviling planet with weapons systems based in the United States, or on offshore aircraft carriers, or even on military bases dotted across the globe, no less via a series of delivery vehicles from outer space. The resistance in Iraq has made this point staggeringly clear: We smote—and given our fundamentalist administration that word is surely on target—Saddam Hussein's regime with our techno-best and from its ruins arose an armed opposition centered in but not limited to Sunni Iraq. 5,000 armed men, if you believe the Pentagon, up to 50,000 if you believe a recent CIA report; all Baathist "bitter-enders" and al Qaeda warriors from elsewhere, if you believe Don Rumsfeld or the President; up to 23 different mostly home-grown resistance groups if you believe various foreign journalists. But the most curious thing is that no one in Washington or among our military and civil administrators in Baghdad quite knows who the armed opposition actually is and they tend to identify themselves mainly through roadside bombs and suicide bombers.

This is either some kind of bleak miracle, or an illusionist's trick. After all, it took years in Vietnam against a powerful southern insurgency backed by the militarily strong and determined North Vietnamese regime backed in turn by the Earth's other superpower, the USSR, and for good measure by Mao's China with which it shared a border, with copious supplies flowing in from abroad and sanctuary areas in bordering Cambodia and Laos, before a desperate American president even began considering calling up the reserves. In Iraq, against relatively lightly armed, no-name insurgent forces of a few thousand or tens of thousands, without a significant power behind them, without sanctuaries, or major supply channels (other than the copious arms already cached in the country), with largely homemade bombs and small numbers of fanatical individuals willing to turn themselves into suicide weapons, the mightiest military power on earth has already been stretched to the breaking point. Its leaders, scouring the planet for new recruits, are having trouble finding enough troops to garrison an easily conquered, weak, and devastated country.

The foreign legions they've managed to dig up—a few thousand Spaniards and Poles, hundreds of Bulgarians and Thais, handfuls of Mongolians, Hondurans, and the like—add up modestly indeed, when you consider who's asking for a hand. And even our own version of the Gurkhas, the British who, thanks to Tony Blair, have shipped out sizeable numbers of troops to garrison the—at present—more peaceable Shiite southern regions of the country, turn out to be doing their much needed work for sixpence and a song. Their cut of the Iraqi pie looks beyond modest. Like a child with a roomful of toys, all the Bush administration knows how to say is: "Mine."

A Global Enron Moment

In a sense, our new Rome already lies in ruins without even an enemy fit to name to oppose us. And the true face of our home-grown regime in Washington is ever more visible.

The visages on display aren't those of an emperor and his administrators, proconsuls and generals, but of so many dismantlers, strip-miners, and plunderers; less Augustus, more Jesse James (the real one, not the movie hero).

They may be building weapons for 2050, but they're plundering in Iraq and at home as if January 1, 2004 were the beginning of the end of time. Having ushered into office the Halliburton (vice-)presidency, we now have a fitting "empire" to go with it. While empires must to some extent spread the wealth around, our proto-imperialists turn out to have the greed level and satiation point of so many malign children. Other than "must" and "mine," the words they—and their corporate companions—know best, it seems, are "now," "all" and "alone." It's a vocabulary that doesn't contain a future in it, not the sort of vocabulary with which to rule the world.

No matter how many times we insist that all we carry in our baggage train is "freedom" and "democracy" for the oppressed nations of the Earth, those elsewhere can see perfectly well that our saddlebags are full of grappling hooks and meat cleavers. Bad as 2003 was for us, it may not be long before it's looked upon as their global Enron Moment.

2003 was the year our emperor's men decided to use up as much as they could as fast as they could, though thanks to our underachieving media, this can hardly be grasped here. The sad thing is that they are dismantling us and what matters most to us in our country, including our liberties—and all under the deceptive name of "national security." They have an unerring eye for the weak and vulnerable and, on spotting them, set upon them like so many highwaymen.

Unfortunately, as representatives of insecurity rather than security, they have let loose forces for which they feel no responsibility. We are a nation of adults, living largely in denial, led by overgrown, malign children excited by the thought of sending other people's actual children, a whole well-led army of them, including the older "weekend warriors" of the reserves and the National Guard, off to do the impossible as well as the unjust. And this is happening in part because—I believe—they don't imagine war as carnage, but are energized by an especially shallow idea of war's "glory," just as the President has been thoroughly energized by the ludicrous idea that his is a "war presidency."

The term "chickenhawks," often used by critics, hardly catches this. It's true that Bush's first moments after the September 11 attacks—now buried by media and memory—were ones of flight, and so, undoubtedly, of shame and humiliation (which helps account for at least some of the exaggerated macho posturing—"bring 'em on"—that followed). Instead of stepping forward to lead a shocked nation in crisis by heading for Washington, he was shunted from a children's classroom in Florida westward to safety.

What "chickenhawks" doesn't catch, however, is both the immature mock solemnity and the fun of war play for them, something they first absorbed in their childhoods on screen and carry with them still. War for them—as they avoided anything having to do with either the Vietnam War or opposition to it—remains, I believe, a matter of toy soldiers, cowboys-and-Indians games, and glorious John Wayne-style movies in which the Marines advance, while the ambushing enemy falls before them and the Marine hymn wells up as The End flashes on screen.

In a similar way, the neocon utopians who dreamed up our distinctly unpeaceful Pax Americana in deepest, darkest Washington and out of whole cloth seem to have imagined global military domination as something akin to the board game Risk. They too were, after a fashion, Risk managers, seeing themselves rolling the dice for little weapons icons (most of which they controlled), oil-well icons (which they wanted) and strategic-country icons (which they needed). They were consummate game players. It just so happens our planet isn't a two-dimensional gameboard, but a confusing, bloody, resistant, complex place that exists in at least three dimensions, all unexpected.

I mean if you think I'm kidding—about children playing games—just remember that we have a President who, according to the *Washington Post*'s Bob Woodward, keeps a "scorecard" in his desk drawer with the names/faces and personality sketches of al Qaeda adversaries (and assumedly Saddam) and then X's them out as they're brought in "dead or alive." Think tic-tac-toe here.

The president and his men, in short, have been living in a fantasy world that makes *The Lord of the Rings* look like an exercise in reality. Even before the Iraq war, this was worrisome to the adults who had to deal with them. This is why there was so much opposition within the top ranks of the military before the war; this was why there was no Pentagon planning whatsoever for the post-war moment (hey, you've just won the Iraq card in your game, now you fortify and move on); this was why, for instance, General Anthony Zinni, Vietnam veteran and former CentCom commander, who endorsed young George in the 2000 race, went into opposition to the administration; this is why a seething "intelligence community" has been in near revolt after watching our fantasists rejigger "intelligence" to make their "turn" come out right; this is why our great "adventure" in the Middle East pitched over into the nearest ditch.

2004 should be a fierce holding action for them. The question is—as with Richard Nixon in 1972—can they make it through to November before the seams start to tear. They might be able to. But here's the thing: Sooner or later, the children will leave the stage and some set of adults will have to start picking up the pieces. If the 2004 election is theirs, however . . . well, some things, our planet included, can get too broken to fix.

He Said It . . .

"Support for Saddam, including within his military organization, will collapse at the first whiff of gunpowder."

—Richard Perle, 2002

DO CHENEY, PERLE AND WOLFOWITZ—THE CHICKEN HAWKS WHO DREAMT UP THIS WAR—REGRET ONCE AVOIDING THE DRAFT? GOSH, NO!
7-31
DOES BUSH REGRET SKIPPING HIS LAST YEAR OF NATIONAL GUARD DUTY? MY GOODNESS, NOT AT ALL!
DO I WISH I COULD SKIP THE LAST YEAR OF MY GUARD DUTY SO I COULD GO HOME? JEEPERS, YES!
www.doonesbury.com
PERMISSION TO KEEP THIS UP DENIED.
SHOULD YOU STUFF IT? GOSH YES!

Quiz

Paul Slansky

Who is John Brady Kiesling?

(a) The Christian conservative who withdrew his nomination to Bush's Advisory Council on H.I.V. and AIDS after it became known that he referred to AIDS as "the gay plague."
(b) The commentator who said, referring to Bush's plan to eliminate taxes on stock dividends, "This isn't even trickle-down economics. It's mist-down economics."
(c) The State Department diplomat whose resignation letter said, "Until this administration it had been possible to believe that by upholding the policies of my president I was also upholding the interests of the American people and the world. I believe it no longer."
(d) The White House aide, known for his calm disposition, about whom Karl Rove said, "I'd use the word 'sweet' if it didn't make me look odd."

Answer: (c)

Halliburton isn't the only big company making a bundle on Iraq.

Making Money on Terrorism

from *The Nation* (2/23/04)

William D. Hartung

We all know that Halliburton is raking in billions from the Bush Administration's occupation and rebuilding of Iraq. But in the long run, the biggest beneficiaries of the Administration's "war on terror" may be the "destroyers," not the rebuilders. The nation's "Big Three" weapons makers—Lockheed Martin, Boeing and Northrop Grumman—are cashing in on the Bush policies of regime change abroad and surveillance at home. *New York Times* columnist Paul Krugman was on target when he suggested that rather than "leave no child behind," the slogan Bush stole from the Children's Defense Fund, his Administration's true motto appears to be "leave no defense contractor behind."

In fiscal year 2002, the Big Three received a total of more than $42 billion in Pentagon contracts, of which Lockheed Martin got $17 billion, Boeing $16.6 billion and Northrop Grumman $8.7 billion. This is an increase of nearly one-third from 2000, Clinton's final year. These firms get one out of every four dollars the Pentagon doles out for everything from rifles to rockets. In contrast, Bush's No Child Left Behind Act is underfunded by $8 billion a year, with the additional assistance promised to school districts swallowed up by war costs and tax cuts.

The bread and butter for the Big Three are weapons systems like the F-35 Joint Strike Fighter (Lockheed Martin), the F/A-18 E/F combat aircraft (Boeing/Northrop Grumman), the F-22 Raptor (Lockheed Martin/Boeing) and the C-17 transport aircraft (Boeing). Northrop Grumman is also a major player in the area of combat ships, through its ownership of the Newport News, Virginia and Pascagoula, Mississippi, shipyards. All three firms are also well placed in the design and production of targeting devices, electronic warfare equipment, long-range strike systems and precision munitions. For example, Boeing makes the Joint Direct Attack Munition (JDAM), a kit that can be used to make "dumb" bombs "smart." The JDAM was used in such large quantities in the wars in Iraq and Afghanistan that the company has had to run double shifts to keep up with Air Force demand.

The Bush nuclear buildup—large parts of which are funded out of the Energy Department budget, not the Pentagon—is particularly good news for Lockheed Martin. The company has a $2 billion-a-year contract to run Sandia National Laboratories, a nuclear weapons design and engineering facility based in Albuquerque. Lockheed Martin also works in partnership with Bechtel to run the Nevada Test Site, where new nuclear weapons are tested either via underground explosions—currently on hold due to US adherence to a moratorium on nuclear testing—or computer simulations. Late last year, Congress lifted a longstanding ban on research into so-called "mini-nukes"—nuclear weapons of less than five kilotons, about one-third the size of the Hiroshima bomb. It also authorized funds for studies on a nuclear "bunker buster" and seed money for a multibillion-dollar factory to build plutonium triggers for a new generation of nuclear weapons. These new investments will be presided over by Everet Beckner, a former Lockheed Martin executive who now heads the National Nuclear Security Administration's nuclear weapons complex.

The Big Three are also poised to profit from President Bush's plan to colonize the moon and send a manned mission to Mars, both of which are stalking horses for launching an arms race in space. Boeing and Lockheed Martin were already well positioned in the military-space field through major contracts in space launch, satellite and missile defense work, plus a partnership to run the United Space Alliance, the joint venture in charge of launches of the space shuttle. Northrop Grumman bought into the field through its acquisition of TRW, a major space and Star Wars contractor. The new presidential commission charged with fleshing out Bush's space vision is being chaired by Edward "Pete" Aldridge, the Pentagon's former Under Secretary of Defense for Acquisition and a current member of Lockheed Martin's board of directors. Meanwhile, over at the Air Force, the under secretary in charge of acquiring space assets is Peter Teets, a former chief operating officer at Lockheed Martin. His position was created in accordance with the recommendations of the Commission to Assess US National Security Space Management and Organization, an advisory panel that published its blueprint for the militarization of space just as Bush was taking office. The group, which included representatives of eight Pentagon contractors, was presided over by Donald Rumsfeld until he left to take up his current post as Bush's Defense Secretary. Rumsfeld has been dutifully implementing the commission's recommendations ever since.

The Big Three are also wired into numerous other sources of federal contracts for everything from airport security to domestic surveillance, all in the name of fighting what the White House now calls the GWOT (Global War on Terrorism). The $20 billion-plus total that Lockheed Martin receives annually is more than is spent in an average year on the largest federal welfare program, Temporary Assistance for Needy Families, a program that is meant to provide income support to several million women and children living below the poverty line. Under Bush and company, corporate welfare trumps human well-being every time.

One would think that with the military budget at $400 billion and counting—up from $300 billion when Bush took office—all would be well in the land of the military-industrial behemoths, especially since the Pentagon budget is only one opportunity among many. (The budget of the Department of Homeland Security is $40 billion and counting, and the wars in Afghanistan and Iraq have racked up $200 billion in emergency spending to date, over and above normal Pentagon appropriations.) Yet in my discussions with industry representatives at the June 2003 Paris Air Show as well as in their recent behavior, I have detected an unmistakable sense of desperation, a sense that even this embarrassment of riches may not be enough to stabilize these massive companies.

On the desperation front, Boeing is head and shoulders above its rivals. After losing the highly touted "deal of the century"—the $300 billion F-35 Joint Strike Fighter program—to its rival Lockheed Martin in 2001, the company took a huge hit to its commercial-airliner business when air travel plummeted in the wake of the September 11 attacks. A bailout was in order, and the company pulled out all the stops to create one in the form of a deal that would have required the Air Force to lease 100 Boeing 767s for use as aerial refueling tankers. As initially crafted, the deal would have cost $26 billion over a decade, $5 billion more than it would have cost to buy the planes outright. Behind it was a group that included Senator Ted Stevens, who used his clout as chair of the Senate Appropriations Committee to insert an amendment into the Pentagon's budget specifically requiring the lease arrangement; Secretary of the Air Force James Roche, a former VP at Boeing's sometime partner Northrop Grumman; Boeing senior vice president of Washington operations Rudy deLeon, a former top official in Bill Clinton's Pentagon; and House Speaker Dennis Hastert. Like most pork-barrel projects, the deal was a mix of strategic thinking and self-interest. Roche made no bones about the fact that part of the point was to throw some money Boeing's way so that it would remain healthy. What you and I might call a "bailout," folks in the Pentagon call "maintaining the defense industrial base."

Boeing used every possible lever to get the deal done. It hosted a fundraiser in Seattle for Stevens at which Boeing executives threw $22,000 into his campaign coffers. It enlisted Hastert, who had wooed the company to move its headquarters to his home state of Illinois, to weigh in directly with President Bush. Representative Todd Tiahrt, whose Wichita district includes the Boeing plant that would retrofit the 767s for use as tankers, raised the issue so often with Bush that the President nicknamed him "Tanker Tiahrt." Members from Washington State, home of Boeing's main production complex, also lobbied vigorously. Defense Policy Board member and Rumsfeld pal Richard Perle wrote an op-ed in favor of the deal for the

Wall Street Journal—but only after Boeing had invested $20 million in Trireme, a Perle investment firm. Boeing sponsored the 2001 annual dinner of the Jewish Institute for National Security Affairs, a neocon redoubt with which Under Secretary of Defense Douglas Feith was closely associated before joining the Administration. The honorees were the secretaries of the three military services: The Air Force's Roche, Navy Secretary Gordon England (formerly of General Dynamics) and Army Secretary Thomas White (formerly of Enron). The host for the evening was Boeing Washington office head Rudy deLeon.

For once all this influence-peddling may go for naught. The deal is on hold thanks to relentless questioning by Senator John McCain, who has denounced it from the beginning as "war profiteering," and persistent public pressure by good-government groups. The last straw was the revelation that Boeing offered Air Force acquisition official Darleen Druyun a job while she was negotiating the lease deal with the company.

Boeing isn't the only corrupt weapons company; it's just the one that was too desperate for a short-term payoff to cover its tracks. Rumsfeld's preference for industry executives and ideologues of the Perle/Feith variety has created an ethically challenged, politically tone-deaf environment that needs to be opened up to public scrutiny and reform. Some steps are under way. The Pentagon's Inspector General is investigating all Boeing contracts that Druyun was involved in. The Senate Armed Services Committee will hold hearings on the Boeing deal, and McCain has promised hearings on the Pentagon-industry "revolving door."

Much more needs to be done. At the height of World War II, Senator Harry Truman made a name for himself by uncovering profiteering and fraud at companies providing supplies for the war effort. Given the high political and economic stakes in the war on terror, a comparable investigation is in order now. Whether the work is being done in Iraq, Washington or points in between, contracts involving US national security should be opened to true competitive bidding. Profits should be limited, and the books of contractors doing the public's business should be open and available for inspection. Politicians and bureaucrats who are lining their pockets under the guise of fighting terrorism should face criminal penalties, not symbolic fines. The public should demand that all candidates for the presidency and Congress renounce campaign contributions from companies involved in the rebuilding of Iraq, the war in Afghanistan or any of the other far-flung outposts of Bush's war on terrorism.

The culture of cronyism that allows arms-industry executives to pull down multimillion-dollar compensation packages while wounded veterans are shunted into makeshift medical wards has to end. Getting rid of George W. Bush and his gang of neocon profiteers is an excellent place to start. But it's only a start.

DONALD RUMSFELD

with quotes by Donald Rumsfeld;
quizzes by Paul Slansky;
and anagrams

Legend has it that Henry Kissinger—himself no powder-puff—once described Donald Rumsfeld as the most ruthless man he ever met. Rummy served in Congress during the '60s, then worked for the Nixon and Ford administrations. He served as a CEO in the pharmaceutical and technology industries and (often at the same time) held a variety of government posts. He urged the Reagan administration to support Iraq and Saddam Hussein. As GWB's secretary of defense, he helped convince the public that Iraq was a threat to the United States, and has presided over the invasion of Iraq and the chaos that ensued. He also has overseen the capture of his old acquaintance, Saddam Hussein, and proposals for cutbacks in combat troop compensation, and the abuse of Iraqi prisoners.

Donald Rumsfeld

from deal-with-it.org

Gus DiZerega

Donald Rumsfeld has trouble speaking clearly and truthfully to the American people. Until you understand this fact, you will not be able to follow what is happening under his authority as Secretary of Defense.

On May 14, 2003, at a hearing of the Senate's appropriations subcommittee on defense, Rumsfeld said: "I don't believe anyone that I know in the administration ever said that Iraq had nuclear weapons." [1]

Let's see. To paraphrase Bill Clinton, a lot hinges on what "said" means.

George W. Bush informed us in October 2002: "The evidence indicates that Iraq is reconstituting its nuclear weapons program. Saddam Hussein has held numerous meetings with Iraqi nuclear scientists, a group he calls his 'nuclear mujahideen'. . . . his nuclear holy warriors . . . Facing clear evidence of peril, we cannot wait for the final proof. . . . the smoking gun. . . . that could come in the form of a mushroom cloud."

Condoleezza Rice told us: "The problem here is that there will always be some uncertainty about how quickly he can acquire nuclear weapons, but we don't want the smoking gun to be a mushroom cloud." [2]

Indeed, it sounds as if Bush and Rice rehearsed their answers—to scare us all with the threat of an Iraqi nuclear attack. Did they say Iraq had nuclear weapons? Not quite.

1. See: http://slate.msn.com/id/2083532/
2. See: http://www.cbc.ca/news/features/iraq/quotes.html

They said if we didn't go in, we would find out very possibly through a "mushroom cloud." Weasel words at best, with the clear intent to make us think Iraq very likely had nuclear weapons.

Rumsfeld's lies about what Bush and Rice said are not isolated examples. Consider Rumsfeld's claims about Iraq's weapons of mass destruction.

- "We know where they are. They're in the area around Tikrit and Baghdad and east, west, south and north somewhat."—ABC interview, March 30, 2003. [3]

- "I never believed that we'd just tumble over weapons of mass destruction in that country." Fox News interview, May 4, 2003. [4]

- "They may have had time to destroy them, and I don't know the answer." May 27, 2003 remarks at Council on Foreign Relations.

The most charitable interpretation possible is that Rumsfeld is not uncomfortable claiming far more knowledge than he really has. Given the importance of the issues at hand, this is as morally reprehensible as the most bald-faced lie. Certainly these quotations would be cited as evidence of lying if Bill Clinton had said them. Let's apply the same standards to the Radical Right.

3. See: http://www.dod.gov/news/Mar2003/t03302003_t0330sdabsteph.html
4. See: http://www.dod.gov/transcripts/2003/tr20030504-secdef0153.html

But there is, alas, more. For example, *Slate's* Whopper of the Week reported:

> Q: Secretary Rumsfeld, when did you know that the reports about [Iraq seeking] uranium coming out of Africa were bogus?
>
> A: Oh, within recent days, since the information started becoming available.
>
> *—Defense Secretary Donald Rumsfeld, answering a question posed by Sen. Mark Pryor, D.-Ark., at a hearing of the Senate Armed Services committee, July 10, 2003*

But Dr. Mohamed ElBaradei, director of the International Atomic Energy Agency, on March 7, 2003, said this:

> The [International Atomic Energy Agency] has made progress in its investigation into reports that Iraq sought to buy uranium from Niger in recent years. . . . The IAEA was . . . able to review correspondence coming from various bodies of the Government of Niger, and to compare the form, format, contents and signatures of that correspondence with those of the alleged procurement-related documentation.
>
> Based on thorough analysis, the IAEA has concluded, with the concurrence of outside experts, that these documents—which formed the basis for the reports of recent uranium transactions between Iraq and Niger—are in fact not authentic. We have

> therefore concluded that these specific allegations are unfounded.

His statement was reported the next day in the *Washington Post.* [5]

MILITARY INCOMPETENCE

History is littered with examples of successful military attacks ruined by failure to follow through. Future historians may add Rumsfeld's Iraq strategy to the list. Given our overwhelming military superiority over Iraq, Rumsfeld thought we could wage war on the cheap. But destroying opponents is only the first half of the task. The second is the follow through.

Rumsfeld chose to ignore the advice of American generals with experience in military affairs, preferring the fantasies of Paul Wolfowitz and other self-declared experts with no military experience or specialized knowledge of the Middle East. That is why he chose to invade and occupy Iraq with a remarkably small military force. Apparently knowing nothing about military occupations, and confident in his own infallibility, Rumsfeld did not plan for unpleasant contingencies. He placed thousands of American and Iraqi lives hostage to his pet theories.

The result? On Sept. 5, 2003, the *New York Times* wrote:

> An official from the United States Central Command, speaking on condition of anonymity, acknowledged today that the American-led military

5. See: http://slate.msn.com/id/2085434/
For another Rumsfeld lie, see http://slate.msn.com/id/2064740/

operation in Iraq did not have enough troops to heavily guard all 2,700 Iraqi munitions sites that have been identified.

Rumsfeld's theories were wrong.

Rumsfeld and his allies are now claiming that no one could know the outcome of such a risky venture as a war. Yet before the war the following respected organizations predicted trouble and argued for better planning:

- U.S. Army War College
- Center for Strategic and International Studies
- Council on Foreign Relations and the James A. Baker Institute for Public Policy

Rumsfeld and his allies chose not to listen. Despite an almost complete absence of military experience, they imagined their pet theories were far wiser than the experience and knowledge of countless generals, intelligence officials, and other experts on the Middle East and war. Here is the conclusion to the U. S. Army's War College report: "Without an overwhelming effort to prepare for occupation, the United States may find itself in a radically different world over the next few years, a world in which the threat of Saddam Hussein seems like a pale shadow of new problems of America's own making."

The man doesn't learn from experience. Baghdad four months after the US invasion was very far indeed from being back to normal. But this contradicts the fantasy Rumsfeld and his Neoconservative buddies sold to the American people: that the war would be cheap, short, and we would soon exit, leaving a viable democracy behind.

Since the facts on the ground do not support the prewar spin, Rumsfeld has taken a page from his Commander in Chief, and lied.

Consider the following on crime rates in occupied Iraq:

- "You've got to remember that if Washington, D.C., were the size of Baghdad, we would be having something like 215 murders a month."—Donald Rumsfeld, 6/19/2003

- "The Baghdad police don't have official crime statistics, but the number of bodies at the city's morgue says it all. Baghdad is in the midst of an unprecedented crime wave. The city morgue handled 470 gunshot deaths in July."—Associated Press, 8/11/2003

By Rumsfeld's own statistics, Baghdad's administration is a failure. But he won't admit it.

More incompetence

Rumsfeld's apparent inability to think about complex things in context—an absolutely vital ability for anyone responsible for our nation's defense—is sadly demonstrated in Afghanistan, as well.

There, again, Rumsfeld opposed putting adequate troops on the ground to truly pacify the country and make rebuilding possible. It is hardly controversial to observe that postwar rebuilding depends on security. It also requires the early encouragement of labor-intensive projects improving transportation and communication. This helps the country and put wages into the pockets of those who need them. Isabel Hilton writes in *The Guardian*, "But this has not been applied in Afghanistan. Security never came because, when the Taliban fell, the US would not agree to the deployment of the International Security Assistance Force (ISAF) outside Kabul. Why? Because the US defence secretary, Donald Rumsfeld, was already planning the invasion of Iraq and did not want men tied down in peacekeeping." [6]

Worse, Rumsfeld actively strengthened the warlords who are now undermining what little stability the average Afghan might have gained from the end of the Taliban. Human Rights Watch reported that "In most parts of the country, security and local governance has been entrusted to regional military commanders—warlords—many of whom have human rights records rivaling the worst commanders under the Taliban. . . . American military forces have maintained relationships with local warlords that undercut efforts by U.S. diplomats and aid agencies to strengthen central authority and the rule of law."

For example, with backing from the US, Ismail Khan seized Western Afghanistan and the city of Heart. He rules through torture, beatings, intimidation, and a ruthless police, with women and girls continuing "to suffer extreme forms of discrimination, including many Taliban era practices that are now being revived." Donald Rumsfeld described Ismail Khan as "an appealing person. . . . He's thoughtful, measured and self-confident." [7]

The Pentagon prefers to pay the warlords to run the

6. See: http://www.guardian.co.uk/afghanistan/comment/story/0,11447,1009459,00.html
7. See: http://www.alternet.org/story.html?StoryID=14552

country outside Kabul, dressing up the exercise with a loya jirga in which 80% of those "elected" were warlords. Washington sources report that when Karzai appealed to Rumsfeld for support to confront one of the most notorious warlords, Rumsfeld declined to give it. The result has been that reconstruction is crippled, political progress is non-existent and human rights abuses are piling up. [8]

When more and more Americans begin returning from Afghhanistan in body bags, you can thank Donald Rumsfeld.

PENNY-WISE, POUND-FOOLISH

As the monthly overhead for the occupation has risen to a whooping four billion dollars per month, Rumsfeld's men proposed saving $35 million dollars per month (less than 1%), out of the imminent danger pay and family separation allowance approved by the Bush administration in April. The imminent danger pay of $225 per month was scheduled to drop to $150 a month, and the family separation allowance to drop from $250 to $100 a month. At the same time Halliburton and other corporations receive no-bid cost-plus contracts worth billions. [9]

Public reaction was so strong that Rumsfeld and his allies backtracked, saying they didn't really mean it. Well, then, why did they say it? Particularly, why did they say it while American troops were fighting and dying?

RUMSFELD AS ABOVE CRITICISM

As Rumsfeld's incompetence becomes harder to deny, he

8. See: http://www.truthout.org/docs_03/080303C.shtml
9. See: http://www.commondreams.org/headlines03/0814-02.htm

has taken the same tactic as used by John Ashcroft: criticism is evidence of disloyalty. His point is clear, though again, he left himself wiggle room, just in case anyone called him on his charge:

> To the extent that terrorists are given reason to believe he might, or, if he is not going to, that the opponents might prevail in some way, and they take heart in that, and that leads to more money going into these activities, or that leads to more recruits, or that leads to more encouragement, or that leads to more staying power, obviously that does make our task more difficult.

In other words, the problem is not any shortcoming in Bush's policies, but rather Bush's domestic critics. This again is a lie, and this one is unambiguous. Almost none of the critics have called for our withdrawal. Rumsfeld's critics have pointed out that he has botched the aftermath, not that we should simply go home. They have called for us to do a good job. This will not give any comfort at all to the Baathists or Al Qaeda. They would prefer the current incompetence.

ANAGRAM

Donald Henry Rumsfeld
Fondly handles murder.

He Said It . . .

"Some have argued that the nuclear threat from Iraq is not imminent—that Saddam is at least five to seven years away from having nuclear weapons. I would not be so certain. And we should be just as concerned about the immediate threat from biological weapons. Iraq has these weapons."

—Donald Rumsfeld, 9/18/02

"I never said imminent threat, and I don't know anyone who did say imminent threat."

—Donald Rumsfeld, 2/6/04

Quiz

Paul Slansky

Three of these statements were uttered by George W. Bush. Which was spoken by Defense Secretary Donald Rumsfeld?

(a) "The war on terror involves Saddam Hussein because of the nature of Saddam Hussein, the history of Saddam Hussein, and his willingness to terrorize himself."
(b) "For those who urge more diplomacy, I would simply say that diplomacy hasn't worked."
(c) "There are known knowns. These are things we know that we know. There are known unknowns. That is to say, there are things that we know we don't know. But there are also unknown unknowns. There are things we don't know we don't know."
(d) "Republicans and Democrats stood with me in the Rose Garden to announce their support of a clear statement of purpose [to Saddam]: You disarm or we will."

Answer: (c)

Rumsfeld's Personal Spy Ring

from Salon.com (7/16/03)

Eric Boehlert

During last fall's feverish ramp-up to war with Iraq, the Pentagon created an unusual in-house shop to monitor Saddam Hussein's links with terrorists and his allegedly sprawling arsenal of weapons of mass destruction. With direct access to Secretary of Defense Donald Rumsfeld's office and the White House, the influential group helped lay out, both to administration officials and to the press, an array of chilling, almost too good to be true examples of why Saddam posed an immediate threat to America.

Six months later, with controversy mounting over the administration's handling of war intelligence, the small, secretive cell inside the Pentagon is drawing closer scrutiny and may soon be the subject of a congressional inquiry to determine whether it manipulated and politicized key intelligence and botched planning for postwar Iraq.

"The concern is they were in the cherry-picking business—cherry-picking half-truths and rumors and only highlighting pieces of information that bolstered the administration's case for war," says U.S. Rep. Ellen Tauscher, D-Calif., a member of the House Armed Services Committee.

The Pentagon's innocuously named Office of Special Plans served as a unique, handpicked group of hawkish defense officials who worked outside regular intelligence channels. According to the Department of Defense, the group was first created in the aftermath of Sept. 11 to supplement the war on terrorism; it was designed to sift through all the intelligence on terrorist activity, and to focus particularly on various al-Qaida links. By last fall it was focusing almost exclusively on Iraq, and often leaking doomsday findings about Saddam's regime. Those controversial conclusions are now fueling the suspicion that the obscure agency, propelled by ideology, manipulated key findings in order to fit the White House's desire to wage war with Iraq.

"Everything we've seen since the war has confirmed intelligence community suspicions about its [the Office of Special Plans'] sources of information," says Greg Thielmann, who ran military assessments at the State Department's Bureau of Intelligence and Research until he retired in October. "The rosy assumption about troops being greeted with flowers and hugs—that came from that stream of intelligence. The assurance that they knew exactly where the weapons of mass destruction were, or that Iraq was ready to employ chemical and biological weapons in battle within 45 minutes of an order—all of those stories have proven wrong."

Those alarming allegations, and the subsequent failure to find any weapons of mass destruction, have created a firestorm over intelligence that has forced the Bush administration on the defensive in recent days. The controversy may soon focus attention on the Office of Special Plans, which has been raising hackles among intelligence professionals for the last year. Former CIA counterterrorism chief Vince Cannistraro refers to the office dismissively as "the bat cave."

Thielmann is still unclear why the civilian-run office was formed. "Do they [staffers in the Office of Special

Plans] have expertise in Iraqi culture?" he asks. "Are they missile experts? Nuclear engineers? There's no logical explanation for the office's creation except that they wanted people to find evidence to support their answers [about war]."

Currently, the Senate Intelligence Committee is holding closed-door hearings about the intelligence gathering for Iraq. But the House Appropriations Committee, which is weighing the Department of Defense's nearly $400 billion annual budget request, may soon sign off on an inquiry specifically looking into the Office of Special Plans. It would be triggered by a survey and investigation, or S&I, request. The appropriations committee has at its disposal a unique arm of investigators, sort of an in-house General Accounting Office staff.

"What we're asking for is not a determination of wrongdoing," says Scott Lilly, minority staff director for the House Appropriations Committee. "But just routine information about appropriated funds that we ask all the time."

The initial request, made by the ranking Democrat on the Appropriations Committee, Wisconsin Rep. David Obey, could lead to more sensitive questions about the office.

"There have been serious allegations made and he [Obey] thinks our committee has responsibility to determine if they're true," says Lilly. "If there's evidence that the office of Secretary of Defense got itself involved in extracurricular intelligence operations that generated misinformation, that's serious and something we'll try to see doesn't happen in the future."

The House inquiry, though modest in its scope, would

mark another setback for the Bush administration as it comes under increasing political pressure to explain gathered intelligence on Iraq, why so much of it appears to have been badly off the mark, and whether the White House knowingly misled the country about the need for an unprecedented preemptive war.

For the last week, in what the *Washington Post* on Tuesday officially labeled a "feeding frenzy," the White House has been trying to explain why bogus information, long ago discredited by intelligence experts, about Saddam Hussein's alleged effort to secure uranium from Niger for his nuclear weapons program, made it into this year's State of the Union address.

On Monday, Bush defended the use of intelligence and insisted: "When all is said and done the people of the United States will realize that Saddam Hussein had a weapons program." But before the war, the White House insisted Saddam had actual weapons, not simply "programs," which was why Iraq was supposed to be a grave, imminent threat to the United States.

According to a recent *Newsweek* poll, 45 percent of Americans say the Bush administration misinterpreted intelligence reports about Iraq; 38 percent think it deliberately misled the country.

To date, no weapons or significant evidence of weapons programs have been located, which itself is remarkable. "One year ago, no serious person would've thought we'd have 150,000 troops combing the country and still not be able to find the poison gas," says John Pike, an intelligence expert and director of GlobalSecurity.org.

Pike describes the Office of Special Plans as "Rummy's war room." Other critics are convinced the operation was manipulating information, and worse, disturbing the peer-review method within the intelligence community. "There's a formal, well-established intelligence process in Washington, which Rumsfeld apparently wanted to circumvent" by creating the office, says Thielmann. "Their operation was virtually invisible to us; I don't remember seeing any of their intelligence information." He says the Office of Special Plans "had no status in the intelligence community."

"It was not a neutral, transparent link in the intelligence chain," adds Steve Aftergood, senior research analyst for the Federation of American Scientists, a nonprofit organization that monitors national security policy. "It was staffed by people with a distinct perspective on events, so it was logical to assume that perspective would be reflected in the work."

Operating under the command of Rumsfeld, the office was the brainchild of his top deputy Paul Wolfowitz, and directly overseen by Undersecretary of Defense for Policy Douglas Feith. Together, the top three Pentagon civilians make up the most hawkish, neoconservative wing of the administration. In fact, all three had been calling for Saddam's removal years before the current war on terrorism.

Critics are also somewhat dumbfounded that Rumsfeld, with access to the Defense Intelligence Agency, which already has a reputation for its often alarmist intelligence analysis, felt the need to create yet another, separate, intelligence office. "Nobody ever said we don't have enough resources at the DIA," says Rep. Tauscher.

The premise behind the office seemed to be that career analysts inside the intelligence community, and specifically the CIA, were not grasping the hard realities about Iraq and its weapons of mass destruction, and that a fresh set of eyes examining much of the same information could make critical links.

Wolfowitz told the *New York Times* last year that there is "a phenomenon in intelligence work that people who are pursuing a certain hypothesis will see certain facts that others won't, and not see other facts that others will."

The current tension over intelligence is simply the resumption of a battle fought during the Cold War when conservatives such as Rumsfeld, Wolfowitz and Feith accused the CIA of underestimating the military dangers posed by the Soviet Union. (Following the Soviet Union's collapse, it became clear the CIA had been more accurate in its estimates than the hawks had been.) Since the Sept. 11 terrorist attacks and the onset of the war on terrorism, the ideological battle has simply shifted to the Middle East.

Last month Feith held a rare press conference to try to stem the criticism surrounding the office. "This suggestion that we said to them [analysts], 'This is what we're looking for, go find it,' is precisely the inaccuracy that we are here to rebut," he said. "I know of nobody who pressured anybody."

But since that attempted preemptive strike, the questions have only grown louder and more pointed about what the self-described "cabal" at the Pentagon was up to, and why, if its Iraqi leads were solid, it felt the need to end-run the intelligence establishment.

The White House's desire last year to gather damning Iraqi intelligence was driven home by Vice President Dick Cheney, who made three separate, and highly unusual, trips to the CIA before the war where he conferred with analysts and reportedly urged them to dig up better information about Saddam's alleged nuclear weapons program. Cannistraro says the meetings were unprecedented: "The vice president going to the CIA? Cutting ribbons and giving speeches, yes. But sitting down with analysts and going over the intelligence? I've never heard of that." Typically, if members of the executive branch have intelligence queries they contact the National Security staff, which has offices right inside the West Wing.

In retrospect, Cannistraro says it's clear "the decision was made within a couple of months of Sept. 11 to get rid of Saddam Hussein. But the administration had to find rationale to do it. So they set up a secretive group through Feith which started producing information on Iraq that was more compatible than the CIA."

A distinguishing characteristic of the office seemed to be the extraordinary access and influence given to Ahmad Chalabi, the exiled leader of the Iraqi National Congress. A darling of Beltway neocons, Chalabi has been viewed over the years with suspicion by the State Department and the CIA, which recognize the obvious political agenda behind his desire for the U.S. to overthrow Saddam—he'd be installed as Saddam's successor. The CIA and State Department have also been wary of some of the Iraqi defectors Chalabi produced who allegedly detailed Saddam's deadly arsenal. By contrast, Chalabi reportedly enjoyed unprecedented access at the Pentagon's office. According to some reports, the information and allegations he and his fellow defectors made about Saddam were passed up to Rumsfeld and Bush, with no review by outside intelligence professionals. The information was often shared with the press as well, helping to build a public case for war.

But the trick with dealing with defectors, says Cannistraro, is that "you have to understand how to vet them and what their motivations are. Otherwise they're just going to give you exactly what you want to hear." He says the Office of Special Plans never asked defectors the tough questions. "The level of naiveté was extraordinary."

Meanwhile, Rumsfeld's spy office is also coming under new scrutiny for its questionable job of planning for a postwar Iraq, a country that nearly three months after the toppling of Saddam remains mired in all sorts of political, legal and humanitarian chaos.

Last weekend, Knight-Ridder newspapers reported the Office of Special Plans "dominated planning for postwar Iraq" and yet "failed to prepare for the setbacks that have erupted over the past two months." Further, Knight-Ridder reported, "the Pentagon [civilian] leaders didn't develop extensive plans, the officials said, because they believed that Iraqis would welcome U.S. troops with open arms and that Washington could install a favored Iraqi exile as the country's leader. And, when their envisioned scenario collapsed amid violence and disorder, they had no backup plan."

"There is no postwar planning I can see that reveals any level of accomplishment," says Tauscher, who notes the U.S. cost of the war was recently doubled to $4 billion per month.

For now, though, the focus is on the office's role in gathering intelligence on Iraq—and on the pending congressional survey and investigation request, which needs bipartisan support to move forward. Democrats Obey, the ranking member of the Appropriations Committee, and Rep. John Murtha of Pennsylvania, ranking member of the defense appropriations subcommittee, have signed on. Now they need Rep. Jerry Lewis, R-Calif., the defense subcommittee chairman, and the Appropriations Committee chairman, Rep. Bill Young, R-Fla., to do the same.

According to Young's spokesman, S&I requests are "very seldom" denied. And last week the Wall Street Journal reported Lewis would agree to the inquiry, while, according to the Capitol Hill publication Congress Daily, Young indicated he too would support the bipartisan request. But to date, neither man has formally agreed to the inquiry.

"We have a request letter we're negotiating with Republicans," says Lilly, the Democratic staffer on the Appropriations Committee. "We're trying to keep this bipartisan because that's the only way to get to the bottom of this quickly and effectively."

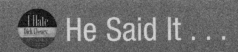

He Said It . . .

"Death has a tendency to encourage a depressing view of war."

—Donald Rumsfeld, 12/12/03

Quiz

Paul Slansky

Who said what?

1. "In the corporate world, sometimes things aren't exactly black and white when it comes to accounting procedures."
2. "[Osama bin Laden is] either alive and well or alive and not too well or not alive."
3. "How many Palestinians were on those airplanes on September 9th? None."
4. "First of all, let's get one thing straight: crack is cheap. I make too much money to ever smoke crack. Let's get that straight. O.K.?"

(a) George W. Bush
(b) Dan Quayle
(c) Whitney Houston
(d) Donald Rumsfeld

Answers: 1 (a), 2 (d), 3 (b), 4 (c)

The Poetry of D. H. Rumsfeld

from Slate.com (4/02/03)

Hart Seely

Secretary of Defense Donald Rumsfeld is an accomplished man. Not only is he guiding the war in Iraq, he has been a pilot, a congressman, an ambassador, a businessman, and a civil servant. But few Americans know that he is also a poet.

Until now, the secretary's poetry has found only a small and skeptical audience: the Pentagon press corps. Every day, Rumsfeld regales reporters with his jazzy, impromptu riffs. Few of them seem to appreciate it.

But we should all be listening. Rumsfeld's poetry is paradoxical: It uses playful language to address the most somber subjects: war, terrorism, mortality. Much of it is about indirection and evasion: He never faces his subjects head on but weaves away, letting inversions and repetitions confuse and beguile. His work, with its dedication to the fractured rhythms of the plainspoken vernacular, is reminiscent of William Carlos Williams'. Some readers may find that Rumsfeld's gift for offhand, quotidian pronouncements is as entrancing as Frank O'Hara's.

And so *Slate* has compiled a collection of Rumsfeld's poems, bringing them to a wider public for the first time. The poems that follow are the exact words of the defense secretary, as taken from the official transcripts on the Defense Department web site.

The Unknown

As we know,
There are known knowns.
There are things we know we know.
We also know
There are known unknowns.
That is to say
We know there are some things
We do not know.
But there are also unknown unknowns,
The ones we don't know
We don't know.

—Feb. 12, 2002,
Department of Defense news briefing

Glass Box

You know, it's the old glass box at the—
At the gas station,
Where you're using those little things
Trying to pick up the prize,
And you can't find it.
It's—

And it's all these arms are going down in there,
And so you keep dropping it
And picking it up again and moving it,
But—

Some of you are probably too young to remember those—
Those glass boxes,
But—

But they used to have them
At all the gas stations
When I was a kid.

—Dec. 6, 2001,
Department of Defense news briefing

A Confession

Once in a while,
I'm standing here, doing something.
And I think,
"What in the world am I doing here?"
It's a big surprise.

—May 16, 2001, interview with the New York Times

Happenings

You're going to be told lots of things.
You get told things every day that don't happen.

It doesn't seem to bother people, they don't—
It's printed in the press.
The world thinks all these things happen.
They never happened.

Everyone's so eager to get the story
Before in fact the story's there
That the world is constantly being fed
Things that haven't happened.

All I can tell you is,

It hasn't happened.
It's going to happen.

—Feb. 28, 2003,
Department of Defense briefing

The Digital Revolution

Oh my goodness gracious,
What you can buy off the Internet
In terms of overhead photography!

A trained ape can know an awful lot
Of what is going on in this world,
Just by punching on his mouse
For a relatively modest cost!

—June 9, 2001, following European trip

The Situation

Things will not be necessarily continuous.
The fact that they are something other than
perfectly continuous
Ought not to be characterized as a pause.
There will be some things that people will see.
There will be some things that people won't see.
And life goes on.

—Oct. 12, 2001,
Department of Defense news briefing

Clarity

I think what you'll find,

I think what you'll find is,
Whatever it is we do substantively,
There will be near-perfect clarity
As to what it is.
And it will be known,
And it will be known to the Congress,
And it will be known to you,
Probably before we decide it,
But it will be known.

—Feb. 28, 2003,
Department of Defense briefing

ANAGRAM

Donald Rumsfeld
Me? Droll? Adds fun.

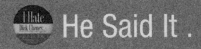

He Said It . . .

"I believe what I said yesterday . . . I don't know what I said, but I know what I think and, uh . . . I assume it's what I said."

—Donald Rumsfeld

Quiz

Paul Slansky

Three of these statements were made by George W. Bush. Which one was made by Donald Rumsfeld?

(a) "I think war is a dangerous place."
(b) "First, let me make it very clear: poor people aren't necessarily killers. Just because you happen to be not rich doesn't mean you're willing to kill."
(c) "The true strength of America happens when a neighbor loves a neighbor just like they'd like to be loved themselves."
(d) "Stuff happens."

Answer: (d)

Don Rumsfeld Meets the Press

from *The Nation* (11/17/03)

Calvin Trillin

With condescending smile, so tight,
He seems to take a great delight
Explaining to the press this fight,
As if they're kids who aren't too bright.
When wrong he needn't be contrite:
Don't might and arrogance make right?

JOHN ASHCROFT

with a quote by John Ashcroft;
a cartoon by Stuart Carlson;
and anagrams

John Ashcroft—who believes that the best way to protect the American way of life from religious fanatics is to eliminate the civil liberties that define the American way of life—is himself a religious fanatic. He's also a pompous bore, a dyed-in-the-wool doofus who writes songs about soaring eagles and forces his Justice Department underlings (as he clearly considers them) to sing them. He's easy to mock, but he is dangerous.

The Fundamental John Ashcroft

from *Mother Jones* (March/April 2002)

David Corn

A Washington showdown loomed. For weeks, a small number of lawmakers and pundits had been sniping at Attorney General John Ashcroft and the Bush White House over the administration's plan to try, and possibly execute, foreign terrorists in secret military tribunals. As the detractors gained momentum, Senator Patrick Leahy (D-Vt.), chairman of the Senate Judiciary Committee, firmly requested Ashcroft's presence before his committee.

When Ashcroft took his place in the crowded hearing room in early December, many of those present anticipated an explosion. But the attorney general skillfully deflected most queries, claiming the administration would not use the tribunals and other new powers indiscriminately. Then he went on the offensive: Critics who "scare peace-loving people with phantoms of lost liberty only aid terrorists, for they erode our national unity and diminish our resolve," he declared. The journalists in attendance winced. Here was the attorney general of the United States, in wartime, effectively calling his opponents traitors. But no one on the committee challenged Ashcroft on this point. After the hearing, he walked away smiling, while a frustrated Democratic senator muttered, "Finally, the real John Ashcroft."

Sept. 11 reconfigured the political hierarchy in Washington. President Bush lost his smirk and became a somber wartime leader. Secretary of Defense Donald Rumsfeld morphed into a media darling, and Secretary of

State Colin Powell returned to prominence. But more than any other cabinet official, John Ashcroft was transformed-and reborn. After seven months as a mostly low-profile attorney general, he reemerged as a pugnacious, crusading politician, fully in keeping with his past as one of the Senate's most passionately conservative members. He threw himself into the war on terrorism with the same zeal that had fueled his fierce opposition to abortion and gun control. And now, with his power and prominence enhanced, he is poised to confront a string of other hot-button issues, from physician-assisted suicide to the future of the Internet.

Chosen by President Bush to win points with social conservatives, the attorney general seemed disengaged in his first months in office, disappointing his allies on the right. Many liberals were relieved to see him seemingly biding his time, and not acting like the zealot they had depicted during a bitter confirmation battle.

But after Sept. 11, Ashcroft became absorbed, if not obsessed, with his new mandate: Find the terrorists, stop them, and make sure this never happens again. He pushed forward with a series of bold measures that alarmed his critics and even unsettled some fellow conservatives. Within the administration, he emerged as the hardest of the hardliners, serving as the president's spear catcher for controversial initiatives like the military tribunals and the suspension of due process for noncitizens caught in the terrorism investigation. Once a critic of expanding the federal government's police powers, he now argued that the administration could be trusted to wield such powers wisely. A year earlier he had warned that using secret evidence in immigration proceedings violated the rights of the accused; now he ordered that certain immigration hearings be conducted in secret. And when critics, including some Justice Department and FBI officials, challenged his approach, his response echoed the president's post-Sept. 11 declaration to the world: You're either with us in the fight against terrorism, or against us.

As a senator, Ashcroft had often cast issues in stark terms, drawing political inspiration from his Pentecostal faith. Now his uncompromising style was once again on display as he dismissed calls for caution and negotiation—in the fight against terrorism and, increasingly, on other fronts.

Since Sept. 11 Ashcroft has made high-profile policy moves on several matters of intense concern to conservatives. He has taken on voter-approved laws in California and Oregon, cracking down on clinics that dispense medical marijuana and on physicians who help terminally ill patients commit suicide. He has reversed long-standing department positions on affirmative action; ordered federal agencies to hold back on public-information requests even in routine cases; and signaled a willingness to give industry a break on antitrust issues. In the coming months, he is expected to continue steering the Justice Department rightward while lending an increasingly powerful voice to the interests of social conservatives on a range of issues—from hate-crime legislation to the Bush administration's judicial appointments.

"I am concerned that as events arise, we will see more of his mindset, which is far more authoritarian than libertarian," says Roger Pilon, director of the libertarian Cato Institute's Center for Constitutional Studies. "That he does not support government for purposes that liberals support does not mean that he is antigovernment. He just has his own agenda for expansive government."

The defiant attorney general who testified before his former colleagues in December was far different from the embattled nominee who had appeared before the same committee for his confirmation hearings 11 months earlier. In the fall of 2000, Ashcroft's bid for reelection to the Senate from Missouri had been defeated under weird, and demeaning, circumstances. His challenger, Mel Carnahan, had died in an airplane crash, and Carnahan's widow had agreed to take the seat if her deceased husband outpolled Ashcroft. The dead man defeated the living incumbent. Six weeks later, President-elect Bush named Ashcroft his choice for attorney general.

The announcement set off the new administration's only major confirmation fight. Ashcroft had been the religious right's favorite senator; in 1998 his voting record had put him in second place on the John Birch Society's legislative scorecard, in a tie with North Carolina's Jesse Helms. As recently as 1999, he had flirted with running for president, with Pat Robertson as one of his top boosters. Liberal groups made defeating Ashcroft's nomination a priority, and they pressed their allies in the Senate to bring him down. The two-day confirmation hearing was a tense affair. Democrats grilled Ashcroft on his past actions and positions—his efforts to criminalize abortion and even contraceptives such as the morning-after pill; his resistance to school desegregation orders in Missouri; his smear campaign against a Missouri Supreme Court justice nominated for a federal judgeship; his supportive words for a magazine published by racists.

During the hearing, Ashcroft was conciliatory, if

unapologetic. He portrayed himself as an inclusive fellow who repudiated "racist ideas." He maintained that despite his fervent opinions on guns and abortion, he would not seek to remake laws that displeased him. It was a Joe Friday performance: He would be A.G. just to enforce the law, ma'am. Ashcroft won confirmation by a vote of 58-42—the narrowest margin of any Bush appointee. Nearly half of his former colleagues had slapped him in the face.

The ordeal cast a shadow over Ashcroft's first months in office. "He was genuinely shocked and hurt," says one top Justice official. In the wake of the confrontation, the attorney general seemed to have decided it was best to avoid giving his critics fresh ammunition. Department insiders wondered what he wanted to accomplish at Justice, if anything. He surrounded himself with political staffers from Capitol Hill and rarely reached out to veteran officials. "He and his people didn't trust anyone who was career," recalls one longtime department lawyer. "They viewed all career people as the enemy. Usually that happens at the start of a new administration, but people get over it. They didn't get over it." Among many in the department a consensus formed: Ashcroft was running the place like a senator's office, where a few people control all the action and the boss is cushioned from much of the outside world.

And there was another similarity: his schedule. He often headed home to Missouri on Thursday afternoons and would not be in the office on Mondays. "Things piled up," says a senior department official. "When you have a job like this, it fucks up your life. Ashcroft was going home on weekends." One Friday early in Ashcroft's tenure, a top department official and an FBI agent flew to Missouri to have their boss sign a top-secret wiretap application connected with a terrorism investigation. Department gossip about the incident reached the *Washington Post,* which reported that "Ashcroft wasn't pleased to see [the pair] standing in front of his house. And there they stood in the cold while Ashcroft sat in his pickup to read and sign the documents."

Not that Ashcroft wasn't up to the job. "People can underestimate him," says a Justice Department lawyer who has briefed him. "He is smart. He's a fast read. He can understand an issue and the political dynamics of it right away. He's not like Reno, who wanted endless briefings." But he was not keen on establishing a game plan of his own. "His attitude was, 'What does the president want me to do, and I'll do it,'" the lawyer recalls.

As one senior Republican Senate aide puts it, "Ashcroft had one job: He had been picked to shore up Bush's right flank." If that was so, perhaps he could get away with punching a clock at the Justice Department. According to Terry Eastland, publisher of the conservative *Weekly Standard* and a former public affairs director at the department, "He was seen as someone bored with certain aspects of the job and thinking about another run for office."

Even an unmotivated attorney general has to render important decisions, though, and Ashcroft did not fail to stir some controversy. In a letter to the National Rifle Association last May, he asserted that the Second Amendment "clearly protects the right of individuals to keep and bear arms"—reversing the Justice Department's long-standing view that the Constitution grants only a collective right to bear arms. (The NRA cheered and placed Ashcroft, a longtime member, on the cover of its magazine.) He presided over the first federal executions in four decades, maintaining that a department study had found no evidence of racial bias in the application of the death penalty (an interpretation that was challenged by death-penalty foes). He held daily Bible study and prayer meetings in the office and praised the "vision" of an evangelist who had called on the nation to "select Christians to rule us."

Still, Ashcroft's performance was not that of a full-fledged religious-right crusader. He allowed department employees to have a gay pride celebration. He angered antiabortion activists by ordering the US Marshals Service to protect a Wichita abortion provider who was the target of protests. He disappointed affirmative action opponents when, in a key Supreme Court case, his attorneys supported a federal Department of Transportation program favoring minority-owned businesses. And when FBI director Louis Freeh resigned last June, Ashcroft opposed the choice of some conservatives, Bush campaign lawyer George Terwilliger, and successfully pushed for the appointment of Robert Mueller III, a nonpolitical former US attorney.

"Those who tried to portray him as a wide-eyed radical weren't borne out," says Clifford May, a Republican strategist. On Capitol Hill, according to a senior Senate Republican aide, "Ashcroft and the Justice Department was not at the top of anyone's agenda. He was doing a fine job in not creating problems. He didn't stand out, and that was not a bad thing."

But Ashcroft's supporters on the right were worried. "There was increasing concern that he wasn't playing as high profile a role as conservatives thought he would," recalls Tom Jipping, an official at the Free Congress

Foundation. "We were wondering why not. We were hoping he'd get around to it."

On the morning of Sept. 11, John Ashcroft and four aides were in the air, flying to Milwaukee in a government jet. A call came in on the attorney general's secure phone. He hung up and said, "Our world has changed forever."

His perhaps more than most. Ashcroft, the less-than-fully engaged attorney general, was now in charge of the largest criminal investigation in the nation's history. His department—which oversees the FBI, the Immigration and Naturalization Service, US Attorneys' offices, the Bureau of Prisons, and the Drug Enforcement Administration—was command central for efforts to detect and disrupt future plots. In the weeks after the attacks, and during the subsequent anthrax crisis, Ashcroft appeared before the TV cameras at all hours, often with the FBI's Mueller at his side, offering updates and reassurance about the administration's initiatives. The fleshy bags beneath his eyes became more pronounced. There would be no more four-day workweeks.

"It seems harsh to say, but prior to Sept. 11, I wouldn't have expected such a powerful reaction from Ashcroft," remarks one department official. "It quickly was evident that he took his new responsibilities very seriously."

If Ashcroft had entered the Justice Department without an agenda, he possessed one now. "We got speeches from him about not missing anything," recalls another Justice attorney. "He was a man with a cause. You could feel it in the building. To him, the job became terrorism, terrorism, terrorism. He was devastated by the attacks. It happened on his watch."

In sync with the White House, Ashcroft set the tone for

a new style of federal law enforcement: This was war, and war required extreme measures. A week after the attacks, he issued a directive allowing the federal government, in certain instances, to detain noncitizens indefinitely without charges. Critics warned that the audacious step—along with Ashcroft's announcement that the government would monitor conversations between inmates and their lawyers in certain instances—eroded due process and divided the population between citizens and noncitizens, a distinction not noted in the Constitution. But Ashcroft was unmoved. "It is difficult for a person in jail," he noted, "to murder innocent people or to aid or abet in terrorism." This, in other words, was not a time to get hung up on legal niceties.

Nor was it a time for lengthy public or congressional debate. The White House legal counsel's office and the Justice Department's Office of Legal Policy, which Ashcroft had staffed with archconservative policy wonks, hastily drew up the USA Patriot Act—a bill that called for far-reaching changes in federal law enforcement. It gave the FBI new authority to search homes and offices without probable cause and to monitor phone conversations and email. It permitted grand juries to pass confidential information to the CIA, a step that could erode the prohibition against domestic spying by the agency. It afforded federal investigators greater access to business, bank, credit, and medical records, and it affirmed the government's right to detain noncitizens without charges.

The bill set off protests from civil libertarians, including some of Ashcroft's supporters on the right. At one of the weekly Washington meetings hosted by conservative strategist Grover Norquist, an attendee asked the group of

100 or so for a show of hands from those happy with the bill. Only two hands went up. "No one knows which of the things in the legislation will end up being dangerous," says Norquist. "You have 6 million noncitizens in this country. That's an awful lot of people who can be woken up with a knock on the door at night."

Sept. 11 had not only energized Ashcroft; it had caused a shift in his political priorities. In the past he was associated with the civil libertarian wing of the conservative movement, the folks who were upset about Ruby Ridge and Waco, who were leery of awarding law enforcement extra powers. In a 1997 op-ed, he scoffed at government attempts to monitor the Internet to combat crime: "We do not provide the government with phone jacks outside our homes for unlimited wiretaps. Why, then, should we grant government the Orwellian capability to listen at will and in real time to our communications across the Web?"

But since the attacks, he has demonstrated little sympathy for such concerns. "I understand what happened after 9/11," Norquist says. "Ashcroft shouts down the hall—'Get me all the antiterrorism stuff we need'—and they throw out all the stuff they've been trying to do for years. I wish that Ashcroft would have been more strict when the staffers came in and said, 'Here are the 100 things we need.' But that didn't happen."

Even in the law enforcement community, some argued that Ashcroft was going too far. When he considered a plan to relax restrictions on FBI spying on U.S. religious and political organizations, top Justice and FBI officials criticized the move. The rules, they pointed out, had been imposed after the J. Edgar Hoover era to prevent the kind of domestic surveillance that had given the bureau a bad name. "This came out of the White House and Ashcroft's office," a senior FBI official told the *New York Times*. "There are tons of things coming out of there these days where there is absolutely no consultation" with the FBI.

Several prominent FBI alumni also blasted Ashcroft's cast-a-wide-net approach to the terrorism investigation, which led to the detention of some 1,200 people, only a dozen of them suspected of having any links with Al Qaeda. The mass arrests were part of a fundamental shift in the bureau's strategy. In the past, the FBI would identify suspected terrorists, move to forestall any immediate threat of violence, then watch the suspects in hopes of cracking an entire cell. Ashcroft's approach, the critics noted, might jeopardize the kinds of investigations that had prevented previous attacks. "We used good investigative techniques and lawful techniques," warned Reagan-era FBI director William Webster, "and we did it without all the suggestion that we are going to jump all over people's private lives."

Ashcroft drew the most fire, however, over the administration's plan to set up secret military courts. Using the tribunals had not been his idea: The executive order creating them had been drawn up in the White House, and the Pentagon, not Justice, was charged with working out the details. But it was Ashcroft who enthusiastically defended the measure and tangled with right-wingers aghast at the broad sweep of the president's order. Ashcroft's foes included US Rep. Bob Barr (R-Ga.), who warned that the plan "takes your breath away," and conservative columnist William Safire, who accused Bush of assuming "dictatorial power" because he was misadvised by a "frustrated and panic-stricken attorney general."

"Ashcroft seemed to relish going up against his critics," one Justice Department official notes. "He could be sincerely self-righteous in his role as America's protector." As he was preparing for his appearance before the Judiciary Committee—the one in which he would accuse unnamed critics of aiding terrorists—Ashcroft led 90 federal prosecutors on a nighttime tour of Washington's monuments. The point, he said, was to "dedicate ourselves to the wisdom and knowledge of the founders, who were dedicated to justice."

Ashcroft's new confidence hasn't been limited to the war on terrorism. In recent months he has ordered brassy initiatives in a number of controversial areas. In November, he instructed the Drug Enforcement Administration to revoke the drug-prescription licenses of physicians who provide medication to help terminally ill patients die—a measure directed at Oregon's law legalizing physician-assisted suicide, but with nationwide implications. "Ashcroft was trying to wipe out physician-assisted death with one single edict and no hearings, and no consultations with physicians or patients organizations," complains Ryan Ross of the Hemlock Society, a right-to-die advocacy group. The state of Oregon and several patients took Ashcroft to court, and a federal judge issued a temporary stay on the DEA order. The matter will likely work its way toward the Supreme Court.

Ashcroft's move against right-to-die legislation was cheered by social conservatives still smarting over Bush's decision last August to allow limited federally funded research on human stem cells, and was seen by some lawyers in the department as a political payback to the religious right. But it also displeased conservative states' rights advocates. On another front, the DEA in October raided two clubs in California that dispense medicinal marijuana to people with AIDS, cancer, and glaucoma. "It was fairly shocking timing to now put resources into a blast at medical marijuana," says a former top-ranking Justice Department official, "and to make the face of drug crime in America an HIV patient in a wheelchair and not a Colombian drug lord." An Ashcroft spokeswoman defended the raids as proof that the department had "not lost our priorities in other areas since Sept. 11."

In a number of less-publicized actions, Ashcroft has been guiding his department away from key positions taken by the Clinton administration. Since 1997 the federal government had been a co-plaintiff in a suit arguing that an unusual physical test used for hiring Philadelphia transit cops discriminated against women, 93 percent of whom failed the test. In October, Ashcroft directed his attorneys to withdraw from the suit. The department also dropped its support of affirmative action programs at the University of Michigan—just a few months after arguing for the Department of Transportation program favoring minorities.

In November, signaling another shift in priorities, the department reached a settlement with Microsoft in the largest antitrust case in two decades. Ashcroft hailed the agreement as "historic," but 9 of the 18 states that were party to the suit refused to go along with the deal, and consumer advocates attacked it as proof that the administration was going soft on antitrust enforcement. (Ashcroft will not be involved in what could be the biggest corporate investigation of his tenure: He has recused himself from the Enron case because he received campaign contributions from the company.)

As Ashcroft heads into his second year in office, he remains a team player following the lead of the White House. But as a revitalized and empowered attorney general with an approval rating near 70 percent, he also has more latitude to head where his natural inclinations direct him. If he didn't know it before Sept. 11, he clearly realizes at this point that the office of attorney general is not a Joe Friday position. The A.G. does not merely enforce the law: He decides how to apply and shape it—and that is a values-driven exercise.

In the months ahead, Ashcroft will have ample opportunity to pursue his values as he encounters an assortment of contentious issues. The FBI is expected to seek additional surveillance powers and perhaps even attempt to influence the shape of the Internet—demanding, for example, that all electronic traffic be forced through easy-to-monitor nodes. The attorney general will also have to decide whether to order more DEA raids on medical marijuana clubs, and how to prosecute the people who run them.

On Capitol Hill, Ashcroft is expected to weigh in as Congress takes up legislation that he vehemently opposed as a senator. Lawmakers who seek to close the loophole that allows gun-show visitors to buy firearms without background checks, or to extend the ban on assault weapons (which expires in 2004), could find a forceful adversary in the attorney general, whose department oversees the Bureau of Alcohol, Tobacco, and Firearms. And as the nation's chief enforcer of civil rights laws, Ashcroft may face a congressional initiative to extend the federal hate-crime law to cover sexual orientation. "Speculation within the department is that the political people will oppose it, but do not want to admit it yet," says one career department lawyer.

Then there's the ultimate prize for social conservatives: a Supreme Court justice who can flip the court's balance to the anti-abortion side. "This is the North Star for conservative activists: who gets into the Supreme Court," notes Terry Jeffrey, editor of the right-wing journal *Human Events*. Anti-abortion advocates, he notes, "look to Ashcroft, whom they consider to be part of their movement, to prevent Bush from making a mistake."

Ashcroft is now in a better position than ever to help his allies on the religious right. Despite some conservative griping about his approach to civil liberties, he remains in good standing in those circles. In December, the Christian magazine *World*, edited by onetime Bush adviser Marvin Olasky, chose him as its "Daniel of the Year," as in the biblical hero, for withstanding "scorn and harassment."

"He was never an insider within the Bush team," notes Marshall Wittmann, director of the Washington office of the conservative Hudson Institute. "But now he's clearly the domestic conservative heartthrob of this administration. He is an evangelical himself, he has been a very strong loyalist to the president, and now he has a general popularity beyond the conservative base of the party. I would suspect that he will have a long tenure within this administration."

Or beyond. "He might mount a comeback run for the Senate, since he lost in a freak occurrence," says May, the GOP strategist. "And since he flirted with a presidential campaign, you can't discount that." In the meantime, as a full-throttle attorney general, John Ashcroft may yet live up to the hopes of his admirers and the fears of his foes.

He Said It...

"Your tactics only aid terrorists, for they erode our national unity and diminish our resolve."

—John Ashcroft, 12/6/01, to critics of the so-called Patriot Act.

ANAGRAM

Department of Homeland Security
They fund, arm modern police state.

John Ashcroft

from Rotten.com

Rotten.com staff

Much like the Nazis in Casablanca, John Ashcroft enjoys a good song—as long as people remember their place.

Even before September 11, Attorney General John Ashcroft was a disaster waiting to happen. An evangelical fanatic with an agenda, Ashcroft was a man with a dream, or perhaps we should call it a vision, or perhaps—as he might say—a mandate from God.

After sitting Senator Ashcroft lost his seat to a dead man, Mel Carnahan—the first time in history such a thing has happened—President George W. Bush decided to rescue Ashcroft. The collective cringe could be heard all across America, from women, gays, blacks, Jews, Muslims, Buddhists, supporters of civil rights, doctors, people who enjoy having sex, Methodists . . .

And if there's anything worse than an attorney general with an apocalyptic messiah complex, it's an attorney general with an apocalyptic messiah complex at a time when *infidels* have declared a holy war on America.

And if there's anything worse than THAT . . . it would have to be an attorney general who writes inspiratational songs and forces his staff to sing them daily; an attorney general whose father anointed him in a messianic ritual when he took office; an attorney general who drafted the biggest rollback of individual rights in American history and is already planning a sequel . . .

Jesus Loves Me . . . But I'm Not So Sure About You

Understanding John Ashcroft starts and probably ends with the Assembly of God, the evangelic Christian sect that spawned him. In his autobiography, Ashcroft said he woke every morning to a "magisterial wake-up call" of his preacher-father's noisy prayers.

Among the Assembly of God's teachings: Homosexuality is evil and causes disease; Christians should not make friends with non-Christians; people should avoid all "sexually suggestive forms of media and entertainment"; speaking in tongues is a necessary component of salvation;

Jesus isn't just coming, he's coming to take over the world; mixed-gender dancing leads to evil and should be avoided; and government and laws should be predicated on the teachings of the Christian bible.

Some verbatim quotes from the Church's teachings include:

- "The spread of oriental religions and the occult in America has brought with it an increase in demon possession similar to that reported formerly by missionaries on foreign fields. All too often there has been too little teaching in this area."
- "All believers who have died will rise from their graves and will meet the Lord in the air, and Christians who are alive will be caught up with them, to be with the Lord forever."
- "The Millennial Reign of Christ when Jesus returns with His saints at His second coming and begins His benevolent rule over earth for 1,000 years. At that time many in the nation of Israel will recognize and accept Him as the Messiah, the Savior who died for them and all mankind."
- "The Assemblies of God calls youth and singles to refrain from all forms of sexual intimacy until marriage. Such actions would include prolonged sessions of kissing, words of unique expression, actions of intimate caressing, and partial or total nudity."
- "Unfortunately, many today mislabel those who speak out against the sin of homosexuality as hatemongers and prejudiced people seeking to oppress and take away the rights of homosexuals. But these

persons view homosexuality from a skewed social perspective devoid of true biblical morality."

• "Generally it is risky for Christians to build deep friendships with those who do not share a spiritual bond in Christ. If the friendship has no deep spiritual unity, it is then based on secular values, material interests, and views of the world. In such instances the negative spiritual toll on the Christian is significant as one's spirit is constantly dulled through repeated exposure to worldviews and ideas. Few Christians are able to live consistent holy lives when unequally yoked in deep friendships with unbelievers."

• "The alarming shift from a Judeo-Christian philosophy to secular humanism as the foundation of American government has created profound problems for all Bible-believing churches. More and more, government is defying biblical principles and interpreting sinful behavior as civil rights, i.e. abortion and homosexuality. The church as the body of Christ is obligated to respond."

Principles in Practice

Sure, you might argue that this sort of doctrinal dissection could be applied to just about any religious person in politics, and you'd be right.

Except that unlike most politicians, Ashcroft fervently believes every word of it and is willing to put that belief ahead of political expediency. It's just our luck that the one principled politician in the history of the United States would have to have principles like these.

"The source of freedom and human dignity is the

Creator," Ashcroft testified to a Bible-thumping audience of religious broadcasters in February 2002. "The guarding of freedom that God grants is the noble charge of the Department of Justice." No, sir! You won't catch John Ashcroft getting blow jobs from interns in the cloakroom! You're much more likely to find him accepting mandates from God in the sort of ritual one associates with the Freemasons.

Every time Ashcroft has stepped up to take a political office, he has been anointed with holy oil "in the manner of King David," as he specified in his autobiography. His father did the job during his terms as a Senator. On one occasion, the 24-hour quickie mart was out of holy oil, so Crisco was substituted at the last minute. When Ashcroft was selected to be Attorney General, reputed porno-purveyor Supreme Court Justice Clarence Thomas did the honors.

The religious significance of anointment (particularly in the context of King David) is a little broader than one would like—the word "Messiah" means "anointed one" in Hebrew, based on Old Testament prophecies, and is also widely considered a signpost relevant to the second coming of Christ.

Another of Ashcroft's highly principled acts involved a crackdown on public nudity. The bare-breasted lady in question was a statue of Justice. Ashcroft ordered curtains hung in the Justice Department's press room in order to remove the giant iron nipple which loomed so salaciously, enticingly, over his head. (Good thing Michelangelo's David wasn't looming back there. Sexual provocation *and* homoerotic subtext is a twofer in the Assembly of God . . .)

Then there's the music (one of the few "fun" things allowed under Assembly precepts). While in Congress, Ashcroft took part in a barbershop quartet called "The Singing Senators," but his commitment to musical excellence didn't end there.

In the post-September 11 environment, Ashcroft decided to inspire his Justice Department employees by starting each day with song. But such godless standards as the "Star Spangled Banner" just wouldn't suffice. Ashcroft wrote his own song, "Let the Eagle Soar," and forced his hapless subordinates to join him in a daily caterwaul of defiance to such outmoded concepts as "separation of church and state":

"Let the eagle soar,
Like she's never soared before.
From rocky coast to golden shore,
Let the mighty eagle soar.
Soar with healing in her wings,
As the land beneath her sings:
'Only god, no other kings.'
This country's far too young to die.
We've still got a lot of climbing to do,
And we can make it if we try.
Built by toils and struggles
God has led us through."

When interviewed by a British paper, an anonymous Justice Department lawyer summed up her objections to this cruel and unsusual practice thusly: "Have you heard the song? It really sucks."

A Self-Starter

But Ashcroft's crusade doesn't start and end with making an ass out of himself in harmless and amusing ways. The Attorney General is deadly serious about his job.

When the conservative with a messiah complex took office, a lot of people were understandably concerned, based on his track record, that these would be dark years in such areas as abortion rights, gay rights, civil rights, affirmative action, anti-trust, environmental and corporate crime, and so on. Amazingly, Ashcroft managed to give us *bigger* problems to worry about.

After 9/11, Ashcroft flew like a bat out of heaven to "repurpose" the Justice Department for what he perceived as a new and excitingly apocalyptic reality. Ashcroft's enthusiasm couldn't be contained. He was so eager to start his crusade that he didn't even bother to consult with his boss before making the announcement.

"Defending our nation and defending the citizens of America against terrorist attacks is now our first and overriding priority," Ashcroft said in early November 2001, as he laid out his plan to reorganize the department for the voracious Washington press corps.

The *new* Justice Department would no longer bother with such trivial tasks as enforcing and interpreting federal law, ensuring the rights of citizens, protecting consumers and keeping rein over big business. Terrorism was now Job One, and Jobs Two through Eleven as well.

A couple days later, CNN's Larry King asked Ashcroft whether he had discussed this sweeping reorganization plan with Bush before announcing it. Whoops! Ashcroft carefully explained that Bush "noted" the announcement after the fact. "I don't want to say that the president and I have conferred about every aspect of this," he said.

And really, why would the president want to micro-manage a little project like a total re-invention of America's federal justice system? He's a busy man!

PATRIOT GAMES

Ashcroft's greatest—uh, let's go with "highest profile"—accomplishment to date was the rolling back of individual rights by several decades, under the guise of fighting terrorism.

The provisions of the PATRIOT Act taken as a whole are enough to make civil libertarians scream; the average citizen can usually find at least one provision worthy of alarm. Sponsored by the Bush administration, the PATRIOT act gave sweeping new powers to Ashcroft and his department, including:

- The right to freely monitor the activities of political and religious groups without a criminal pretext.
- New restrictions on open hearings and the public's right to receive information through the Freedom of Information Act.
- The ability to stamp down on the dangerous menace of librarians who tip off the media to federal subpoenas of borrowing records.
- Permission to monitor conversations between lawyers and suspects, on those increasingly rare occasions that suspects are allowed to have lawyers.
- The ability to detain Americans in prison indefinitely without trial or criminal charge.

Not satisfied with the most sweeping police powers

ever granted to an Attorney General, Ashcroft set his flunkies to work drafting "PATRIOT II," also known as the "Domestic Security Enhancement Act of 2003," a vast expansion of the vast expansion of his powers. The Justice Department's wish list for PATRIOT II would enhance domestic security by:

- Dramatically loosening restrictions on secret government surveillance of citizens, including on phones, e-mail and bank accounts.
- Adding a "deport at will" option allowing the Justice Department to circumvent inconvenient immigration laws.
- Expanding terrorism investigations to allow the Department to revoke the rights of anyone within about six degrees of separation of an actual terrorist act.
- Criminalizing the use of encrypted e-mail.
- Increasing the list of federal death-penalty crimes.
- Allowing the government to desecrate the graves of deceased victims of terrorism without permission from families.
- Restricting access to information about corporate pollution and environmental crimes. This would, incidentally, not only prevent private citizens from researching toxins in their backyards but would even restrict the ability of local governments to get information about environmental crimes in their own neighborhoods.

With all these powers, you would think that Ashcroft would have a long list of convictions to brag about, but no such luck. Americans have yet to see a single conviction in a U.S. court for any crime directly related to the Sept. 11 attack. They nailed one guy for selling false ID's to the hijackers,. but he pleaded guilty. Crazy shoe bomber Richard Reid pleaded guilty.

Ashcroft has yet to even convict "20th hijacker" and raving lunatic Zacarias Moussaoui, *who is representing himself.* Moussaoui's court filings, handwritten on legal paper, tend to run along such lines as "Ashcroft must be sent to Alexandria jail so I can torture him. After all torture is now part of the American way of life," complaints about his lack of Internet access and requests to travel abroad in search of evidence which will exonerate him.

Moussaoui's trial has been indefinitely postponed because the defendant called witnesses who are currently being held incommunicado and without charge by the federal government, which doesn't want to cough them up.

John Ashcroft may be one hell of a singer, but he's been legally outmanuevered by a madman with virtually no knowledge of the U.S. justice system—even as Ashcroft is angling to ask for an incease in his *already* unprecedented power to subvert due process and constitutional protections. What's wrong with this picture?

TIMELINE

9 May 1942	John Ashcroft born, Chicago IL.
1964	Graduates Yale University.
1967	Law degree, University of Chicago.
1984	Elected Governor of Missouri.
Nov 1994	Elected to U.S. Senate.
16 Oct 2000	Governor of Missouri, Mel Carnahan dies in a plane crash.

Nov 2000	John Ashcroft loses his Senate seat to a dead man, Mel Carnahan.
22 Dec 2000	George W. Bush announces he will appoint John Ashcroft as U.S. Attorney General.
26 Oct 2001	Ashcroft's *Patriot Act I* signed into law.
11 Feb 2002	Ashcroft's office confirms that U.S. Attorney General John Ashcroft did indeed say, "Islam is a religion in which God requires you to send your son to die for him. Christianity is a faith in which God sends his son to die for you." They appended a claim that this statement is taken out of context, but does not explain in what type of context such a statement might be appropriate or not highly offensive.
7 Feb 2003	*Patriot Act II* leaked.
15 Sep 2003	In a speech before the National Restaurant Association, Attorney General John Ashcroft declares: "No one believes in our First Amendment civil liberties more than this administration."
4 Mar 2004	Attorney General John Ashcroft is admitted to George Washington University Hospital for treatment of gallstone pancreatitis.

REJECTED OPTIONS FOR CONCEALING the SEMI-NUDE SCULPTURES AT the U.S. JUSTICE DEPT.:
LARGE BAND-AID
PASTIES
PATRIOTIC BIKINI TOP
BURQA
NOW THAT'S MY KIND OF COVER-UP!
ASHCROFT
CARLSON
MILWAUKEE JOURNAL SENTINEL · UNIVERSAL PRESS SYND.

1/31

I Hate
Dick Cheney...

ANAGRAM

The US Attorney General John Ashcroft
He channels for rage, hate; not joy, trust.

Victory

from www.billmon.org (8/11/03)

Billmon

From *The New York Daily News*, Aug. 6 2003:

> Attorney General John Ashcroft is hitting the road to rally support for the 'Victory Act', which would further expand his powers . . . Ashcroft will start pushing the Vital Interdiction of Criminal Terrorist Organizations Act later this month in a 10-day, 20-state 'Victory tour'.

From *1984* by George Orwell:

> 'Victory Mansions' were old flats, built in 1930 or thereabouts, and were falling to pieces . . .
>
> From somewhere at the bottom of a passage the smell of roasting coffee—real coffee, not 'Victory Coffee'—came floating out into the street . . .
>
> 'Where can we meet?'
> ''Victory Square', near the monument.'

Winston sat in his usual corner, gazing into an empty glass. Now and again he glanced up at a vast face which eyed him from the opposite wall. BIG BROTHER IS WATCHING YOU, the caption said. Unbidden, a waiter came and filled his glass up with 'Victory Gin'.

CONDI AND COLIN

with a cartoon by Aaron McGruder;
and anagrams

Many Americans during the early months of the Bush presidency viewed National Security Adviser Condoleezza Rice and Secretary of State Colin Powell as moderates. The wishful thinking ran like this: If Bush and his other cronies prove as stupid and angry as they seem, Condi and Colin will keep things from getting out of hand. It didn't work out that way, did it? The national security adviser and the secretary of state continue to provide a gloss of respectability to the administration's arrogant and dangerous foreign policy. Colin and Condi have shown themselves to be opportunists of the worst sort—the sort who know better, but are willing to trade their integrity for a piece of the action.

Condoleezza Rice

from deal-with-it.org

Gus DiZerega

Condoleezza Rice arrived in Washington a respected authority on Russian politics. But power is a strong drug. It has undermined the integrity of many and Dr. Rice can be counted among its victims.

After 9-11, Rice spread the false story that Bush was flown to Oklahoma after the attack because "intelligence" indicated the White House and Air Force One were also targets. There was no such intelligence. [1]

Then she testified the U.S. government had never anticipated an attack by an airliner. We now know the Bush administration received and ignored many such warnings. Joe Conason writes "in fact there had been many warnings of exactly such tactics—most notably during the summer of 2001, when Western intelligence services set up anti-aircraft batteries around the Genoa summit to protect the President." [2]

Rice served as a shill for Bush's attack on Iraq. She began warning us that the aluminum tubes were only for the production of atomic weapons and that we

1. See: http://www.observer.com/pages/story.asp?ID=7632
http://www.cbsnews.com/stories/2002/09/10/60II/main521483.shtml
http://slate.msn.com/id/1008371/

2. See: http://www.buzzflash.com/interviews/2002/07/25_Joe_Conason.html
http://www.indybay.org/news/2003/08/1632318_comment.php
http://publish.portland.indymedia.org/en/2003/07/268897.shtml

risked an atomic attack. On CNN's "Late Edition" Rice said the tubes "are only really suited for nuclear weapons programs, centrifuge programs." She also said, "The problem here is that there will always be some uncertainty about how quickly he can acquire nuclear weapons, but we don't want the smoking gun to be a mushroom cloud." [3]

Rice also spread the allegation that Iraq had tried to purchase "yellowcake uranium" from Niger, another untruth. She appears to have been a primary reason Bush included it in his State of the Union address. On July 11, 2003, Rice told the press aboard Air Force One: "Had I known that there was a forged document here, would I put this in the State of the Union? No."

Actually, "Yes." If they believed what they were saying, why did the U.S. refuse for months to turn over their 'proof' to the International Atomic Energy Agency (IAEA)? When the IAEA did get the "evidence" they quickly found out the documents were crude forgeries. Given all the other misrepresentation, errors, untruths, and lies, this is not evidence of carelessness, but instead a campaign for war, regardless of the evidence. [4]

This interpretation becomes even stronger considering that Stephen Hadley, Rice's deputy, disclosed that two CIA memos and a phone call from CIA Director George Tenet had persuaded him to take a similar passage about Iraq and uranium out of a presidential speech three months before the State of the Union address. According to an AOP report, "Hadley said one of the memos casting doubt

3. See: http://www.cbc.ca/news/features/iraq/quotes.html
4. See: http://www.commondreams.org/news2003/0716-05.htm

on the intelligence was sent to Rice. She doesn't recall reading it, the NSC's spokesman said."[5]

Humor helps at this point, and Brad DeLong gives us a refreshing dose while discussing Rice's handling of the uranium issue. Writes DeLong (an economist at Berkeley):

> I knew that intellectual standards at Stanford are low, but this is ridiculous. Ex-Stanford professor and provost Condoleezza Rice complains that it is not fair for her to be tested on footnotes that she did not know were there:
>
> > With Mallets Toward One (washingtonpost.com): Meanwhile, reporters keep hounding the administration over President Bush's use of the bogus Iraqi uranium procurement allegation. They pestered national security adviser Condoleezza Rice last week on Air Force One. When an intelligence agency demurs from a consensus view in an assessment, it "takes a footnote," Rice explained. The State Department's Intelligence and Research (INR) office doubted the story about Iraq trying to buy uranium from Niger, she said, and that "standard INR footnote was 59 pages in the back," so she and Bush didn't know . . .
>
> Condi: You know those little superscript numbers you occasionally see in the text? Those are called "footnote numbers." For every footnote in the back, there is a number. That's how you know that if you are a serious rather than a casual reader of National Intelligence

5. See: http://www.truthout.org/docs_03/072903F.shtml

Assessments, you are supposed to turn to the back of the report and read the footnote.

And, yes, professors, graduate students, and Assistants to the President for National Security are *always* responsible for material in the footnotes.[6]

Rice is a liar, incompetent, or both. You decide.

RUTHLESSNESS

In the uproar over the falsehoods in Bush's State of the Union address, Rice first tried to blame George Tenet, director of the CIA. "Maybe someone knew down in the bowels of the agency, but no one in our circles knew that there were doubts and suspicions that this might be a forgery," she said. But as early as October, 2002, Tenet personally warned Rice's deputy, Steve Hadley, not to use the Africa/uranium claim.

Here Rice crossed another ethical line, where dishonesty became ruthlessness. For Tenet, if anyone in the inner circles of Bush's power, had tried to warn the government *not* to use the uranium claim.

CLINTON AND RICE ON ENGLISH

Rice appeared on Fox News to explain the yellowcake debacle. In a statement that would have done Bill Clinton proud, Rice said, "The statement that (Bush) made was indeed accurate. The British government did say that. Not

6. See: http://www.j-bradford-delong.net/movable_type/2003_archives/001770.html
For more silliness from Rice, see also: http://www.dailyhowler.com/dh091003.shtml

only was the statement accurate, there were statements of this kind in the National Intelligence Estimate." In other words, rather than telling us that Iraq was guilty of these actions, which is what we all foolishly thought he said, Bush was essentially giving a school report, telling us that the British government had made claims about Iraqi guilt. Imagine that. How foolish of us.

But, why then did Tenet "take the blame" by stating the uranium yellowcake ore statement should not have been included in the president's speech? After all, all Bush was doing was reporting on a British report. Why did Bush, Rice, and Rumsfeld try and confuse us by saying first that Bush's assertion was not accurate and then saying that it was? The answer is simple, and not pretty. [7]

AND BEFORE 9-11?

Rice told the public in May 2002 that a pre 9-11 intelligence briefing for the president on terrorism contained only general warnings and historical information. Nothing specific. But according to the Congressional report on 9 11, Bush's briefing a month before the suicide hijackings included, as an AP story reported, "recent intelligence that al-Qaida was planning to send operatives into the United States to carry out an attack using high explosives." AP adds "The White House defended Rice, saying her answers were accurate given what she could state publicly at the time about still-classified information." Yeah.

AP continued, " The Sept. 11 congressional investigators underscore their point three times in their report, using nearly identical language to contrast Rice's answers with the actual information in the presidential briefing."

Basically, the White House had explicit reports that Al Qaida was planning an attack, that they planned to use planes to fly into major buildings.

The president's daily briefing on Aug. 6, 2001, contained "information acquired in May 2001 that indicated a group of bin Laden supporters was planning attacks in the United States with explosives," the report stated.

Rice "stated, however, that the report did not contain specific warning information, but only a generalized warning, and did not contain information that al-Qaida was discussing a particular planned attack against a specific target at any specific time, place, or by any specific method." More tricky language—the report did not tell her that four aircraft were to be hijacked on 9-11, and that the four targets were the two WTC towers, the Pentagon, and whatever the fourth would have been. But most of us would expect that less specific reports would have led to heightened security.

At a May 2002 press briefing, Rice said that "I don't think anybody could have predicted that these people would take an airplane and slam it into the World Trade Center, take another one and slam it into the Pentagon; that they would try to use an airplane as a missile, a hijacked airplane as a missile."

AP writes the congressional report states that "from at least 1994, and continuing into the summer of 2001, the Intelligence Community received information indicating that terrorists were contemplating, among other means of attack, the use of aircraft as weapons."

The Bushies resorted to their most frequently given

7. See: http://www.webleyweb.com/tle/libe232-20030803-02.html

reason for lying to us: national security. "Dr. Rice's briefing was a full and accurate accounting of the materials in question without compromising classified material that could endanger national security," National Security Council spokesman Sean McCormack said. How keeping this information from us helped any security but the election possibilities of the White House is difficult to grasp. The entire story is even worse, but check for yourselves. [8]

8. http://www.truthout.org/docs_03/072903F.shtml
For more, see: http://www.truthout.org/docs_03/073103C.shtml

ANAGRAM

National Security Advisor Condoleezza Rice
Crazed, overzealous, idiotical cretin annoys.

Colin Powell once enjoyed the respect of Americans in both parties; these days both sides hold him in contempt. What happened?

The Tragedy of Colin Powell

from Slate.com (2/19/04)

Fred Kaplan

Is Colin Powell melting down?

It's hard to come up with another explanation for his jaw-dropping behavior last week before the House International Relations Committee. There he sat, recounting for the umpety-umpth time why, back in February 2003, he believed the pessimistic estimates about Iraqi weapons of mass destruction. "I went and lived at the CIA for about four days," he began, "to make sure that nothing was—" Suddenly, he stopped and glared at a Democratic committee staffer who was smirking and shaking his head. "Are you shaking your head for something, young man back there?" Powell grumbled. "Are you part of the proceedings?"

Rep. Sherrod Brown, an Ohio Democrat, objected, "Mr. Chairman, I've never heard a witness reprimand a staff person in the middle of a question."

Powell muttered back, "I seldom come to a meeting where I am talking to a congressman and I have people aligned behind you, giving editorial comment by head shakes."

Oh, my.

Here is a man who faced hardships in the Bronx as a kid, bullets in Vietnam as a soldier, and bureaucratic bullets through four administrations in Washington, a man who rose to the ranks of Army general, national security adviser, chairman of the Joint Chiefs of Staff, and secretary of state, a man who thought seriously about running for president—and he gets bent out of shape by some snarky House staffer?

Powell's outburst is a textbook sign of overwhelming stress. Maybe he was just having a bad day. Then again, he's also been having a bad three years.

As George Bush's first term nears its end, Powell's tenure as top diplomat is approaching its nadir. On the high-profile issues of the day, he seems to have almost no influence within the administration. And his fateful briefing one year ago before the U.N. Security Council—where he attached his personal credibility to claims of Iraqi WMD—has destroyed his once-considerable standing with the Democrats, not to mention our European allies, most of the United Nations, and the media.

At times, Powell has taken his fate with resigned humor. Hendrik Hertzberg wrote in *The New Yorker* last year of a diplomatic soiree that Powell attended on the eve of war, at which a foreign diplomat recited a news account that Bush was sleeping like a baby. Powell reportedly replied, "I'm sleeping like a baby, too. Every two hours, I wake up, screaming."

At other times, though, Powell must be frustrated beyond measure. One can imagine the scoldings he takes from liberal friends for playing "good soldier" in an administration that's treated him so shabbily and that's rejected his advice so brazenly. That senseless dressing-down of the committee staffer—a tantrum that no one with real power would ever indulge in—can best be seen as a rare public venting of Powell's maddened mood.

The decline of Powell's fortunes is a tragic tale of politics: so much ambition derailed, so much accomplishment nullified.

From the start of this presidency, and to a degree that no one would have predicted when he stepped into Foggy Bottom with so much pride and energy, Powell has found himself almost consistently muzzled, outflanked, and humiliated by the true powers—Vice President Dick Cheney and Secretary of Defense Donald Rumsfeld. (Bureaucratic battles between Foggy Bottom and the Pentagon have been a feature of many presidencies, but Powell has suffered the additional—and nearly unprecedented—indignity of swatting off continuous rear-guard assaults from his own undersecretary of state, John Bolton, an aggressive hard-liner who was installed at State by Cheney for the purpose of diverting and exhausting the multilateralists.)

One of Powell's first acts as secretary of state was to tell a reporter that the Bush administration would pick up where Bill Clinton left off in negotiations with North Korea—only to be told by Cheney that it would do no such thing. He had to retract his statement. For the next nine months, he disappeared so definitively that *Time* magazine asked, on its cover of Sept. 10, 2001, "Where Is Colin Powell?"

The events and aftermath of 9/11 put Powell still farther on the sidelines. He scored something of a victory a year later, when Bush decided, over the opposition of Cheney and Rumsfeld, to take his case for war against Iraq to the U.N. General Assembly. But Powell's attempts to resolve the crisis diplomatically ended in failure.

Once the invasion got under way, the principles of warfare that he'd enunciated as a general—the need to apply overwhelming force on the battlefield (which, during the last Gulf War, was dubbed the "Powell Doctrine")—were harshly rejected (and, in this case, rightly so—Rumsfeld's plan to invade with lighter, more agile forces was a stunning success, at least in the battlefield phase of the war). Powell's objections to Ariel Sharon's departure from the Israeli-Palestinian "road map" were overridden by a White House where Elliot Abrams had been put in charge of Middle East policy. Powell's statements on the Middle East came to be so widely ignored—because no one saw them as reflecting U.S. policy—that Bush sent Condoleezza Rice to the region when he wanted to send a message that would be taken seriously. When Bush dispatched an emissary to Western Europe after the war to lobby for Iraqi debt-cancellation and make overtures for renewing alliances, he picked not Powell but James Baker, the Bush family's longtime friend and his father's secretary of state.

Ian Bremmer, president of the Eurasia Group, a political risk-assessment firm, notes that Powell has scored significant policy achievements on China, Georgia, and the India-Pakistan dispute. But these are issues over which neither Cheney nor Rumsfeld has much at stake—politically, ideologically, or financially.

There have also been occasions, on higher-profile

topics, when Powell has broken through the barricades and advanced his positions. He (and Condi Rice) persuaded Bush, over Rumsfeld's opposition, to implement the U.S.-Russian accord reducing strategic missiles. However, he couldn't stop the president from pulling out of the Anti-Ballistic-Missile Treaty.

Last September, Powell met with President Bush in the Oval Office to make the case for presenting a new U.N. resolution on the occupation of Iraq—and to announce that the Joint Chiefs agreed with him. This was a daring move: Rumsfeld opposed going back to the United Nations; Powell, the retired general, had gone around him for support. Even here, though, Powell's triumph was partial, at best. Bush went back to the United Nations, but the resulting resolution did not call for internationalizing political power in Iraq to anywhere near the degree that Powell favored.

Similarly, Powell has had a few successes at getting Bush to participate in negotiations with North Korea over its nuclear-weapons program. (Cheney and Rumsfeld oppose even sitting down for talks.) Yet Bush has declined to adopt any position on what an acceptable accord, short of North Korea's unilateral disarmament, might be. More than a year into this perilous drama, the fundamentals of U.S. policy haven't changed at all.

Powell has also won the occasional battle—or, more accurately, has been on the winning side—when his position converges with Bush's vital political interests. For instance, against the advice of Cheney and Rumsfeld, Bush will probably turn over at least some political control in Iraq to the United Nations. He will do so not because Powell has advised such a course, but because the presidential election is coming up and Bush needs to show voters that he has an exit strategy and that American soldiers will not be dying in Baghdad and Fallujah indefinitely.

If there is a second Bush term, Powell will almost certainly not be in it. News stories have reported that he'll step down. He has stopped short of quitting already not just because he's a good soldier, but because that's not what ambitious Cabinet officers do in American politics. Those who resign in protest usually write themselves out of power for all time. They are unlikely to be hired even after the opposition party resumes the Executive Office because they're seen as loose cannons.

Powell, who at one point might have been an attractive presidential candidate for either party, has fallen into a double-damned trap. He can't quit for reasons cited above; yet his often-abject loyalty to Bush, especially on the Iraq question, makes him an unseemly candidate for a future Democratic administration.

He seems to have launched a rehabilitation campaign, to escape this dreaded state. Last month, after David Kay resigned as the CIA's chief weapons inspector and proclaimed that Iraq probably didn't have weapons of mass destruction after all, Powell told a reporter that he might not have favored going to war if he'd known there were no WMD a year ago. He almost instantly retracted his words, as all internal critics of Bush policies seem to do.

Powell's best option, after January, may be to abandon his ambitions for further public office, nab a lucrative job in the private sector, and write the most outrageous kiss-and-tell political memoir that the world has ever seen.

ANAGRAM

'A Soldier's Way'—Colin Powell
Really sad, low policies now.

Colin Powell and 'The Power of Audacity'

from *The Nation* (9/22/03)
Eric Alterman

One of the problems with the media coverage of this Administration is that it requires bad manners. I don't mean the kind of bad manners usually associated with reporters: shouting over one another, elbowing a colleague to get closer to one's interview subject or even quoting an anonymous source reporting that so-and-so really isn't up to the job. Rather, to be an honest, objective and fair-minded reporter of the Bush Administration's policies requires pointing out repeatedly and without sentimentality that just about all the men and women responsible for the conduct of this nation's foreign (and many of its domestic) affairs are entirely without personal honor when it comes to the affairs of state. This simply isn't done in respectable journalism, and the Bush people understand that. Arthur Miller, speaking at a Nation Institute dinner last year, termed the willingness to use this kind of knowledge "the power of audacity."

The preceding, while a bit baldly stated for most, would be considered arguable, but not outrageous, to many mainstream journalists with regard to Bush, Cheney, Rumsfeld and their militant minions in the Pentagon and NSC. But what of Colin Powell? Widely considered to be a man of uncommon personal integrity and a voice of reason in presidential war councils—perhaps the only such voice—Powell remains the thin reed upon which men and women of good will here and abroad pin their ever-declining hopes. A war hero, a member of a minority who is known to be more moderate, thoughtful and generally sensible on pretty much everything than the President and the rest of those who serve him, it was Powell, after all, who fought the good fight for a multilateralist approach to foreign policy in Iraq and elsewhere.

When Powell went before the UN Security Council in February 2003, reporters treated his accusations against Saddam Hussein as if akin to tablets passed down by Moses from the mountaintop. A study by Gilbert Cranberg, former editorial page editor of the *Des Moines Register,* discovered a nearly perfect storm of wide-eyed credulity in coverage of the speech. We heard and read of "a massive array of evidence," "a detailed and persuasive case," "a powerful case," "a sober, factual case," "an overwhelming case," "a compelling case," "the strong, credible and persuasive case," "a persuasive, detailed accumulation of information," "a smoking fusillade . . . a persuasive case for anyone who is still persuadable," "an accumulation of painstakingly gathered and analyzed evidence," so that "only the most gullible and wishful thinking souls can now deny that Iraq is harboring and hiding weapons of mass destruction." "The skeptics asked for proof; they now have it." "Powell's evidence," we were told, was "overwhelming," "ironclad . . . incontrovertible," "succinct and damning . . . the case is closed." "Colin Powell delivered the goods on Saddam Hussein." "If there was any doubt that Hussein . . . needs to be . . . stripped of his chemical and biological capabilities, Powell put it to rest."

And yet the slightest scrutiny of the text would have revealed this certainty on the part of the Fourth Estate to be completely inappropriate. Powell employed all kinds of weasel words in his address that should have set off alarm bells in any first-year journalism student. Over and over, Cranberg notes, he attributed his charges to the likes of "human sources," "an eyewitness," "detainees," "an Al Qaeda source," "a senior defector," "intelligence sources." At a meeting at the Waldorf Astoria just before his talk, reported by the *Guardian*, Powell complained to British Foreign Secretary Jack Straw that the claims coming out of the Pentagon—particularly those made by Deputy Secretary Wolfowitz—could not be substantiated (Straw denies that the meeting took place). Powell allegedly told the Foreign Secretary that he had just about "moved in" with his intelligence staff to prepare for his speech but had left his briefings "apprehensive," fearing that the evidence might "explode in their faces." A *U.S. News & World Report* story describes the Secretary of State throwing the documents in the air and declaring, "I'm not reading this. This is bullshit!"

But the good soldier read it anyway. His worst fears would soon be realized, however, when the British Foreign Office was forced to admit that a considerable portion of its Iraq dossier—upon which Powell had decided to rely quite heavily—had been lifted, verbatim, from dated academic sources and even included a portion that was plagiarized from a journal article by an American graduate student. What's more, it turned out that the dossier did not even purport to prove what Powell insisted it did. Recently, the Hutton Commission in England discovered an e-mail from Tony Blair's chief of staff to his boss, explaining that the dossier "does nothing to demonstrate he [Saddam Hussein] has the motive to attack his neighbours, let alone the west. We will need to be clear in launching the document that we do not claim that we have evidence that he is an imminent threat." In recent weeks, Charles Hanley, an Associated Press reporter, subjected Powell's claims to thorough investigation in light of what was known at the time as well as later revelations. It is a tough-minded assessment, and just about nothing in Powell's presentation survived. (You can find it at www.commondreams.org.) Every one of those reports quoted above was, in other words—to borrow Powell's term—"bullshit."

In a truly nutty editorial published in June, *Washington Times* editors observed that "86 percent of Americans continue to be certain, or at least believe it is likely, that before the war Iraq not only had the facilities to develop weapons of mass destruction, but that it also possessed biological or chemical weapons." The editors were arguing that Americans don't care that their leaders deliberately misled them to convince them to enter this apparently never-ending quagmire, and so neither should the media. It's quite a trick: Lie to the American people and then fall back on the fact that they bought the lies to demonstrate that truth really doesn't matter anyway. It is in this and only this Alice-in-Wonderland universe that a dishonest propagandist like Colin Powell may be considered an "internationalist," a "moderate" and, sadly, a "man of honor."

AND WE'RE BACK WITH SECRETARY OF STATE COLIN POWELL. MR. SECRETARY, YOU WERE EXPLAINING HOW IRAQ IS A GREATER THREAT THAN NORTH KOREA?
© 2003 Aaron McGruder/Dist. by Universal Press Syndicate
YES. EVEN THOUGH NORTH KOREA ACTUALLY HAS NUCLEAR WEAPONS, IS CURRENTLY MAKING MORE, AND COULD HAVE THE CAPABILITY TO STRIKE THE U.S. IN THE NEAR FUTURE, IRAQ IS MUCH MORE DANGEROUS.
1/9
www.ucomics.com www.boondocks.net
AND ... THAT ACTUALLY MAKES SENSE TO YOU?
GIMME A BREAK, ALL RIGHT? THEY MAKE ME SAY THIS STUFF ...

Colin Powell, Alas

from *The Nation* (11/17/03)

Calvin Trillin

His memory of war was strong.
No Sissy Hawk, he'd fought the Cong.
He knew that bunk on nukes was wrong.
But, still, he chose to go along.
Of him, they'll sing the saddest song:
"But, still, he chose to go along."

NORTON, GRILES AND COMPANY

with a quote by Gale Norton;
a quiz by Paul Slansky;
a cartoon by Tom Toles;
and an anagram

The Bush administration's mishandling of foreign policy and the economy overshadow the fact that its members have declared open season on the environment. Secretary of the Interior Gale Norton and her deputy Steven Griles have allowed their friends in the polluting industries to trash the planet in pursuit of profit. These so-called stewards of the land are enough to make us pine for the days when the brutal and clownish Reagan interior secretary James Watt (Norton's former mentor) enforced (or failed to enforce) environmental policy.

Sale of the Wild

from *Vanity Fair* (September 2003)

Michael Shnayerson

Gale Norton smiles a lot—pretty much all the time. She likes to wear jeans and work shirts, and make press appearances in the great outdoors, against backdrops of natural beauty.

Today's setting is a farm in North Carolina. Trailed by a few local reporters, the secretary of the interior inspects a wetland restored by a feisty widow with help from the U.S. Fish and Wildlife Service, one of Interior's eight agencies. "Projects like this one are the future of conservation," Norton, 49, says from a lectern, brought down for the occasion. Citizens and the government, working together.

Rigid rules—which is to say the body of environmental regulations adopted in the U.S. over the last 33 years, starting with the Clean Air Act of 1970—are out of fashion. Partnership is in.

It's an appealing approach when applied to landowners restoring wetlands. Less so, perhaps, when extended to the extractive industries—coal, oil, gas, and timber—that want to exploit the natural riches of public lands and build power plants that pollute national parks.

When President Bush nominated her to his Cabinet, two and a half years ago, Norton stirred widespread outrage among environmental activists—the "enviros" or, as Bush once called them, the "green, green lima beans." She was, after all, a protégé of James Watt, the gleefully anti-environmental secretary of the interior under President

Ronald Reagan. Before joining Watt in Washington, she had worked as lead attorney for his Mountain States Legal Foundation, trying to weaken environmental laws that hindered landowners. As Colorado's attorney general, she argued before the U.S. Supreme Court that the Endangered Species Act should not prevent landowners from destroying habitat, even if species went extinct as a result.

Despite this, Norton was confirmed to run the department, which oversees more public land than any other: 20 percent of the U.S. in all. Then an odd thing happened. To the enviros' surprise, no Watt-like battle cries emanated from the secretary's corner office at 18th and C Streets. Norton just . . . smiled and invoked her new catchphrase—"the four C's": "consultation, cooperation, and communication, all in the name of conservation." She repeated it so often that it began to madden even her own staffers. Yet, as she did, the great ship of Interior began to turn.

The change in course is part of a larger shift throughout the Bush administration. The president has made future energy needs a top priority. Unfortunately, massive drilling on public lands is deemed necessary to meet them. Inside his agencies, "preservation" has become a dirty word—a word that gets you transferred if you insist on it in a land-use plan instead of proposing to auction mineral rights to the highest bidder.

Overseeing the shift are several dozen top Bush appointees who, like Norton, once worked as lawyers or lobbyists for the extractive industries, hammering away at environmental laws. Now they hold high posts in the agencies they once attacked: not just at Interior but also at Agriculture (which includes the U.S. Forest Service), the Environmental Protection Agency (E.P.A.), and less obvious enclaves, such as the Justice Department and the Office of Management and Budget, which affect environmental policy, too—controversial cases are dropped, environmental programs deemed uneconomical. The "politicals," as they're known in Washington, were named to these jobs with the enthusiastic approval of their industries, as payback for campaign contributions: $48.3 million in all to the G.O.P. during the 1999-2000 election season from mining, timber, chemical, and manufacturing interests, oil and gas, and coal. Every administration rewards its friends, but never has there been such a wholesale giveaway of government agencies to the very industries they're meant to oversee. The results have seemed staggering, and not just to groups such as the Sierra Club. The mainstream Republicans for Environmental Protection recently rated the Bush administration in eight areas of environmental concern. Six of the eight grades were D's. A seventh—on energy policy—was an F. Farm policy got the highest grade: B-.

Happily for Bush, most voters of both parties, distracted by 9/11, Afghanistan, and Iraq, remain oblivious to the story. Environmental news comes and goes, and no one connects the gathering dots to see the big picture. One of the few aspects to resonate of late is the resignation in June of E.P.A. administrator Christie Whitman. People are more colorful than policies, and Whitman was seen as the only environmental moderate of any influence in the Bush administration. In her resignation statement, she played the loyal soldier, pleading the need for a personal life after two grueling years in Washington. Was she, in fact, unwilling to accept the White House's doctoring of an about-to-be-released "report card" on the environment she'd commissioned in 2001? A section linking global warming to smokestack and tailpipe emissions was cut to a few paragraphs by White House officials, *The New York Times* determined. The final version declared global warming a "scientific challenge."

If so, the report was but the latest in a long line of defeats for Whitman, starting with Bush's abrupt dismissal of the Kyoto Protocol on greenhouse-gas emissions. Instead of being allowed to prepare her own plans for domestic policy and present them to the White House, one E.P.A. insider explains, Whitman was summoned to the White House, time and again, to have plans presented to her. "She was sitting across the table from people at the White House who know these industries, starting with (Vice President) Cheney," says the insider. "She was powerless."

At least the E.P.A.'s new, lower standards for pollutants may be reversed by a future administration, and air and water may improve. When unspoiled land is opened to development, however, it's changed—forever. That's why what's happening at Interior is so distressing to many of the department's own employees. "Every time you turn around here," says one insider with a sigh, "there's a decision that makes you wince. The only body that stops us is Congress. But now it's all in the same party, so there's no check there. So they're just getting away with it all."

Because public lands stir such strong feelings, the politics at Interior are more complex than at the E.P.A., and more subtle. Norton is the department's public face, upbeat and reassuring. Behind her is the deputy secretary, said by many to be the department's real head, running it day to day. Like all of her top officials, J. Steven Griles pays earnest lip service to Norton's "four C's." But coming from him, the mantra sounds like a lullaby crooned by a salivating bear.

Griles, 54, is a big, broad-shouldered former lobbyist for coal, oil, and gas who now wields extraordinary power behind the scenes. He's charming and gregarious, tough, canny, hot-tempered, and sometimes bullying. He's also very smart, though not quite smart enough to have kept from getting enmeshed in several seeming conflicts of interest. His story is his own, and yet, at the same time, it's something larger.

It's the story that connects the dots.

The Interior Department building stands like a fortress not far from the Washington Monument, overlooking the forested hills that rise unexpectedly south of the Mall. Inside, the main corridors are as wide as tennis courts and two blocks long. W.P.A. murals depict scenes from the department's disparate realms: engineers building a dam, cowboys and Indians on the plains. Along with Fish and Wildlife, Interior's eight agencies include the National Park Service and the Bureau of Land Management (B.L.M.); the latter manages 262 million acres of public land, mostly in the West, that have been designated for "multiple use," a term encompassing both conservation and development. In all, Interior employs 70,000 people, overseen by fewer than 50 "politicals," most of whom are on the sixth floor.

Norton's office is immense: a vast oak-paneled realm with chandeliers and facing sofas, ornately framed oil paintings, and brass doorknobs with a buffalo motif. The decor, to be sure, pre-dates the current secretary, and Harold Ickes, secretary of the interior under F.D.R. and Harry S. Truman, is responsible for the room's dimensions:

the story has it that he measured all of Roosevelt's other Cabinet secretaries' offices, then called for his own to be a foot longer and wider than the largest of them.

Griles's office is at the opposite end of the same wing. He can reach it only through adjoining offices, however, because poised in front of his closed door is a stuffed, full-grown Alaskan grizzly bear, standing upright with its long teeth bared and front claws extended, ready to pounce. Griles heard that it was gathering dust in a Fish and Wildlife archive building and had it brought up. "He's great, isn't he?" Griles says with a grin. "Children love him."

Covering the walls inside are framed pictures of Griles with various top Republicans, including President Reagan: this is not the former lobbyist's first tour at Interior. On this day in early June, his career in public service hangs on an investigation under way by the department's inspector general, but if Griles is worried he gives no sign of it. He has a politician's penchant for touching your arm, or clapping a hand on your shoulder, as he makes a point, and leaning in close to create an instant bond. Mention golf and you're friends for life. Staffers pride themselves on how much golf they play with the deputy secretary, who seems happy for any excuse to get away from meetings at the Interior Department.

Meetings are what got Griles in hot water: dozens of them, beginning within days of his confirmation, in July 2001, with ex-clients and associates linked to issues from which he'd recused himself because of his former lobbying activities. "Griles doesn't seem to understand how bad it looks," says Kristen Sykes, the Interior Department watchdog for Friends of the Earth, who got the calendars through the Freedom of Information Act, "when he continues to keep company with these special interests."

Just as upsetting to the enviros was the arrangement the deputy secretary made upon his confirmation to distance himself from the lobbying firm he'd created. Griles sold the client base of J. Steven Griles & Associates for $1.1 million to another firm, National Environmental Strategies (N.E.S.), in which he had had a principal interest. N.E.S. also happens to do business in the same Washington office suite that J. Steven Griles & Associates did. N.E.S.'s founder, Marc Himmelstein, one of Griles's best friends, committed to buy the client base in four annual payments of $284,000, beginning in 2001. So the deputy secretary is receiving a major outside income from his former business colleague, who continues to represent Griles's former clients. Those clients are principally coal, oil, and gas companies.

One might reasonably ask what the value of a lobbyist's client base is without ongoing representation of those clients' interests, and ongoing payments by those clients for same. But as Griles testily observes when asked, the arrangement was fully disclosed at the start of his tenure and approved by Interior Department lawyers. And the subsequent meetings with ex-clients, he says, were of a general nature, not on the "particular matters" from which he'd recused himself. All this is what the inspector general is reviewing.

As deputy secretary, Griles oversees Interior's whole range of red-hot issues—excluding, ostensibly, the ones from which he's recused himself—and so he's quick to react to two that have stirred deep dismay of late, not only among enviros but also in the Bureau of Land

Management's ranks. Last April, Interior's lawyers chose to settle with the state of Utah in a suit involving wilderness designation of 250,000 acres of B.L.M. land. Basically, they agreed to abandon Clinton-era efforts to afford the land ultimate protection—no development. It's a complex story that most Americans chose to ignore, but it's extraordinarily important.

Utah, like all western states, where most of Interior's public lands lie, bridles at federal oversight of any kind. It particularly resented the Clinton administration's decision to keep recommending more areas of B.L.M. land in Utah for wilderness designation, after the expiration of a congressionally mandated period in which the B.L.M. was ordered to consider all its lands for such protection. The period had begun in 1980 and ended in 1993. Clinton's B.L.M. felt that two Republican administrations, loath to alienate their western political base, had dragged their feet on the matter. So the Democrats earmarked about 2.6 million Utah acres as wilderness. These were only recommendations; Congress retained the power to make the actual designations.

An earlier court challenge by Utah of the Clinton administration's policy had failed. But with the new case, Norton's Interior chose to cave. As a result, the 2.6 million acres in Utah that might have qualified for designation cannot be considered. "They're more vulnerable," says one B.L.M. insider. And that's the catch. "Once they're developed, they can't be protected as wilderness." Worse, Norton declared that the Utah case sets a national precedent. With that one decision, more than 220 million acres of B.L.M. land across the West and Alaska can no longer be considered for wilderness designation by this process.

Only the 23 million acres proposed to Congress before October 1993 are still eligible.

"What occurred," says Griles of the Clinton-era B.L.M. officials, "was they continued a process that was not authorized by the statute. That's what the settlement says, that's what the judge authorized, and that's what we agreed with." Other top politicals at Interior are quick to add that three million acres in Utah were set aside before 1993 and Congress has yet to take action on them. Also, they say, any of the department's lands can still be "managed" as wilderness within standard land-use plans. But these are the same politicals who are calling for more energy development in those plans.

This decision was kept quiet by Norton, Griles, and a tight circle of top politicals until it was issued, with little publicity. "The wilderness decision was a huge shock to all of us," says one department insider. So was the related revival by Interior of RS2477, an 1866 mining-road law; now western states are claiming ownership of thousands of miles of old "roads," many of them overgrown trails on federal lands, to thwart even the agreed-upon wilderness recommendations. "It was done entirely in the secretary's office," says a congressional staffer. Which makes sense, the staffer adds dryly. "If the word gets out, you'll generate controversy and lose control."

These moves are all too typical. Whenever possible, agency rules are "streamlined" and "modernized" without fanfare. Time passes. Public-comment periods end. Unnoticed, policies shift. The soothing euphemisms are taken directly from the playbook of Republican political consultant Frank Luntz. So are the names of multi-agency programs too big to slip under the radar. "Healthy Forests" is the administration's dubious new campaign to fight forest fires by engaging large timber companies as "partners." The companies will clear decades of undergrowth that does act as kindling for fires; as compensation for this unprofitable work, however, they get to punch roads into pristine wilderness in order to take out very profitable—and irreplaceable—old-growth trees. "Clear Skies" states stirring goals for reducing smokestack emissions; left unstated is that these goals are lower than those the administration inherited.

Control and the secrecy needed to exercise it are seen as the hallmarks of Norton and Griles's Interior Department, according to many of their civil-service employees. "It's a culture," says one, "of mistrust." "There are a lot of policy changes and decisions being made by a select few, very carefully," says another, "without any input or data from career professionals."

"They came in being critical right away: 'This is what we're going to do; this is what you're not doing,'" explains one high-ranking Fish and Wildlife official. "And because of the lack of trust, there was a disconnect between politicals and field people."

At the B.L.M., where the balance between conservation and development is most delicate, the politics have been nastiest. "The only career people at B.L.M. the politicals trusted were a few who had come in as Republicans," says one insider. As a result, "the morale at B.L.M. is probably the poorest it's been in 20 years."

Martha Hahn, the B.L.M. state director for Idaho, with 24 years' experience in the agency, claims she was one casualty. When Hahn took a hard line on grazing rights, she says, she ran afoul of powerful Idaho senator Larry

Craig—the same Senator Craig who distinguished himself recently by holding up some 850 military promotions in order to get a few promised planes for an Idaho military base. Craig turned to Griles, says Hahn. Craig's office denies any role in the situation. By letter, Griles informed Hahn that she was being transferred—to New York Harbor, as executive director of the National Park Service. "There hadn't been one before," Hahn says, "and there isn't one now. It was just a position to threaten people into. I had no verbal communications with him, which is what the rules require. The letter just said, 'You accept this or you resign.'" Hahn resigned.

"That's a very distorted story," Griles says with a pained look. "I've known Martha—I knew her when she was a B.L.M. ranger in Moab." The transfer, he says, was not punitive. "It's what the Senior Executive Service (or S.E.S., a B.L.M. corps of elite civil-service employees) is intended to allow to occur. The purpose of the S.E.S., when it was set up, was to have this layer of qualified people who were the best managers. They could go from one department to the next and take the understanding and influence. After a point, you need new blood, new ideas. That's what I try to do with the S.E.S. Re-invigorate it. Give them new challenges."

Hahn's former supervisor, Nina Hatfield, confirms that S.E.S.-ers do get transferred with each new administration. But transfer by letter, she admits, "just doesn't happen." She calls Hahn "smart and professional." Since her resignation, Hahn has become a lightning rod for discontent. "People are feeling helpless, and very scared," she says. "I get lots of phone calls from colleagues. What they ask is: How can I survive this?"

By "this," what the insiders mean is not just the secrecy, or the centralization—field officers now have to route even the smallest decisions, such as whether to close a road in elk-hunting season, to Washington for approval—but the raw push to give industry and western states whatever they want.

In Utah, for example, oil and gas exploration has been proposed for the Dome Plateau, a 36-square-mile swath of red-rock canyon, as well as for the much larger and more remote Book Cliffs, which overlaps with seven areas on the list for wilderness designation. The latter was approved despite 25,000 public comments opposing the decision—and objections from the E.P.A. In Montana, the B.L.M. has approved plans for natural-gas drilling in Missouri River Breaks National Monument. In Texas, oil drilling has been stepped up at Padre Island National Park; the heavy trucks that daily service this project's 156-foot drilling derrick roll across beaches that serve as the main nesting grounds for the imperiled Kemp's-ridley sea turtle.

These are the small projects.

Most Americans know that last April the Bush administration came within four votes of opening the 19-million-acre Arctic National Wildlife Refuge (ANWR) to drilling after two decades of bitter debate. Because it's a refuge, ANWR is governed by Fish and Wildlife at Interior, so it's within Griles's domain. Fewer know that Alaska also contains the nearly untouched 23.5-million-acre National Petroleum Reserve-Alaska (N.P.R.-A.), which was set aside by Congress in 1923 for future emergency use only. When ANWR was established by President Jimmy Carter in 1980, a compromise allowed Congress to review its status in the future; that's why it's stirred high-profile brawls ever since. But the N.P.R.-A. is B.L.M. land, so no such fight is needed. And because it's B.L.M. land, it, too, is within Griles's domain.

All told, the B.L.M. is proposing to lease more than nine million acres for oil exploration in Alaska in the next few years—all of it outside ANWR. "Industry's top request is for us to keep sales on a predictable schedule and provide them ample time for planning," Griles told an Alaskan audience last fall. "We are committed to do this."

As Mr. Inside, Griles does far fewer press events than Norton, but this morning he's scheduled to paddle a canoe with inner-city kids on Washington, D.C.'s Anacostia River and look in on a new-park ceremony. Like Norton, he uses a private elevator that goes from the sixth floor down to the parking garage, where a car and driver are waiting.

Griles is a short distance and a long way from the town of Clover in Southside, Virginia, where his father worked as a small-time tobacco farmer. But this outing reminds him that his father took an interest in children with disabilities—"took them fishing, put them in boats, things like that"—during the six months of the year when he wasn't working. Griles did a lot of fishing with his father, too, and a lot of hunting and horseback riding, until his father's untimely death at 51 from emphysema. He still rides whenever he can, and rafts canyon rivers.

Griles started working for the state right after college, monitoring the coal industry. "I was the guy who kept insisting that the laws of the state of Virginia be changed to increase the environmental controls," he says, but that's not how some others remember him.

"I found Steve to be extremely pro-industry," recalls

Frank Kilgore, a lawyer who worked in the 1970s for mining reform. "No matter what evidence you showed him about people having their houses blown apart, or rocks through the roof, or private cemeteries or water supplies destroyed by stripping, it didn't seem to make any impression on him . . . He was always pretty up-front that he was an industry man—and get out of the way."

When reform came with a federal surface-mining act in 1977, which finally set pollution standards and forced companies to restore ravaged land, Virginia fought it up to the Supreme Court. A decision was still pending in 1981 when Griles was nominated, reportedly with a good word from Virginia senator John Warner, to join the Reagan administration as deputy director at the newly formed Office of Surface Mining (O.S.M.) in James Watt's Interior Department. Griles says he came with a mission to make "cookie-cutter rules" more flexible. But several ex-colleagues say his mission was to do whatever he could to defang the O.S.M. on behalf of his home state.

The Supreme Court ruling on the surface-mining act came not long after Griles's arrival in Washington, while a number of Carter-era appointees were still packing their bags. "One of my staff attorneys came down yelling, 'We won!'" recalls a Carter-appointed Interior lawyer who had worked to get the surface-mining act passed. The vote to strike down Virginia's challenge was unanimous. The lawyer recalls hearing the news while fielding a phone call from Griles. "'Steve, we just heard—we won!'" the lawyer recalls telling him. "There was this silence, then a very cold voice, 'What do you mean, we won? We lost.'" (Griles denies having said this.)

Griles soon alienated the O.S.M.'s inspectors by slashing

their ranks, though, in fairness, he had no choice. New laws called for a gradual transfer of federal oversight to the states, which meant letting go federal inspectors so that states could hire their own. But according to an ex-colleague, he tended to cut or transfer especially those inspectors who acted with the most vigilance. "He'd say, 'What the hell are you doing writing this up?'" recalls one inspector. "We were scared to death. He was going to protect the coal companies; that's the sense we've always had."

One manager, Jack Spadaro, incurred Griles's wrath by having inspectors close a mining company called Dal-Tex for flagrant environmental violations. Spadaro says that Griles, through an intermediary, directed him to reverse the order. Spadaro refused. "Griles then had two people in his human-resource division . . . figure out a way to get me fired," he recalls. Spadaro, who until recently worked as a superintendent at the Mine Safety and Health Administration's National Mine Academy in Beckley, West Virginia, says he was charged with "insubordination" and with making an improper phone call that cost the government 82 cents.

"I had a meeting with him face-to-face, when I was first charged with insubordination," Spadaro recalls. "I went through the violations that had been written at Dal-Tex and explained why I would not vacate them. He became enraged, his face got red, he was almost spitting. I've never seen anything like it. I knew then that this was a different kind of animal." Spadaro was merely suspended for 30 days, not fired. He says he spent $23,000 over the next two years appealing the suspension. "But I won."

By the early 1980s much of the easy coal had been taken, so companies were motivated to try a new method:

blasting off the tops of mountains to get to the coal seams deep within. The only problem was what to do with the obliterated mountaintop. The Clean Water Act set strict rules for what mining companies could dump as "fill" into valley streambeds, and how they could do it. "In the Carter administration, we required them to truck it down and put it in four-foot compacted lifts," explains one inspector. With Griles's promotion in 1983 to deputy assistant secretary of the interior for lands and minerals management, says the inspector, the rules were basically ignored. "Mining operators could push or shove fill from the top of a hollow and let it flow right down to the streambed, transported essentially by gravity."

"Griles more than anyone is the person who was responsible for the relaxation of enforcement efforts that allowed mountaintop removal to proliferate in the 1980s and 1990s," says Spadaro. "More than anyone else in the country. And I'm an expert. I know what I'm talking about, and I know how the rules were weakened dramatically under Griles."

As Reagan's second term wound down, Griles took a job at United, an energy company that happened to have, among other holdings, the Dal-Tex operation. By then he had met Marc Himmelstein, a voluble lobbyist who was about to form his own firm, the previously mentioned National Environmental Strategies, or N.E.S. In 1995, Griles formed J. Steven Griles & Associates and began sharing Himmelstein's office space in downtown Washington. The two firms also shared clients and focused on two of the same issues: coal mining and a new method of producing natural gas called coal-bed methane.

By the mid-1990s producers of natural gas had sensed

a bonanza just waiting to be prized from the Powder River Basin in Wyoming and Montana. They had known that huge reserves of methane could be drawn from the coal-rich basin. But new technology had made the process economically feasible, and the demand for natural gas had soared. Wyoming began leasing state-owned land, and many private landowners joined in. Much of the mineral reserves, however, lay in B.L.M.-controlled lands, and the B.L.M. was getting nervous.

Natural gas might be "clean fuel," but getting it out of the ground in this way is dirty business. Putting in a well brings new roads, tractor-trailer rigs, heavy power lines and pipes, noisy well pumps, and compressor stations across open ranchland. Worse, the process brings huge quantities of underground water to the surface. Much of the water in the Powder River Basin is salty enough to harden the clay soil, kill crops it flows over, and contaminate streambeds. (A top political at Interior questions that: "I've never heard of a situation where you can contaminate the environment with water," he says.) By January 2000 the B.L.M. decided it needed thorough studies of coal-bed methane before allowing the drilling of a projected 39,000 wells in the basin on either side of the Wyoming-Montana line. The lobbyist who helped persuade Congress to free up $3.5 million for the Montana study was one Steve Griles. (Part of that money, he says, was to fund inspectors on the ground.) For the Wyoming study, industry paid. Clinton-era B.L.M. director Tom Fry sanctioned the arrangement when no other monies seemed forthcoming.

"I've struggled with that," Fry admits, "because you can move to the front of the line if you want to pay for it. I've always thought the government should pay. But industry does pay." Western Gas Resources, one of Griles's former coal-bed-methane clients, contributed to industry's share of the payment to a Colorado consulting firm called Greystone, which began doing the environmental-impact study. Greystone, as it happens, is now a client of N.E.S.

"I didn't have anything to do with Greystone," Griles says. "The oil and gas companies chose to do that. I was not representing them on that. They made their own independent judgments."

During the 2000 election, a number of Griles's coal-bed-methane clients were moved to make significant contributions to the G.O.P. Devon Energy gave $45,000 during the campaign season, and its principals gave some $25,000 more. Western Gas gave $16,000, and Yates Petroleum $50,000. More would flow in after Bush was elected. Did the donors have some reason to hope that with a Bush victory their lobbyist would go to Interior, just in time to shepherd the environmental-impact statement through and steer them leases worth billions of dollars? Griles calls that "a conspiracy theory that has no basis, and paranoia with no foundation." He says he had no idea how much each of his former clients gave to the G.O.P. "I never asked them to give to anybody . . . I never was consulted, and never was involved."

In his confirmation hearings of May 2001, Griles fielded tough questions from Senator Ron Wyden (Democrat, Oregon), among others. But the rest of the Energy and Natural Resources Committee seemed distracted, and Griles was approved by an 18-to-4 vote. He signed a letter of recusal on August 1, 2001, pledging to sell his interest in his lobbying firm to N.E.S. within 90 days of his appointment and to recuse himself for a year from "any particular matter" involving his former clients. Over the next month Griles would seem to take rather a broad view of what the word "particular" meant.

Numerous meetings with former clients followed. One visitor was Hal Quinn, senior vice president of the National Mining Association, a former lobbying client of Griles's. Griles says that the talk was strictly social. Undeniably, though, Quinn had a problem. On August 21, a Kentucky citizens group, claiming violations of the Clean Water Act, filed suit in federal court to block the Army Corps of Engineers from issuing permits to coal operators who were burying streams with mountaintop fill.

In the 20 years since Griles first involved himself with the practice, mountaintop mining had turned once forested hills into barren moonscapes across much of coal country. According to figures the government itself would soon produce, from 1992 to 2002 more than 1,200 miles of streams had been damaged in the four-state area of Kentucky, Tennessee, West Virginia, and Virginia, and more than 700 miles of streams had been buried. From 1985 to 2001 some 6,700 valley fills for mountaintop mining were approved, allowing the shearing off of some 380,500 acres of forest cover. "This devastation is unprecedented in this country," declares Joe Lovett, a lawyer who handled the citizens' lawsuit that stopped the industry in its tracks. "It's the kind of thing you can't imagine ever happening." The coal companies wanted to keep up the practice as long as it was profitable, but to do so they felt the E.P.A. would have to broaden its definition of the word "fill."

The decision was the E.P.A.'s, as part of the environmental-impact statement the agency began readying on the issue.

But Interior's Office of Surface Mining had a say, and so did Fish and Wildlife, because of aquatic life in the streambeds. "We sent up 18 pages outlining why we felt the rule was flawed, why we felt it was violating the Clean Water Act and it would have a profound effect on the environment in Appalachia," reports one Fish and Wildlife career official in the field. "Those comments were basically excised when they arrived in D.C."

Griles says with a laugh that he never saw the Fish and Wildlife comments. "The thing you need to know is that N.E.S. never represented the National Mining Association on anything to do with those issues . . . never represented a single company on mountaintop mining." But in October 2001, Griles sent a letter to four federal agencies, calling for E.P.A.'s environmental-impact statement to "focus on centralizing and streamlining coal mine permitting," even as it dealt with "minimizing or mitigating environmental impacts." The next month, he met with representatives of Beech Fork Processing, the very company that figured in the citizens' suit over mountaintop mining. Between September and December 2001, he had at least eight meetings with government officials from other agencies on the issue.

On May 3, 2002, the E.P.A. and the Army Corps of Engineers announced a new definition, right along the lines of what the National Mining Association had advocated. Within days, U.S. District Court judge Charles H. Haden II, who had ruled against the industry before, struck down the new definition. "Fill" was waste, he reiterated, prohibited by the Clean Water Act.

For Lovett and the coal-country residents he represented, this was a triumph, but a short-lived one. The government and the industry appealed to the U.S. Court of Appeals for the Fourth Circuit, heavily stacked with conservative judges. In January 2003, the appeals court overturned Judge Haden's ruling.

Since then, about 100 permit applications for mountaintop mining have piled up, according to one federal official.

The E.P.A. has the power to block those permits, as defined by Congress in the Clean Water Act. But in the draft environmental-impact statement finally published last May, the E.P.A. grants Interior's Office of Surface Mining a greater role in the decision-making process. "It appears the primary goal of the . . . draft E.I.S. was streamlining the permitting process, rather than minimizing environmental impacts," declares a bitter June letter from 19 members of Congress to outgoing E.P.A. secretary Whitman and other federal officials. The Office of Surface Mining is, as it happens, run by Jeffrey Jarrett, a Griles crony from the Reagan years.

Another victory for coal happened more quietly, with a bit of help from Griles but more from two other top Interior officials. Peabody Energy, the world's largest coal company, had proposed not long after Bush's election to build the biggest coal-fired electrical plant in America in a generation. Unfortunately, the site it had in mind was roughly 50 miles west of Kentucky's Mammoth Cave National Park, a UNESCO World Heritage Site and international biosphere reserve.

Set as it is in Kentucky coal country, Mammoth Cave already has the worst visibility of any national park in America. But the 1,500-megawatt Thoroughbred Generating Station proposed by Peabody seemed certain to worsen the white, sulfurous haze that settles over the park on even the sunniest days. According to initial estimates submitted by Peabody to park officials, Thoroughbred would generate some 20,000 tons of sulfur dioxide a year—a significant amount. According to park officials, no emission-reducing scrubbers were proposed for its stacks. (A Peabody spokesman says scrubbers were planned from the beginning.) Thoroughbred was to be a "merchant" plant, selling much of its electricity outside the state.

E-mails over the next 17 months between the park's staff and the National Park Service's Air Resources Division in Denver tell a disturbing story. (The e-mails were F.O.I.A.'d by the Natural Resources Defense Council.) There was concern not only about sulfur dioxide but also about mercury and acid depositions from the facility that might contaminate park streams and soil, endangering fish and plants. But the National Park Service staffers could wrangle hardly any concessions from Peabody. By September 2001 the two sides were at a standoff.

That month, a meeting was held in Washington to move things along. Present were National Park Service director Fran Mainella and Griles. Griles's presence was unusual in itself. But Mammoth Cave's Bob Carson, participating by speakerphone, was more surprised to learn that Peabody representatives were at the meeting, too. He'd been at the National Park Service for more than 20 years and had never heard of a "source"—i.e., a potential source of pollution—sitting in on a meeting in Washington about its own project. Clearly, Peabody had a lot of political clout, Carson thought.

Despite the meeting, months of tussling followed. By late January 2002 a Denver staffer wrote to a colleague in exasperation, "It seems to me that we should not be making concessions (another 'C' word?) to an applicant that has been uncooperative . . . Instead, I suggest that we be willing to take a tough stand based upon our 'core values.'"

Other park staffers agreed-and back at Interior in Washington their superiors appeared to support them. In February 2002, Fish and Wildlife issued an adverse-impact finding on Thoroughbred.

Just as the adverse-impact letter was going out, a National Park Service staffer found a computer glitch in Peabody's weather data. (A Peabody spokeswoman says her side found the error.) Set right, the model showed the plant would not affect visibility at the park as much as feared. Yet, for the staffers, deep concerns remained about the mercury and acid deposition. Unfortunately, no critical threshold had been established for them, so staffers backed off, fearing a battle they might not win. This was frustrating because park scientist Mark DePoy was convinced that several endangered species unique to the park, including certain mussels in the Green River and two kinds of bats in the caves, might be pushed to local extinction by the plant's emissions. So he sent a formal "may affect" report to Fish and Wildlife, because Fish and Wildlife was in charge of endangered species.

Fish and Wildlife was focused on concerns of its own. By April 2002, Peabody had decided to apply for a permit to build a barge-unloading dock and huge water-supply and discharge structures on the Green River hard by the site of the proposed plant. Fish and Wildlife wanted a formal environmental-impact study done.

Because of Peabody's aggressive stance to date, nobody was surprised when the company's lobbyist Dan Scherder set up a meeting for himself and Peabody executives with Fran Mainella in Washington on August 8. As a result, Carson and the other National Park Service staffers were directed to settle with Peabody. Not long after, Fish and Wildlife's call for a study was rejected by the Army Corps of Engineers. On August 22, 2002, Fish and Wildlife assistant secretary Craig Manson sent the Kentucky Division of Air Quality a letter withdrawing the adverse-impact finding.

What none of the staffers knew was that at critical junctures in these weeks Peabody and a subsidiary had begun making a series of soft-money contributions to the G.O.P.

On July 22, 2002, as Scherder was about to set up his meeting with Mainella, Peabody sent $50,000 to the G.O.P.

As Manson's letter went out, Peabody sent in another $50,000.

On August 28, 2002, after the Army Corps of Engineers rejected Fish and Wildlife's call for a major impact study, Peabody gave $100,000. That same day, Peabody subsidiary Black Beauty, a coal company in Indiana, sent in $100,000.

On September 23, 2002, as Kentucky was processing its air-permit application for the plant, Peabody gave $50,000. The permit was issued by the state of Kentucky on October 12, 2002, contingent on a 45-day E.P.A. review. Two weeks after that, Peabody made another $100,000 contribution. On November 18, 2002, the E.P.A. weighed in with two extremely minor comments on the permit. Peabody had won. (A Peabody spokesman says the contributions were pledged months earlier and were in no way related to Thoroughbred.)

"I don't know anything about that," Manson says when

asked about the contributions. Neither does Griles. "And I will tell you there's not a single political appointee that can tell you whether Peabody even contributed," Griles adds heatedly. "I never knew it."

If coal is king in the Bush administration, coal-bed methane is crown prince. Here, too, Interior has chosen energy over the environment. Here, too, are the fingerprints of Griles.

By the winter of 2002 the Colorado consulting firm Greystone had turned in its draft of the environmental-impact statement on coal-bed-methane drilling on the Wyoming side of the Powder River Basin. "You have to be kidding me," one B.L.M. staffer recalls as the general reaction. "Greystone analyzed what industry wanted: 51,000 wells. And then analyzed the alternative of no wells. It didn't look at anything in between." Nor did Greystone pay more than passing heed to the water and air pollution that coal-bed-methane extraction would cause. "They didn't even analyze things you could do to mitigate the problems," says the staffer. "Coal-bed-methane wells would dump billions of gallons of saline water on the surface of the land. It was ridiculous to think that the environment would be the same. Everyone knows that." (Greystone failed to respond to calls from *Vanity Fair*.)

At Interior, coal-bed methane had become a holy cause. "You hear what Alan Greenspan is saying about natural-gas needs in this country," says one top political. "So where's it going to come from? The critics can't just say, 'We'll conserve.'"

But then came a nasty surprise. Because coal-bed methane had an impact on water and air, the E.P.A. had a right to review Greystone's study. Without warning, Jack

McGraw of the E.P.A.'s Denver office gave the report its lowest rating: an E.U.-3—Environmentally Unsatisfactory. Griles wrote a memo to E.P.A. deputy administrator Linda Fisher, complaining that McGraw, a career official, was about to be replaced by a Bush appointee and as such should not have taken "this significant action." He added, "I hope you will consider the best means of addressing EPA's concerns together versus sending a letter that will create, at best, misimpressions and possibly impede the ability to move forward in a constructive manner."

Griles grimaces with annoyance when the memo is mentioned. At the time, he explains, no bureau heads had yet been confirmed. So the president had asked him to serve not only as deputy secretary but also as acting assistant secretary for lands and minerals, overseeing the B.L.M., among other bureaus.

"That morning," Griles recalls of the genesis of his memo to the E.P.A., "(Land and Minerals Management deputy assistant administrator) Tom Fulton said, 'I can't get E.P.A. to call me back.'" Griles says he called E.P.A. deputy administrator Fisher, who wasn't in. So he had Fulton draft a memo, then he modified and signed it and sent it over, with the express purpose of having the agencies communicate better. "It's not a particular matter," he says. "Nobody benefits by the environmental-impact statement." But in any event, he says, "I never got involved."

Three days after the memo, Griles went to a cookout at the Washington home of his old friend Marc Himmelstein. Also at the cookout were Kathleen Clarke, the new B.L.M. chief, and Rebecca Watson, the new assistant secretary for land and minerals, among other Interior politicals.

"Marc's been a friend of mine for 25 years," Griles says in an aggrieved tone. "There was no business discussed."

Griles must have been aware that he was skirting a line, however, because he insisted, he says, on reimbursing Himmelstein for the costs of the dinner. "Look, I've done this too long, O.K.? I know that you can trip yourself up by not being cautious. I gave him a check."

But the deputy secretary did get tripped up by his memo to Fisher. It provoked 55 pages of in-house documents not released to F.O.I.A. applicants. Around the same time, Griles signed a second letter, in which he specifically recused himself from any matters having to do with environmental—impact statements on coal-bed-methane drilling in Wyoming and Montana. Griles avowed that any questions about matters covered by the recusal agreement would be handled by James Cason, his top assistant, whose office is next to his own.

The murkiness of all these arrangements—Griles's two recusals, the continuing meetings—plus growing rumbles from the press and enviros, was what provoked Senator Joe Lieberman (Democrat, Connecticut) in April to ask Interior's inspector general to conduct his own inquiry not just of Griles but also of how the department deals with conflicts of interest.

Griles is unperturbed. "It's the facts, you know?" he says with feeling, back in his office after the Anacostia River canoe outing with children, "and the facts will come out."

And then, as if to show he has nothing to hide—and because he has to change from his canoe-paddling casual clothes into a suit for a formal ceremony—Griles closes the door to his office and rather disarmingly disrobes down to his underwear.

Who has overseen coal-bed methane since Griles's second recusal? Not the new assistant secretary for lands and minerals. Rebecca Watson, an owl-like lawyer from Montana, also had to recuse herself from the issue. Before coming to Washington, she represented the one coal-bed-methane company that managed to sink wells on the Montana side of the basin before a lawsuit slapped a moratorium on drilling in the state. Redstone Gas Partners (now called Fidelity) has also been, as it happens, a client of National Environmental Strategies.

So the mantle has fallen, ostensibly, to Kathleen Clarke, the new B.L.M. director, who says she started the job in January 2002—three months before Griles's memo to Fisher. A cheerful Utahan with a firm handshake and an open manner, Clarke found herself in the middle of a crossfire between B.L.M. and E.P.A. staffers, appalled by the handling of coal-bed methane, and western constituents pushing for leases. Some of the latter were represented by Marc Himmelstein, who asked for, and received, a meeting with Clarke, as well as one with her chief of staff. She says she wasn't at all bothered by meeting with her boss's former lobbying colleague. "Steve has never put one iota of pressure on me about this issue," she says. "He won't even talk to me about this."

The devastating E.P.A. review might well have triggered a supplemental environmental-impact statement, which would have taken up to a year to complete. "We looked at all our options . . . and chose not to take that course," says Clarke. Instead, more modeling was done, and B.L.M. staffers were told to meet with the E.P.A. "We did meet with E.P.A.," says one B.L.M. staffer. "But we didn't change anything."

"If you read the Montana and Wyoming environmental-impact statements," adds the staffer, "and you envision one picture from those thousands of pages, you see a changed landscape, and a changed way of life. From a rural area of ranchlands to an industrial zone. And all we're required to do is say that. We can disclose that you won't be able to ranch. We're going to totally change your life and you have no power at all. As long as we say that, in effect, we can get away with doing it."

By late fall of 2002, many ranchers in the Powder River Basin were upset. These were the unlucky ones whose land had been purchased through the Stock Raising Homestead Act of 1916. The government had sold surface rights to that land, but retained the mineral reserves beneath. In Wyoming, permits to drill have been granted for more than 14,000 wells, many on these ranchers' properties. Miles of cables and access roads now crisscross their grazing land. Noisy compressors whine all night long; one rancher reportedly was so unhinged by the noise that he shot a compressor into silence. Most of the ranchers had been rock-ribbed Republicans and voted for Bush. Now they found themselves filing lawsuits with the enviros. Where, they had to wonder, did they fit into Gale Norton's vision of partnership and the four C's? "If it takes bringing 200 environmentalists into town and having them live in tents on my creek, I'll do it," said one rancher in High Country News. "I've never been one for siding with the wackos, but things change when you're protecting your home."

As part of due process, the B.L.M. invited public comment on its plans to allow the drilling of approximately 39,000 new wells for coal-bed methane in Wyoming. At the same time, it pushed ahead with plans for about

18,000 more in Montana. Many of the comments were more than 20 pages long. Some ranchers hired soil scientists and hydrologists to do in-depth studies of what extraction of coal-bed methane would do to the land and water. "We responded with equally long letters," says a B.L.M. staffer. "But we ignored the complaints." The only concessions, says the staffer, were to the oil companies. Mike Mottice, Interior's overseer of the project, says, "I think that's a completely inaccurate and unfair representation of what happened . . . We, at a minimum, responded to all the concerns."

This spring, after the public-comment period had ended, the B.L.M. announced its decision on coal-bed methane: roughly 57,000 wells were approved in principle, pending actual permits to drill.

In her speeches, Gale Norton often ticks off a dizzying list of new moneys being spent on conservation, and the figures are impressive. She got an increase in funding for the national refuge system, for example, and another infusion to take on the staggering backlog of maintenance problems in national parks. "We're getting a computer system set up that keeps track of all of the maintenance needs," Norton says. "We're trying to make sure that where we're putting our resources is where the projects really need to be done, as opposed to just the place where the superintendent yells loudest about it." But Destry Jarvis, a former assistant director at the National Parks Service, says this system was initiated in the Clinton administration, and in any event won't come close to wiping out the backlog, which, he observes, candidate Bush vowed to do.

Interior press secretary Mark Pfeifle feels Norton's

conservation initiatives have been ignored in the angry rhetoric of such groups as the Sierra Club and the Natural Resources Defense Council. He may be right, though the list he proffers of more centrist organizations for a balanced view is not an entirely successful gambit—they, too, have plenty of criticisms. "At best, the secretary's record has been mixed," says Paul Hansen, executive director of the Izaak Walton League, half of whose members are hunters. "There is an anti-public-land bias in this administration. The attitude is: we can't manage what we have so we shouldn't get any more . . . Our members are becoming increasingly concerned and upset." Scott Sutherland of Ducks Unlimited applauds Norton's new emphasis on private-public incentive programs for conservation—the partnership theme. "At the same time," he cautions, "we don't want them to think that those . . . are the only solutions needed." Michael Bean of Environmental Defense faults the administration for using "an accounting trick" to fund the incentive programs with money that Congress intended for land acquisition.

Especially troubling is Interior's seeming desire to please off-road-vehicle owners—a relatively small but vocal bunch. Snowmobiles in Yellowstone and Grand Teton National Parks are the most dramatic example: Griles makes an earnest case that new four-cycle machines are much quieter, but why have them at all? Now Jet Skis are being sanctioned in such coastal refuges as Washington State's Nisqually, according to one Fish and Wildlife official. "If off-road vehicles can access a wildlife refuge without harming the ecological value," says Assistant Secretary Manson, "then why not?"

To the extent that Gale Norton's Interior does engage in

conservation, it tends to do so with other agencies, which is how the department connects to some of the more distant dots in the Bush administration's environmental picture.

Endangered species, for example, don't live only on Interior lands. They live on U.S. Forest Service land, too. The head of the service is Mark Rey, a former lobbyist for the American Forest and Paper Association. For endangered species, Rey espouses the virtues of "partnership programs" with landowners, be they farmers or timber companies. So does Craig Manson, who caused a stir last May by declaring that the department had run out of legal funds to wrangle in court with environmental groups pressing to secure protection and critical habitat for one endangered species after another. But he doesn't appear to be too upset about that. He feels strongly that critical habitat does little to help species. "Habitat is essential to the conservation of species," he clarifies. But "critical" habitat often means arbitrary boundaries on private land. Better to work with landowners.

"You have to look close," retorts Jamie Clark, Fish and Wildlife director in the Clinton administration and a wildlife biologist herself. "Is it partnership? Or is it abrogation of their responsibilities?"

Wetlands are another interagency issue: here Interior weighs in, mostly through comments submitted by Fish and Wildlife, but the E.P.A. decides. In 2001, the Supreme Court ruled that certain isolated wetlands were not protected by the Clean Water Act. This year the E.P.A. and the Army Corps of Engineers interpreted the ruling to mean that many more isolated wetlands were no longer protected, either. As a result, about 20 percent of the country's remaining wetlands—or roughly 20 million acres—have become vulnerable to developers. Astonishingly, the E.P.A. is pondering ways to go further, with a "proposed rule-making" of more wetlands rollbacks; this has drawn, to date, 137,000 comments. Even Ducks Unlimited's "conservationist hunters" recently went on record opposing these changes. Julie Sibbing of the National Wildlife Federation says that Interior and Agriculture are strong influences on the E.P.A. in regard to wetlands, especially now, with Whitman gone. "They're the real philosophical pushers behind the rollbacks," she claims.

With both issues—endangered species and wetlands—the phrase "sound science" is often heard these days in the halls of Interior. "Sound science" means getting second opinions, usually from outside government. To government scientists, it often seems a way of ignoring the advice of career civil servants and finding industry-friendly scientists to justify changes that Interior's new, private "partners" want.

"Trying to reach consensus with disparate factions—that isn't science," says Howard Wilshire, a former official with the U.S. Geological Survey, yet another Interior agency. "In science, you don't go for consensus, you go for the truth."

The next frontier in conservation for Norton is water—long-term management of water in the West to deal with drought—and it is here, in a new Interior report called "Water 2025," that nearly all of the themes of her tenure get braided together: development, partnerships, interagency work, sound science, and much talk of the four C's.

Along with general drought in the West, a local drama last year forced Norton to focus on how Interior might deal with water in the future. In the Klamath River basin, which cuts across the Oregon-California border, farmers demanded the right to draw off more water than ever before for irrigation. The U.S. Bureau of Reclamation, yet another agency within Interior, gave the farmers what they wanted, over the objections of career scientists who feared the dangers of a too shallow river for spawning salmon. Last fall, 33,000 salmon died—the largest-ever fishkill in the West. California's Department of Fish and Game concluded the low water flow caused the kill. In mid-July a federal judge agreed, ordering that the administration's ruling must be revised because it violates the Endangered Species Act.

Klamath showed just how fierce and complex the politics of water are, and Norton deserves credit for wading into them. Whatever she decides, one or more factions—ranchers, farmers, fishermen, lawn-watering suburbanites—will be furious. For enviros, a key issue is how much water Interior will fight to reserve for public lands, and here a recent decision seems ominous. Last April, Interior agreed with Colorado's attorney general to reserve a much smaller amount of water than it typically asks for for the Gunnison River, which flows through Black Canyon national park. Rebecca Wodder, president of American Rivers, says the agreed-upon flow is devastating. "The needs of the park and endangered fish downstream are being jeopardized. This outcome . . . is a step towards opening the doors for trans-basin water diversion to Colorado's Front Range."

As yet, "Water 2025" is only an outline. So is the inextricably linked issue of grazing rights, but the direction seems clear. In the Clinton years, Interior Secretary Bruce Babbitt revised old regulations that basically gave ranchers unlimited grazing rights on public lands. His intent was to keep those lands from being overgrazed. An angry National Cattlemen's Beef Association and other livestock groups sued the government, and the case worked its way to the Supreme Court, only to lose in a 9-0 decision. The association's lawyer was William Myers.

William Myers is now chief solicitor of the Interior Department.

Now on the government side, Myers has proposed new regulations that give cattlemen much of what they tried to win in court, including ownership of any improvements they make, such as fences, water wells, and pipelines.

One frustrated B.L.M. insider listened to a speech by B.L.M. director Kathleen Clarke on how she hopes to adapt these changes for her agency, and posted an annotated version on-line. "Once the permittee (rancher) has ownership of these improvements," the critic wrote, "they will have a legal argument that any change in their way of doing business is causing them harm and they therefore have a right to be compensated for that change or loss. Remember, these are public lands!"

Public lands. Threading its way through all these issues is a question that few at Interior appear to have asked. Whose lands are public lands? Do they belong to the states in which they lie, to be cared for or despoiled as those states see fit? Do they belong to the politicals at Interior, to be portioned off in accordance with the desires of an energy-minded White House? Or do public lands belong to all of us?

And if they do, are these the ways that a majority of us want them used?

For all the raw politics that appear to guide so many decisions at Interior, a reporter cannot spend two days at the department, going from one top political's office to the next, without realizing that more is involved here than paybacks and a desire to please western Republicans. The politicals really believe in what they're doing.

They believe in paring federal government and giving more power to states. They believe in doing whatever they can to tap energy reserves on public lands for future needs. They believe that environmental regulations are too restrictive for the country's own good. Most disconcerting, they convey these beliefs with keen intelligence. Every last one of them is, like Norton, well spoken, warm and engaging, considerate and earnest.

The most openly philosophical of the bunch is Lynn Scarlett, assistant secretary of policy, management, and budget. Next to Norton, she's the political most responsible for Big Picture thinking. In her office at the end of a long day, she muses about the National Environmental Policy Act—the cornerstone of environmental law—which requires impact statements and public participation before the building of a power plant, say, or drilling in the Powder River Basin. "You look at that statute, and you read Section 101, the kind of opening salvo, and, by golly, it sounds like the four C's! . . . And yet somehow that grand vision has translated over the years into these hundreds of pages." So, she asks, with more power to answer the question than most, "where are we going to go with the National Environmental Policy Act?"

Increasingly, the consequences of that kind of thinking drive moderates to extremes. "What I can't get over," says former Fish and Wildlife director Jamie Clark, "is their total disregard for legacy. They're making irrevocable, irresponsible decisions. The costs of cleanup will be enormous."

And yet, as she says, "the vast majority of the public, when you try to communicate this to them, cannot believe it can be this bad. Poll after poll shows that people just don't want to believe that this administration is so anti-environment."

One day in May, Gale Norton makes another appearance against a backdrop of natural beauty. This time she's come to the East End of Long Island, New York, to celebrate another private partnership, this one with the Nature Conservancy to help preserve an endangered beach bird, the piping plover.

On a walkway above the Atlantic dunes in Westhampton, Norton smiles warmly and extols the $9.5 million recently allocated for private partnerships to help conserve threatened and endangered species around the country. This is all part, she says to local reporters, of what she's come to refer to as the New Environmentalism. "At the heart of New Environmentalism," she says earnestly, "is a recognition that . . . we have in many ways reached the limits of what we can do through government regulation and mandates."

A local reporter, lulled by Norton's opening paragraphs, looks up suddenly at that last sentence. Has she heard what she thinks she heard?

Frowning, she puts pen to paper and begins to write.

She Said It . . .

". . . a really ugly addition to the state capitol."

—Gale Norton, describing a wheelchair ramp required by the Americans With Disabilities Act. Norton as Colorado's attorney general considered suing to block construction of the ramp.

WE CUT DOWN THE TREES, THEN WE GRAZED AWAY THE GRASS, THEN WE STRIPPED OUT THE MINERALS AND SOLD OFF THE WATER.
NOW WE'RE DOWN TO BEDROCK CONSERVATIVE VALUES.
NORTON
TOLES
© 2001 THE BUFFALO NEWS
PRICE OF EVERYTHING, VALUE OF NOTHING?

2-1-01

Who should run the Department of Energy? Not Spencer Abraham.

From Senator "Lunkhead" to Energy Czar: A Year in the Life of Spencer Abraham

from Counterpunch.org (4/17/02)

Jeffrey St. Clair

When Spencer Abraham toiled as the junior senator from Michigan, he wanted desperately to do away with the Department of Energy, a federal outpost that the Republicans have railed against since its creation under Jimmy Carter. In his six years in the senate, he never missed a chance to vote to abolish the department and to accuse its administrators and employees of an hysterical range of misdeeds, from treason (Wen Ho Lee) to using the banner of environmentalism as a cover for bringing about a new age of solar socialism.

Abraham was trounced in his 2000 senate reelection bid and, rightfully thinking that his prospects for employment in the private sector might be bleak, he faxed his frail resumé (highlighting his stint as part of Dan Quayle's brain trust) to the Bush transition team—meaning, as in all other matters of import, Dick Cheney. When word came that Bush and Cheney were set to offer Abraham the post as the nation's energy czar, Abraham reportedly threw something of a tantrum. Apparently, he had his heart set on the slot at the Department of Transportation, where, no doubt, he believed he could do some major league damage for the captains of industry in Detroit and Dallas.

But time heals all wounds. Now that he finds himself in charge of the DoE, Abraham seems to have become entranced by its political utility. The Energy Department, Abraham soon discovered, was not some green bunker plotting the solar conquest of the energy market. No. It was a clearinghouse for the oil and nuke industry, a kind of federally-endowed lobby, which occasionally dispensed token handouts to the energy conservation crowd. In recent years those tokens have gotten smaller and smaller.

Let's review Abraham's first year directing the energy policy of Big Oil's newest favorite administration (recall that the last one wasn't all that bad for the likes of Arco and Chevron). At the top of the list is the ceaseless maneuvering to break open the Alaska National Wildlife Refuge to exploration and drilling. The Refuge (only the pro-drilling claque insists on calling it ANWR, which sounds frightfully like an oil company moniker) sits on the arctic tundra in the northeastern corner of Alaska. Long a prize of the oil lobby, the Refuge is the last unsullied swath of coastline in the American arctic, home to polar bear, wolves, caribou, salmon, raptor nesting colonies and the Gwich'in tribe.

Even though by bureaucratic right the Arctic Refuge is part of Interior Secretary Gale Norton's empire, Spence Abraham made the transfer of the wildlife refuge to the oil industry the top priority on his energy agenda. Upon reflection, it wasn't a particularly smart move, even if higher-ups like Cheney were telling Abraham to go for it.

But Spence isn't the brightest bulb in the Bush cabinet. Indeed, during his tenure in the senate Abraham was known by senate staffers—the biggest gossips on the Hill—as being jovial but clueless. One Republican senate staffer told CounterPunch they referred to Abraham as "Senator Lunkhead"—that's a certain kind of distinction in a chamber populated with the likes of Rick Santorum and Sam Brownback.

Drilling in the Arctic Refuge is a battle that Abraham simply can't win. And mightier men than he have tried, from James Schlesinger (the first energy secretary under Carter, now a pimp for Big Oil) to the arch-villain himself, James Watt. It's the third rail of environmental politics, the Death Star for Big Oil's deepest desires. The Big Green groups are likely to capitulate on everything from the Everglades (witness the recent sell-out by National Aubudon Society on Jeb Bush's developer-friendly plan) and Superfund to ancient forests and the Endangered Species Act. But they will not relent on the Arctic Refuge. Why? Easy: it's the biggest fundraiser they've ever come across and they'll fight to the death to keep it. (That also means, of course, that many of these green groups want the Refuge to remain perpetually at risk of development.)

Last week in a desperate attempt to secure enough votes to override a senate filibuster of the bill to open the refuge, Abraham played the Iraq card, alleging that Saddam Hussein's threat to cut off oil sales to Israel's allies necessitated opening the refuge to Exxon and Chevron. Of course, Abraham didn't explain Saddam's threats would have the slightest impact on US oil supplies, which have maintained an embargo against Iraqi crude since the Gulf War.

Even former CIA head and Iraq hawk James Woolsey didn't buy that one. "The bottom line is that we'll be dependent on the Middle East as long as we are dependent on oil," said Woolsey, who served as Director of the Central Intelligence Agency from 1993 to 1995. "Drilling in ANWR is not a recipe for America's national security. The only answer is to use substantially less petroleum."

But Abraham wasn't through. He had a bad hand, but he was determined to play all his cards anyway. The secretary hatched a scheme with Senator Frank Murkowski to lure the votes of Democratic senators by proposing to add a bailout for steelworkers to the energy bill. While the measure may have attracted the attention of some Dems from the steelbelt, it foundered when conservative Republicans condemned it as a boondoggle for big labor. After six years in the senate, you'd have thought that Abraham would have at least learned to check these kinds of vote swaps over with Trent Lott first and not simply take the word of Murkowski, who is deranged on the subject of oil drilling in the Arctic.

Earlier this week Abraham's department came up with another stupid idea: blame it on the Indians. The DoE launched a despicable attack on the Gwich'in, the Arctic tribe that has opposed drilling in ANWR out of concern for the impacts on fish and wildlife, particularly caribou, that they depend on for sustenance. Abraham dredged up a 20-year old exploration arrangement on the Venetie Reservation outside the small town of Arctic Village, signed off on by some tribal members. The exploration site was not in caribou habitat and proved to be lacking in oil reserves, but Abraham went out of his way to portray the impoverished tribe as a band of duplicitous hypocrites in the press, as if hypocrisy were a moral defect unknown to Big Oil.

For their part, the Gwich'in remain undeterred. The

Refuge is a centerpiece of their spiritual cosmology, revered as "the sacred place where life begins."

"We depend on the caribou, as Gwich'in people, for food, clothing, medicine, tools and spirituality," says Sandra Newman, a council member for the Vuntut Gwich'in First Nation. "And in return, the caribou depend on us to take care of the land for them so they can continue to be free."

[It was all for nothing. On Thursday April 18, the pro-drilling forces fell 14 votes short of invoking cloture. But true to his nature, Abraham vows to fight on.]

At the same time Abraham was bashing the Gwich'in, he was going to bat for the big boys in Detroit, helping to defeat once again new fuel efficiency standards for American automobiles. Under the rosiest scenario, the oil reserves under the Arctic Refuge will yield roughly 3.2 billion barrels. And it would take 10 years for that oil to reach the pump, and even when production peaks—in 2027—the refuge would produce less than 2 percent of the oil Americans are projected to use. By contrast, Detroit automakers have the technology right now to boost fuel economy standards to at least 40 miles per gallon. By phasing-in that standard by 2012 the nation could save 15 times more oil than the Arctic Refuge is likely to produce over 50 years.

When tougher fuel efficiency standards came up for a vote before the senate in mid-March, Abraham was there to denounce the measure and lobbying senators to defeat the package. He was so persuasive that fourteen Democrats jumped over to his side, including Baucus-MT, Bayh-IN, Breaux-LA, Byrd-WV, Carper-DE, Cleland-GA, Conrad-ND, Dorgan–ND, Feingold-WI, Kohl-WI, Levin-MN, Lincoln-AR,

Milkulski-MD, Miller-GA, Nelson-NE, and Stabenow-MI. [Nearly all of these Democrats were certified as good greens by the League of Conservation Voters and the Sierra Club's political action committee.)

Then there's Abraham's cozy relationship with Enron, a bond forged during his senate term that continues to this very day despite the company's leprous reputation. Even after the Enron scandal blew up, the DoE and the State Department have continued to go to bat for the energy conglomerate, particularly on the issue of the Dabhol natural gas plant in Maharashtra State, India. This monstrosity was neither needed nor wanted by the Indian people, but came about through a combination of bribes and arm-twisting, led by Frank Wisner, Jr (son of the famous CIA official and suicide) who served as Ambassador to India under Clinton and then made a bee-line for Enron's board. When the plant predictably went under, Enron begin desperately badgering the Indian government to cover its estimated $200 million in loses. Cheney and Abraham were recruited to do the shattered company's bidding. And they did, even as India was being recruited as a fellow traveler in Bush's war on terror. To its credit, the Indian government told the Bushies to take a hike.

But the defense of Big Oil is never done, a loss for one is a loss for all. Thus, a couple of weeks ago, the Bush team was still going to bat for Enron, as the State Department and the DOE warned the Indian government once again that its failure to "live up to its contractual agreements" on the Dabhol plant might limit future investments in the nation by US energy firms. A prospect that the Indian people (if not the government) must be greeting with a sigh of relief.

[By the way, just how phoney was Enron? This nugget gives a pretty good idea. It seems that the company ran a mock trading floor in its Houston headquarters, complete with desks, flat-panel computer displays and teleconference rooms. The idea was to fool visitors and prospective investors into believing that Enron traded commodities full-time, in a kind of 24/7 frenzy. In fact, the equipment was only hooked up internally, and the employee-"traders," who appeared to be frantically placing orders, were merely talking to each other—no doubt about how they could unload the soon-to-be-worthless Enron shares clogging up their 401K plans.]

On the nuclear front there's Yucca Mountain, the austere stretch of Mojave desert 100 miles north of Las Vegas where the DoE and its masters in the nuclear industry want to dump the radioactive waste that is piling up relentlessly at the nation's commercial nuclear reactors. During the 2000 campaign, Bush pledged to Nevada voters that he would hold firm against any attempt to make Yucca Mountain the nation's nuke waste dump.

That promise certainly helped Bush win a tight race in Nevada and (along with the Supreme Court) the White House. But it turns out that Bush was just kidding. Within weeks of taking office, the leaders of the nuclear industry were given free access to the White House and the DOE and quickly went about writing a game plan for seizing Yucca Mountain. Anyone who'd taken the time to look at where the nuke industry's political money was flowing couldn't have been surprised at Bush's political pirouette.

A new report by Public Citizen spells it out pretty clearly. The nuclear industry contributed $82,728 to Abraham during the 2000 election cycle, when he was a

U.S. senator, and spent even more money lobbying on issues dear to the industry's bottom line, including the ill-conceived nuclear waste dump proposal. In 2000 alone, leading nuclear energy interests that helped bankroll Abraham's unsuccessful Senate campaign spent more than $25 million to hire some of the highest-powered lobbyists in Washington, D.C., including top officials from the Reagan and Clinton administrations, records show. Eight of the lobbying firms hired made *Fortune* magazine's recent list of the 20 most influential firms in Washington.

But the nuke industry didn't stop there. They also spent more than $25 million lobbying congress and federal agencies on the matter-that's about a half-million a week, every week of the year. The nuclear industry flooded Washington with a strike force of lobbyists, totalling more 53 different lobbying firms, for a combined total of 199 individual lobbyists. This doesn't include the in-house lobbyists working for utilities and other nuclear industries.

And these were no run-of-the-mill K-Street lobbyists. Nearly half of the lobbyists hired by Abraham's top nuclear contributors previously worked for the federal government. The roster includes seven former members of Congress; former acting Energy Secretary Elizabeth Moler, who also was former chair of the Federal Energy Regulatory Commission; Gregory Simon, the chief domestic advisor to former Vice President Al Gore; Haley Barbour, political affairs director in the Reagan White House and former chair of the Republican National Committee; and James Curtiss, who served on the Nuclear Regulatory Commission.

These people can work political magic. For example, only last week, Abraham and Homeland Security head Tom Ridge came to the remarkable conclusion that shipping high-level nuclear waste across the nation by rail and truck presents no special terrorism risk. No wonder Ridge doesn't want to answer any questions during his appearances before congressional committees.

Of course, Ridge does have a point. Terrorism probably isn't the biggest concern when it comes to hauling all that radioactive waste across country. It's much more likely that an American city will be nuked by accident when one of the atomic trains derails and spills its lethal cargo into rivers and neighborhoods and onto streets. In fact, it's damn near a statistical certainty.

Remember, as my friend David Vest points out, this scheme to ship nuclear waste by rail from every corner of the country to the Nevada outback is being hawked by many of the same people who threw a fit over busing kids a few blocks to improve educational opportunities for urban students. And, by and large, they are the same cadre of politicians who want to pull the plug on Amtrak as a burdensome federal subsidy.

Then there's the Bush/Abraham/Cheney energy plan, the creation of which has been the subject of brutal litigation between the White House, the General Accounting Office and environmental groups. Two recently released documents give an idea of how closely the Bush energy plan followed the industry's script:

A March 20, 2001 email from the American Petroleum Institute to an Energy Department official provided a draft Executive Order on energy. Two months later, President Bush issued Executive Order 13211, which is nearly identical in structure and impact to the API draft, and nearly verbatim in a key section.

In March 2001, a Southern Company lobbyist emailed

a DOE official suggesting "another issue" for inclusion in the energy plan: so-called reform of the Clean Air Act and related enforcement actions. The suggestion was incorporated into the energy plan, launching the Administration's controversial effort to weaken the Clean Air Act and retreat from high-profile enforcement actions against the nation's largest polluters, including the Southern Company.

While Abraham, Cheney and the other Bush bigwigs huddled repeatedly over a period of months with the energy elite, environmentalists were largely locked out. Abraham himself met with more than 100 representatives from the energy industry and trade associations from late January to May 17, 2001, when the task force released its report. But when enviros, lead by the corporate-friendly Environmental Defense Fund, asked for a meeting with Abraham, his scheduler, Kathy Holloway, stiff-armed them, saying that Abraham was too busy for a face-to-face.

One of the DOE documents released by order of a federal court on April 10, 2002, shows that the Energy task force gave one of its staff members 48 hours to contact 11 environmental groups to obtain their policy recommendations. The environmental groups were given 24 hours to provide written comments. Another DOE memo notes that staffers should endeavor to closely scrutinize the green's comments and "recommend some we might like to support that are consistent with the Administration energy statements to date."

There was a final blow. In order to print up the oil/nuke energy plan, Abraham chose not to waste a cent from his multi-billion dollar drilling budget. Instead, he plundered $135,615 from the DOE's mothballed solar, renewables and energy conservation budget to produce 10,000 copies of the White House energy plan released last May. The solar funds were even raided to pay for the Administration's energy lobbyist Andrew Lundquist's air ticket to Alaska to strategize on drilling in the Arctic Refuge.

But Abraham's going to have to find a new printing account next year, because those funds probably won't be around much longer. The energy plan that the solar funds financed the printing of calls for slashing the renewable energy program by more than 50 percent.

Maybe old Spence has a sense of irony after all.

Quiz

Paul Slansky

Which headline did *not* appear in a major daily newspaper during 2002?

(a) "BUSH PREPARES MAJOR EASING OF INDUSTRY POLLUTION RULES"
(b) "BUSH PLAN GIVES MORE DISCRETION TO FOREST MANAGERS ON LOGGING"
(c) "EPA PROPOSES TO EASE RULES ON CLEAN AIR"
(d) "REPUBLICANS MOUNT CAMPAIGN TO RENAME ALZHEIMER'S 'REAGAN'S DISEASE'"

Answer: (d)—it appeared in *The Onion*

TOM DELAY AND OTHER CONGRESSIONAL VERMIN

with quotes by Tom DeLay;
and a quiz by Paul Slansky

The Bush administration expects slavish obedience from Republicans in Congress. That's where the likes of House Majority Leader (and former Republican House Whip) Tom DeLay come in. DeLay and other congressional misleaders punish heretics with an inhuman zeal worthy of the Spanish Inquisition. It's tempting to label these modern-day brutes ideologues or zealots, but their cruelty seems unrelated to principle. True, they cite the principles of strength and courage and sacrifice, but they cite them in service of their own greed for yet more power.

He Said It . . .

"I have seen these liberal psychologists and sociologists talk about there is no need for the man in the family. The woman can take care of it. A woman can take care of the family. It takes a man to provide structure. To provide stability."

—Tom DeLay, as quoted in *Roll Call*, 2/10/04

". . . a great opportunity to bring God back into the public institutions of the country."

—DeLay, on Bush's "faith-based initiatives," 7/10/01

"You see, I don't believe there is a separation of church and state."

—DeLay, 7/10/01

Most politicians are unduly influenced by donors, but the depth and breadth of DeLay's corruption and ruthlessness almost defy belief.

Tom DeLay's Axis of Influence

from *AlterNet* (5/10/02)

Stephen Pizzo

> "It is well known that Enron lavished money and attention on political figures all over the nation's Capitol. But for an insight into how carefully the company cultivated members of Congress, look no further than its efforts to please Representative Tom DeLay." (*The New York Times*, Jan 16, 2002)

By the time Enron collapsed, its tentacles had penetrated deep into our federal government. No investigation into just how deep would be complete without a comprehensive examination of House Majority Whip, Tom DeLay.

In researching this story, it quickly became apparent that Tom DeLay's deep and personal involvement with Enron was not an exception but part of a pattern of controversial relationships that reach back to DeLay's earliest days in Congress.

All these relationships were consistent with a far-right, free-market, anti-regulatory philosophy that DeLay has raised to nearly religious status and upon which he has created a lucrative and ruthless power base.

Among other discoveries, we found a startling contrast between the wholesome, born-again, pro-family image DeLay portrays to voters back home in Sugarland, Texas, and the controversial causes and companies he backs in Washington.

A closer examination of Tom DeLay seems particularly important now, not so much because of his Enron entanglements, but because of his pending political promotion. With the announced retirement of House Majority Leader, Dick Army, (R-Tex) Tom DeLay is widely expected to ascend to that important post, making him the second most powerful person in the House of Representatives.

From Bugs to Bureaucrats

When Tom DeLay came to Congress in 1984 as the Republican representative from Sugarland, Texas, he was widely dismissed as a lightweight. A quirky little man with squinty eyes and a hayseed drawl, he was quickly tagged with the unflattering description, "that little bug-killer from Texas."

But by his second term in office, the former owner of Albo Pest Control had wiped the smirks off those Yankee faces and earned a few more impressive nicknames. His friends call him "The Hammer," a title he earned for his never-take-no-for-an-answer lobbying style.

His enemies, defined as anyone to his political left, had come to know him as both ruthless and effective. They had lots of names for him too: "The Prince of Darkness," "The Exterminator" and "The Meanest Man in Congress."

DeLay's critics no longer dismiss him as a joke. His policies and positions on social, environmental and regulatory issues are extreme and far to the right of the mainstream. And, DeLay sees no difference between the personal and the political. Attacking DeLay's policies will elicit the same ruthless counter-attacks as a personal affront.

Nothing like DeLay's laissez-faire policies have been heard in Congress since the earliest days of America's industrial revolution when robber baron industrialists saw cheap labor as an indispensable ingredient for growth. A financial journalist (who asked that his name not be used in this report) described DeLay's free-market policies this way:

> If there were a capitalist equivalent of the Taliban, Tom DeLay would lead it. He has hijacked a kind of Reaganesque free-market rhetoric to turn back the clock on such laws as those protecting workers and the environment, and those that require transparency in business dealing. His policies have enriched and benefited a handful of powerful corporate and political insiders who in turn, have fueled his political machine.

Millions of words have been written over the last decade detailing Tom DeLay's many controversial friends and policies—most recently his strong ties to Enron. But even the most shocking of these revelations has failed to stop or even slow his rise to power within his party and Congress.

Tom DeLay has become the Teflon Don of the radical-right of his party. Undamaged by criticism, legal challenges and ethics complaints, DeLay has only grown bolder over the years. While few in Congress respect Tom DeLay, most fear him—and with good reason. Anyone who crosses Tom DeLay quickly learns there is a price to pay.

> This whole thing about not kicking someone when he is down is BS—Not only do you kick him—you kick him until he passes out—then beat him over

> the head with a baseball bat—then roll him up in an old rug—and throw him off a cliff into the pounding surf below!!!!! (E-mail between two Tom DeLay staffers)

Reading those words, one would think one were listening in on a pair of John Gotti lieutenants rather than employees of the House Whip. The message was unmistakably clear—if you get in The Hammer's way, you get hammered.

Viral Marketing: Spreading the Influence

Once safely ensconced as GOP Majority Whip, DeLay and his closest aides began to move their operations outside government—much the same way Enron moved partnerships offshore. Some things they had planned could lead to ethics problems if conducted out of DeLay's Capitol Hill office.

So, DeLay facilitated the migration of several trusted former aides to key lobbying positions. Outside government, these DeLay lieutenants would be unencumbered by House ethics rules.

Inside government, DeLay turned his attention to finding ways to buy the kind of political support on The Hill he could not win with honest debate. Using so-called "leadership political action committees," DeLay was legally able to launder corporate campaign contributions to individual Republican members of Congress.

> (DeLay) is the financial godfather of congressional Republicans, overseeing the collection of nearly $30 million in campaign funds in 1999 alone . . .

> The whip—enforcer of party discipline among 221 House Republicans—is, in fact, a former pest exterminator who has used his relentless energy, formidable political skill, charm, intelligence and cunning to rise to power. (*The Washington Post*, May 2001)

Buckle Up. It's a Bumpy Ride

In the first installment of this story we will chronicle DeLay's relationship with Enron. From there, we follow the trail back in time to sweatshops in the North Pacific, Indian casinos in Mississippi, South Africa's apartheid government and a mob hit in Miami. Each story involves DeLay personally or members of his "kitchen cabinet." Taken as a whole, these tales draw a picture of a person whose extremist views on religion, society, business and government place him at the outer fringe of mainstream thought.

TOM DELAY AND ENRON

Tom DeLay learned early in his political career that the best way to control people is with favors, particularly money. In 1994 he inaugurated his first "leadership PAC"—Americans for a Republican Majority (ARMPAC). It was created to raise money which DeLay could then parcel out to House members he wanted to influence. ARMPAC would preach DeLay's anti-regulatory mantra. The money raised would be used to reward those who supported DeLay and punish those who opposed him.

Even some Republicans were concerned that the money would be used in ways to steer their party into radical territory. "He's not above using his Whip organization to pursue rolling back EPA and OSHA to the nth degree," said Rep. Christopher Shays (R-Conn) at the time. "I think he believes it's a Republican cause."

But, DeLay was not swayed by those he viewed as too tied to big government. Nor was he at all concerned how his PAC activities might appear to anyone else. In fact, one of DeLay's most disarming devices is his candor. Rather than try to sugarcoat his policies he revels in embellishing them and confirming his critics' worst fears. "We have a new strategy for regaining the high ground," DeLay said. "We need to raise enough money to tell our story."

"Our story" translated to a convergence of DeLay's radical laissez-faire philosophy and the desires of various industries to be freed from any regulations that cost them money.

> DeLay employs a number of vehicles to direct money to candidates: his own reelection campaign fund; his leadership political action committee, Americans for a Republican Majority; the National Republican Congressional Committee, the GOP's House campaign committee; the Restore Our Majority Program, a fund designed to funnel money to endangered incumbents; and in a more indirect way, the Republican Issues Majority Campaign. (*The Washington Post*)

Enron Gave DeLay's PAC the Breath of Life

Enron hosted ARMPAC's first fundraiser. It was held in Enron's hometown of Houston, Texas and raised $280,000 for DeLay's new leadership PAC. Subsequent disclosures show that Enron and its executives gave early and often. Ken Lay contributed $50,000 to ARMPAC, Enron Vice Chairman, Joseph Sutton, contributed another $25,000. The full extent of Enron's financial support for DeLay's PAC may never be known since reporting such contributions became mandatory only in 2000.

In 1994, DeLay formed "Project Relief," another favorite of Enron. Project Relief represented hundreds of corporations and trade groups seeking regulatory relief of one kind or another. Project Relief (chaired by the father of Microsoft, founder Bill Gates fought for a moratorium on federal regulations and the adoption of risk/benefit measures for future regulations. Adopting a risk/cost formula would mean that if a company could show that complying with an environmental rule would cost them too much, they could dodge it.

When the U.S. Senate stopped Project Relief, DeLay vowed to fight on. He lashed out at the Environmental Protection Agency, his least-favorite federal agency. Since his days as a pest exterminator back in Texas, trimming the EPA's powers had become nothing less than a jihad for Tom DeLay. His language was characteristically intemperate, employing a reference to Nazism commonly used by right-wing militia groups:

> The EPA, the Gestapo of government pure and simple, has been one of the major claw hooks that the government maintains on the backs of our constituents. (*National Journal*, March 2, 1996)

No company could be more supportive of that goal than Enron. The company had already become one of the most notorious polluters in Texas, having received generous "grandfathering" relief under Gov. George W. Bush's administration. But the company had operations and subsidiaries in many states and the EPA was a source of constant irritation.

Ken Lay and his wife, Sharon, became regular fixtures on DeLay's FEC disclosures as well as his PACs. Enron pumped more than half a million dollars into ARMPAC for DeLay to use to reward House members who supported his anti-regulatory agenda. DeLay personally received nearly $29,000 in contributions from Enron and another $18,100 from Enron's accountants, Arthur Andersen.

Despite all the talk of The Hammer's powers of persuasion, DeLay's real power flows from his control of ARMPAC money. In 1997-98 he shoveled over $389,000 to Republican candidates. The next year $879,000 was parceled out by DeLay to compliant Republican candidates. The hammer, it appears, has a golden handle.

"I worked harder than anybody else," DeLay told reporters with his usual swagger. "I raised more money than anybody else. I was smarter than anybody else . . . Once I sink my teeth into something, I don't turn loose until I win."

Enron also helped DeLay move key aides into positions in the private sector where they could further both DeLay and Enron's interests. In 1998 Enron secured a lucrative $750,000 consulting gig for two of DeLay's closest aides. The money would be used for a secret "grassroots" campaign—spearheaded by Enron—to deregulate energy markets.

The DeLay/Enron scheme began with a meeting at Tom DeLay's Texas home. When Enron lobbyists asked how best to proceed, DeLay noted that Enron could begin by giving his Chief of Staff, Ed Buckham (who at that very moment was forming his own consulting company, the Alexander Strategy Group) and Karl Gallant, a consultant to DeLay's ARMPAC, the contract to manage the campaign.

Both men, members of DeLay's unofficial Kitchen Cabinet, were veterans of stealth political operations. Gallant had recently worked on a propaganda campaign for the tobacco industry and he quickly devised a similar campaign plan for Enron.

An outline for the plan was faxed to Tom DeLay's Washington office. It was printed on Alexander Strategy letterhead complete with Ed Buckham's name in print. The only problem was that Alexander Strategy's CEO was still in the employ of the federal government at the time. Buckham was still serving as Tom DeLay's chief of staff. It was a serious mistake and one they moved quickly to obscure. Gallant said the memo had been just a mock up and that they had used Alexander Strategy stationery by mistake.

But it was clear that Enron had been calling the shots the whole time.

> There was a lot of high-level contact between Buckham and Enron," said a source close to the situation. "It was known among the (Whip's staff) that Buckham was trying to maneuver to get a big contract with Enron. It made a lot of people uncomfortable, but you would pay if you challenged Buckham. (*Roll Call*, Feb. 24, 2002)

A month later when Buckham finally went off DeLay's

federal payroll he was immediately put on the payroll of DeLay's ARMPAC. And Alexander Strategy Group was, as Enron promised, awarded the $750,000 contract to drum up support for electric power deregulation—a goal that Enron believed would open the $300 billion a year electric markets to Enron.

The stealth campaign would operate out of an energy consortium dubbed, "Americans for Affordable Electricity"—a name that Californians would find bitterly ironic just three years later. While other energy producers signed onto the campaign, Enron was calling the shots.

> We envision an aggressive field force operating under the direction of Enron and capable of engaging the opponents (of deregulation) wherever necessary. Additionally, this would put in place an operation capable of addressing state regulatory and legislative issues of concern to Enron. (From the memo generated on Alexander Strategy Group letterhead)

Once funded and in operation Alexander Strategy Group put DeLay's wife, Christine on its payroll. She reportedly pocketed a net "salary" of $40,000. Christine DeLay is a retired schoolteacher. What she did for her salary is unclear. According to Alexander Strategy Group, she neither lobbied for the company nor did she show up for work there. Why then were they paying her? The company says Alexander Strategies wrote the checks to Christine DeLay as a "bookkeeping convenience" for ARMPAC.

Americans for Affordable Electricity's lobbying assault—directed by Buckham and Gallant—swung into action. DeLay's legislation to deregulate electric markets quickly earned the nickname "The Enron Bill" among members of the House. And DeLay earned another nickname: "Dereg."

> The connection (Americans for Affordable Electricity) between DeLay and Enron offers a glimpse into how the Texas lawmaker and the corporate giant combined forces behind closed doors to deliver a bare-knuckled political punch aimed at breaking a legislative logjam frustrating efforts to deregulate the $300 billion-a-year electricity market, a top goal of both Enron and DeLay. (*Roll Call*, 2002)

Enron's leadership of AAE had critics among other member companies who viewed Enron's position on deregulation as too radical. And, they began to have questions about Buckham and Gallant, whom Enron had imposed upon them. A few months into the program the other companies had had enough of Buckham and Gallant's bare-knuckle Enron tactics and fired them.

"Hiring them was a mistake," a former AAE member said. "Enron was the eagle in this fight and the rest of us were geese."

But Gallant and Buckham were DeLay and Enron's men and they were not out of work long. Both men were rehired by Enron directly, Gallant for a total of $200,000 and Buckham $370,000.

With all this money flowing to DeLay and his lieutenants, the time had arrived for DeLay to deliver. In 1998, DeLay pushed for energy deregulation legislation virtually crafted for and by Enron. When DeLay introduced the bill, Ken Lay penned a letter lauding DeLay "for his vision." To drum up support for his bill, DeLay hosted a "power summit" in Houston at which Enron's former CEO, Jeffery Skilling, spoke in support of the measure.

> Delay and a cadre of close political advisers operated at the center of an Enron-backed crusade for energy deregulation in the late 1990s. (*Ft Worth Star-Telegram*, Feb. 2002)

Despite all this, many in the energy business considered the bill too radical. It later died a quiet death in committee.

But Tom DeLay could help Enron in ways that did not require the votes of his colleagues on The Hill. For example, in 1999, Enron lost the bidding for a power plant project in the Mariana Islands—a U.S. protectorate in the North Pacific. A Japanese company had been awarded the contract. DeLay stepped in and successfully demanded that the bidding be reopened so Enron could get back into the game. The bidding was reopened and Enron got the contract. DeLay had called in some favors from the island's politicians who owed him—big time.

(More on DeLay's long-standing and controversial ties to the Mariana islands and the Enron power plant deal in the third installment of this report.)

Friends to the End

DeLay remained a friend to Enron to the end. Late in 2001 he threw his full support behind a bill granting big business, including Enron, a massive tax rebate. With Enron's energy Ponzi scheme nearing collapse, Ken Lay was frantic to get the bill passed and signed into law because it would have ensured Enron a $254 million rebate. The fact that Enron had paid no taxes in five years did not seem to matter to DeLay.

The bill did not pass and Enron collapsed leaving thousands of his Texas constituents unemployed and stripped of their retirement savings. But DeLay never apologized for his undying support for the energy giant. Instead, DeLay simply said he was "heartbroken" by Enron's bankruptcy—but not heartbroken enough to return his Enron contributions, as many others in Congress did.

And despite the catastrophic meltdown of deregulated Enron, DeLay remains unapologetically committed to the deregulatory crusade that originally drew him to politics.

DeLay's Judge Dread

When DeLay and other pro-deregulation members of Congress were able to pass measures that weakened regulatory oversight for corporate constituents, federal judges often thwarted their efforts. When the safety of workers, pension funds or the environment are at risk, courts more often than not come down on the side of sensible government regulations.

The threat posed by the Judiciary branch's independence from the Legislative branch quickly became another front in Tom DeLay's deregulatory jihad. When asked by a reporter why he was so riled up at federal judges DeLay explained, "I woke up one day realizing that the judiciary had turned themselves into a regulatory branch."

The first concerted assault on the courts came when the

GOP took control of the House in 1994. DeLay became a fervent supporter of litigation reforms that would ultimately strip shareholders of many of their rights to sue company executives, like Enron's Kenneth Lay.

But DeLay's big stick approach to bringing the judiciary to heel came in 1997. Citing a Supreme Court order forcing the Virginia Military Institute to admit women, DeLay alleged federal judges were exceeding their constitutional authority and it was up to the legislature to rein them in. "We can impeach judges who get drunk," DeLay said at the time, "so why not impeach those who get drunk with power?"

Why not? Well, for starters, the Constitution does not allow the impeachment of judges simply because someone disagrees with their verdicts:

> No serious student of the impeachment provisions can conclude that the Constitution of the United States contemplates impeachment of judges on account of their actual decisions from the bench—their interpretations or their rulings. (Constitutional scholar Terry Eastland)

But this was not a strict constitutional scholar talking. This was "The Hammer," whose solution to an uncooperative, independent judiciary was to intimidate federal judges with threats.

DeLay rejected the idea that the Constitution limits impeachment of federal judges to "high crimes and misdemeanors," the same standard required to impeach a President. Instead, DeLay argued, whenever a judge ruled in ways that "usurped the powers of Congress," he or she should face impeachment. What DeLay was suggesting was a coup d'état by members of Legislative Branch against members of the Judicial Branch. It was precisely the kind of politically motivated intimidation of the judiciary that America's Founding Fathers wished to avoid by putting the judiciary safely outside the political arena.

DeLay's position was closer to one put forth three decades earlier when Rep. Gerald Ford was trying to get Supreme Court Justice William O. Douglas impeached for being too liberal. Back then Ford defended his position this way: "An impeachable offense is whatever a majority of the House of Representatives considers it to be at any given moment of history."

It took the legal wrangling in Florida during the 2000 Presidential race to reveal that DeLay's outrage over judicial activism had its limits. When the Florida Supreme Court ruled in favor of the Gore campaign for a hand recount of contested ballots, DeLay roared that the court had "squandered and violated the trust of the people of Florida in trying to manipulate the results of a fair election." And he vowed, "This judicial aggression must not stand."

But, when the U.S. Supreme Court overturned the Florida court's ruling, handing the victory to Republican George W. Bush in one of the Court's most controversial rulings in history, DeLay expressed pleasure with the ruling.

Some among the imperial judiciary appear more equal than others, in DeLay's view.

It was a double standard that exposed DeLay's anti-judiciary campaign as little more than a naked attempt to weaken the Constitutional independence of the Judicial Branch and replace it with a cowed judiciary more compliant to the wishes and actions of politically driven legislators.

Since "intimating judges" in order to influence their judgments is a crime, DeLay's self-stated goal of doing so might itself have been grounds for impeachment—his own.

DELAY'S GODFATHER

If a person can be judged by his choice of friends, then Tom DeLay should face harsh judgment indeed. Probably no single DeLay insider is more controversial than the man who has been described as DeLay's financial godfather, attorney/lobbyist/fundraiser Jack Abramoff. When DeLay kicked off his political action committee, Americans for a Republican Majority (ARMPAC), Jack Abramoff pledged that he would raise "plenty" for the effort.

And when Jack says "plenty" he means just that. Abramoff routinely raises over $1 million a year for conservative members of Congress, donating up to $250,000 himself. Much of that money ends up in Tom DeLay's PACs. And the route that Abramoff took to become a conservative powerbroker is a strange one indeed.

Abramoff's conservatism stretches back to his college days, when he chaired the GOP's College Republicans in the 1980s. It was there that Abramoff, an orthodox Jew, bonded with evangelical Christian Ralph Reed, who would later go on to lead the Christian Coalition (and then to work for Enron).

Bwana Jack

In 1983, as the South African apartheid regime was fighting for its survival, Abramoff became chairman of the College

Republican National Federation. The group passed a resolution condemning "deliberate planted propaganda by the KGB and Soviet proxy forces" against the South Africa regime. The resolution made no mention of apartheid.

The dawn of the 1990s found Abramoff in apartheid South Africa once again, this time producing an anticommunist thriller film, "Red Scorpion." The film depicted the South African army's fight against "procommunist forces." The film was banned by the United Nations since it violated the UN's embargo on doing business with the racist South African regime.

Abramoff also helped direct the work of The International Freedom Foundation (IFF). The IFF presented itself as a conservative think tank whose stated goal was to "demonstrate the benefits of a parliamentary democracy and expose the failures of a people's democracy." But in explosive testimony before the South Africa Truth Commission, former South African intelligence officers revealed that the IFF was actually part of the apartheid regime's propaganda operations.

According to those who testified, the IFF served as an intelligence gathering and "political warfare" instrument of the government. They testified that the South African government funded the organization to the tune of $1.5 million through 1992 under the code name "Operation Babushka."

According to *Newsday*, which investigated the IFF and reported extensively on it in the wake of the Truth Commission hearings, "The project's broad objectives were to try to reverse the apartheid regime's pariah status in Western political circles. More specifically the IFF sought to portray the ANC as a tool of Soviet communism, thus undercutting the movement's growing international acceptance as the government-in-waiting of a future multiracial South Africa."

It was reported that Abramoff attracted many other Washington conservatives to the IFF's cause, including Rep. Dan Burton (R-IN), Senator Jesse Helms, (R-GA), Rep. Phillip Crane (R-IL) and Rep. Robert Dornan (R-CA)

South African intelligence even voiced satisfaction with the work the IFF did. "They (IFF) were all very good, those guys," testified former South African police official Vic McPheerson, who ran security branch operations for the apartheid regime. "They were not just good in intelligence, but in political warfare."

According to McPheerson, the IFF earned up to half its funding doing "jobs" for South African intelligence. He said the intelligence agency sent their fee payments directly to IFF's Washington office. And while Abramoff's IFF focused on tarnishing the image of Nelson Mandela and the ANC, it also supported the Nicaraguan Contras, defended Ronald Reagan aide Oliver North, and sought a British government investigation of the charity Oxfam for the political support it gave the ANC.

All the US participants involved with the IFF, including Abramoff, deny any knowledge that South African intelligence had funded any of IFF's operations. The IFF disbanded in 1993 when South African president de Klerk pulled the funding for most of the government's clandestine operations.

In 1994, Abramoff had a new lobby-client in Africa: Zairian dictator Mobutu Sese Seko. Sese Seko was a corrupt despot whom the U.S. State Department had designated as one of Africa's "biggest obstacles to democracy."

DeLay and "Casino Jack"

When Republicans gained control of the House, more lucrative prospects opened up for Abramoff. As a member of the Washington lobbying firm Preston Gates Ellis & Touvelas Meeds LLP, Abramoff quickly built a clientele willing to pay big money for help with unpopular causes. Abramoff became a major force in promoting and protecting gambling on Indian reservations. He worked hand in glove with DeLay to successfully block every attempt by Congress to limit the spread of Indian gaming or to tax its exploding revenues.

Gambling proved a very lucrative beat. With American Indian tribes raking in over $10 billion a year in revenue from their combined gambling operations, there was plenty left over to spread around Washington. And who better to spread it than Tom DeLay's friend, Jack Abramoff?

The Choctaw tribe alone has paid Abramoff more than $10 million for his services. It was bargain. In June 2000, the House and Senate passed, without debate, a DeLay-supported bill that turned over thousands of additional acres of land to the tribe.

Historically, American Indians had been a Democratic constituency. Abramoff and DeLay saw an opportunity to change that. The two men were ideological and emotional twins. "You have to be willing to do whatever it takes to win," Abramoff told the *Wall Street Journal*. He was clearly Tom DeLay's kind of guy.

With DeLay's newfound support for all things Indian, Abramoff succeeded in moving tribe contributions to the Republican camp.

> Although American Indians were for many years identified almost exclusively as part of the Democrat coalition, that view has changed. People recognize that Jack Abramoff has been an important part of this transition. (DeLay to the *Wall Street Journal,* July 2000)

In return for his help, DeLay received over $50,000 in contributions from Abramoff and the Choctaws. DeLay, who took only 18 trips in the past five years, made four of those junkets to Choctaw casino/hotels. Abramoff hired two of DeLay's former top advisors to work with his Choctaw clients.

In March 1997, Abramoff's Choctaw clients paid $3,000 in travel and lodging expenses for two DeLay staffers. The staffers listed the junket as a trip "to review and observe the reservation and local economy"—at the tribe's Silver Star Hotel Casino.

The Choctaws have since been granted an unprecedented exemption from scrutiny by federal regulators. The Choctaw became the only tribe allowed to regulate its own gaming operations. That little piece of work earned Abramoff another $2.3 million.

> Republicans expect their piece (of Indian gambling contributions) to grow significantly in 2002. Jack Abramoff, a major campaign donor and fund-raiser for President Bush is one of them. By preaching the GOP's free-market theology, Mr. Abramoff has persuaded five tribes to hire him as a lobbyist—and, he got all five to agree to boost their donations to Republicans. (*Wall Street Journal,* July 2000)

But supporting any form of legalized gambling was not without its risks for DeLay. After all, his public persona was that of a devoted evangelical Christian who supports all that is wholesome and opposes all that is evil. His church-going constituents back in Texas believed that gambling was destructive to families and communities. But thanks largely to Abramoff, the amount of money flowing to DeLay and his PAC from tribes with gambling operations swamped any potential contributions from the Christian right.

Gambling's Bad Karma Comes Home to Roost

The risks involved in backing gambling interests came home to roost for DeLay's friend Abramoff last February, when he and Tom DeLay's former aide, Mike Scanlon, suddenly found themselves smack in the middle of an alleged mob assassination in Miami, Florida.

Abramoff and former Reagan HUD official Ben Waldman had invested in SunCruz, a troubled gambling cruise line based in Florida. Abramoff's other partner in the SunCruz deal, Adam Kidan, was known by authorities to have had business ties to members of the Gambino and Gotti crime families. In 1993 Kidan's mother was murdered in Philadelphia by a mob assassin tied to the Bonanno crime family. His bad luck continued when Kidan's New York business franchise "Dial-A-Mattress" failed. Then in November 2000, he was disbarred as a lawyer by New York State for allegedly misappropriating $100,000 of his stepfather's assets.

Abramoff and his partners signed the deal to purchase SunCruz from its owner, Gus Boulis. Boulis then accused the partners of failing to pay him for his business. He reported that the $5 million check they had given him as a down-payment bounced and that payment of a $20 million promissory note was overdue. Abramoff and Kidan had personally guaranteed the debt as part of the deal.

Kidan responded by reporting to Miami police that Boulis had tried to stab him with a penknife. But Kidan was okay. It would be Boulis who would end up dead. On the night of February 6, 2001, Boulis was gunned down in a blaze of gunfire while driving away from his office. Two cars boxed his car in a narrow ally and he was shot four times. Florida authorities describe it as "a classic mob hit." No one has been charged in the crime, though Florida newspapers have described Kidan as one of the prime suspects.

DeLay's former aide, Mike Scanlon, who had been hired by Abramoff to act as spokesperson for the SunCruz operation, suddenly found himself defending the SunCruz deal and his new boss. Scanlon told reporters that, while Boulis's murder was unfortunate, "Jack's not walking away from this." He went on to protest allegations that Abramoff had any unsavory connections to the gambling underworld. "I do think it's a bit premature to follow a storyline about how a Washington lobbyist fellow, like Jack, now finds himself in this tumultuous world of murder for hire."

> Abramoff and his partners can expect to be contacted soon by homicide detectives, seeking clues as they sift through the complex business dealings between Boulis and his casino antagonists. (*Miami Daily Business Review*, Feb 2001)

Abramoff was never implicated in the crime. But

notwithstanding Scanlon's initial protests, Abramoff quickly shed his interest in SunCruz, signing his 35% share over to the murdered man's estate. The murder flap threatened the wholesome image Abramoff had cultivated for his gambling (he prefers the term "gaming") clients like the Choctaw Indians.

The murder also threatened the mutually lucrative relationship Abramoff had cultivated with the House Whip. With both men now so closely tied to Indian gambling interests—which they maintain were wholesome and crime-free enterprises—the mess over SunCruz was the last thing they needed.

By dumping SunCruz, Abramoff had to abandon another deal he had going in which DeLay could have played a key role. Even as police investigated the murder, Kidan and Abramoff were pushing forward with a planned $100 million junk bond offering to expand SunCruz operations. And where were they planning to expand SunCruz's floating casino operations? To Tom DeLay's favorite place on earth—the US protectorate Mariana Islands in the North Pacific, which DeLay describes this way: "It's like my Galapagos Island."

DELAY'S UNREGULATED PACIFIC "PARADISE"

As Tom DeLay preached his pro-business/anti-regulation theology in the US, his model of perfection was far from the mainland. The U.S. protectorate of the Northern Mariana Islands—14 islands in the North Pacific—have become something of a free-enterprise petting zoo for DeLay and those he wishes to convert to his way of thinking.

At the end of World War II, the U.S. acquired the

islands, which are located off the coast of booming Asia. To encourage development and self-sufficiency Congress exempted the islands from the very kinds of U.S. business regulations and oversight DeLay despised. Even today the island's minimum wage is only $3.05. Other work and safety regulations either do not apply at all or are rarely enforced.

In short, the Marianas embodied many of the key ideals DeLay and other House Republicans were pushing in their 1994 Contract With America.

For Asian sweatshop operators, the Marianas became the Promised Land incarnate. Since the islands were officially U.S. territory, garment factories there were able to tag their products with the coveted "Made in the USA" label. No rules, no regulators, no inspectors, no health and safety laws. What more could a sweatshop operator ask for?

The opportunity was quickly recognized by Asian sweatshop operators like Hong Kong's Tan Holdings, run by garment mogul Willie Tan. Deep in the lush jungles, far from the island's white beaches and luxury hotels, garment factories quickly set up shop. They staffed their factories with workers from China and the Philippines with promises of work in the US. But, workers soon discovered that the work contracts they signed consigned them to near-indentured servitude deep in the Marianas steamy jungles. Wages were low, hours were long. The companies docked workers' pay for housing, food, medical treatments and other charges. The low wages and high deductions made it nearly impossible for workers to save enough money to return home.

None of this was a secret back home in the U.S. In

1998, ABC, CNN, the BBC and the *New York Times* each confirmed reports of forced labor, sex slaves and domestic forced servitude among the Marianas' so-called "guest workers."

According to the US Department of Labor, the indigenous US population of Marianas have an unemployment rate that hovers continuously around 14%. The unemployment rate of the island's 40,000 so-called guest workers on the other hand is only 5%.

Human rights groups, long up in arms over the work conditions on the islands, charged that sweatshop operators did not appreciate it when their female employees got pregnant. Numerous allegations of forced abortions surfaced over the years.

The protests began to reach the ears of Congress. Rep. George Miller, (D-Ca) and others began to demand that US labor and environmental laws be applied to the Marianas. Tom DeLay and his friend Jack Abramoff swung into action and fashioned a vigorous and largely successful counter-attack.

Denying the reports that workers were being mistreated, Abramoff said the Marianas' unregulated environment was in fact a success story and a model for economic development. He said that efforts to regulate the islands' garment factories by some members of Congress like Miller were nothing less than immoral. "These are immoral laws designed to destroy the economic lives of a people," Abramoff said. He went on to compare the proposed laws with the Nuremberg laws that restricted German Jews under the Nazis.

The Marianas became a pedal-to-the-metal cause for DeLay and another cash cow for Abramoff. Abramoff and his team, which now included DeLay's former chief of staff Bill Jarrell, swung into action. They arranged junkets to the islands for scores of Republicans on The Hill. DeLay himself spent New Years Day 1998 in the Marianas with his wife and daughter and his then Chief of Staff, Ed Buckham.

Another of Abramoff's Mariana lobbyists was Patrick Pizzella who, believe it or not, is now serving in the Bush Administration as assistant secretary of Labor. It was Pizzella's job to organize Abramoff's political junkets to the islands

Despite the growing public awareness of work conditions in the islands, Tom DeLay's defense of the status quo remained unshaken. In 1998 DeLay co-authored a letter with House Majority Leader Dick Army (R-TX). The two men, writing to the islands' governor, expressed how "impressed" they were with the Marianas' "commitment to advancing the principles of free markets, enterprise, tax reform and other innovative approaches to governance."

Such high level Washington support was not lost on sweatshop operators. In 1999, a human rights group quoted a Marianas sweatshop operator with an upbeat attitude about Tom DeLay's growing influence in Congress. An investigator for the group posed as an investor who was considering investing in Mariana garment operations. The investigator asked the sweatshop operator about the outlook for Congress applying U.S. workplace rules to the Marianas. The garment factory operator was not worried.

> "I have a real good friend of Tom DeLay," he said, "the Majority Whip. And Tom tell me, as long as we

> are in power they (Democrats in Congress) can't even see the light at the end of the tunnel. So, now it going to be two years, because Tom become real powerful this Congress so guarantee next two years no problem. Tom said if they elect me as majority whip, I make the schedule of Congress. And I'm not going to put it on the schedule. So, Tom told me, forget it, not a chance." (*Contemporary Women's Issues* 1999)

While Abramoff's team wined and dined groups from Washington at luxury Mariana resorts, deep in the jungles the garment factories continued their operations unregulated and unabated. Upon his return from the islands on one such trip a reporter asked DeLay about alleged sweatshop conditions there. "I saw some of those factories," DeLay responded. "They were air conditioned. I didn't see anyone sweating." Delay laughed at his own joke and walked off.

In 1999 the battle moved from the Republican controlled Congress to the courts. A suit filed by human rights groups representing the Mariana guest workers was settled in US District Court. The suit described the Marianas (also known as Saipan) as "America's worst sweatshop, replete with beatings, forced abortions, vermin-infested worker quarters, barbed wire and armed guards where workers put in 12-hour shifts, seven days a week."

The 32 factories that settled the suit were mostly owned by Chinese, Japanese and Korean companies that supplied more than $1 billion a year of "Made in America" garments to some of America's leading retailers and labels.

Nevertheless, DeLay continues to support the current

unregulated Mariana work rules. He has gone so far as to suggest that the United States emulate the way the islands' employers import guest workers from China and the Philippines and suggested that it may provide a model for mainland employers who wish to exploit cheap Mexican labor.

> Returning from a fact-finding trip (to the Marianas) where he played two rounds of golf at the first-class Lao Loa Bay Golf Resort, DeLay blasted critics of what he called Saipan's 'free market success.' He went on to explain how he wants to use a set of Chinese-owned sweatshops on the far-off U.S. territory—factories manned by low-paid Chinese and Sri Lankan indentured servants living in squalor—as a model for Mexican labor camps here on the mainland. (*Dallas Observer/New York Times Group*)

Besides the obvious problems with DeLay's support of poor work conditions in the Marianas, his support has also undercut his own constituents back home. There are about 60,000 apparel workers living and working in El Paso and San Antonio Texas. In fact, Texas ranks third in the nation for its number of garment workers. According to Joe Allen, a garment business consultant, the number of garment jobs is rapidly shrinking as factories close due to low-cost off shore operations like those in the Marianas.

> Tan Holdings is one of the most powerful companies on Saipan. "Workers have fallen ill due to the horrible working conditions they are forced to endure," said Medea Benjamin, a spokeswoman for

> Global Exchange. Drinking water provided workers was contaminated with e.coli and fecal coliform. Ill workers were denied medical treatment and locked in their barracks. Factory officials refused to allow health inspectors in the factory. (*Hong Kong Standard* 1999)

But with millions in lobbying money pouring in from Mariana business interests, DeLay and Abramoff have shown little interest in protecting American jobs. On one trip to the Marianas sponsored by the islands' largest sweatshop operator, Willie Tan, DeLay was effusive in his praise and support.

> On his first night on the island, DeLay was invited to a reception at the posh, beachfront Pacific Islands Club hosted by Will Tan, the powerful garment factory king. "When one of my closest and dearest friends, Jack Abramoff, your most able representative in Washington, D.C., invited me to the islands, I wanted to see firsthand the free-market success and progress and reform you have made," DeLay said. "Even though I have been here for only 24 hours, I have witnessed the economic success . . . (But) You are up against the forces of big labor and the radical left. Dick Armey and I made a promise to defend the island's present system. Stand firm. Resist evil. Remember that all truth and blessings emanate from our Creator." (*Dallas Observer*)

The Marianas account has paid off handsomely for

both DeLay and Abramoff, whose lobbying efforts resulted in more than $8 million in fees over the past five years, some of which inevitably ended up in DeLay's leadership PAC and as personal contributions from Abramoff over the years to DeLay's campaign war chests. DeLay was also able to distribute some of that money to those in Congress friendly to his cause—a fact Abramoff was quick to point out to his client:

"Thanks to past trips the Commonwealth of Northern Marianas has many friends on the Appropriations Committees in Congress," Abramoff wrote to Hong Kong sweatshop mogul Willie Tan. The Tan-controlled newspaper, *Saipan Tribune*, responded with an article lauding Abramoff:

> If [Abramoff's] past success in defending our interests is not enough reason to lock him into a long-term deal, the fact that George W. Bush is now the new President is yet another reason. [Abramoff] was able to defend us by educating powerful Members of Congress and arranging a trip to these islands by the most powerful member, Congressman Tom DeLay. Mr. Abramoff and his team have racked up win after win for these islands. (*Saipan Tribune* 2001 Editorial)

DeLay Gets Enron a Piece of the Mariana Action

Although far from Texas, the Marianas provided DeLay with yet another opportunity to help Enron. When the Marianas put out a call for bids for a new $120 million power plant, a Japanese company was awarded the contract. Enron, attracted by the island's lack of environmental rules, wanted in and complained to DeLay that they had not been given a fair shot at the contract for the power plant.

DeLay responded by calling in some chits from his friends in the Mariana administration—in particular Ben Fital, a conservative politician whom DeLay's former aides, Ed Buckham and Mike Scanlon, helped get elected as the island's representative in Congress. (*The Washington Post* reported that Buckham's lobbying firm, Alexander Strategy Group's representation of Enron's interests in the Marianas won him $50,000 in fees.)

Delay demanded that the power plant bidding be re-opened and that Enron's bid be given new consideration.

And so it came to pass. The bidding was re-opened and Enron was declared the winner. Apparently, free-market mechanisms like open bidding are only good when they favor the right player. Islanders say the bidding was rigged in Enron's favor.

"There were all kinds of political pushes from the top and the side and every way," Vincent Mesa, the island's former manger of the its power utilities, recalled later. "There were all kinds of political interference. They (government officials) didn't want to understand it. They said, 'Just do it! Give Enron the contract.' "

But now with Enron in bankruptcy, the power project has been left to rust in the Pacific sun and the islands are stuck with spotty electric power and lots of debt.

Quiz

Paul Slansky

"This ain't the end of it—we're going to have some more." Who said that, and about what?

(a) George W. Bush, regarding wars in the Middle East.
(b) Representative Tom DeLay (R-Texas), regarding tax cuts.
(c) Vice-President Dick Cheney, regarding obscenely lucrative government contracts awarded to Halliburton.
(d) An unnamed newspaper copy editor, regarding headlines containing the words "cry" (or "cried," or "crying") and "Wolfowitz."

Answer: (b)

Bill Frist

from deal-with-it.org

Gus DiZerega

Bill Frist is Republican Senate Majority Leader. If he doesn't have the basic viciousness of a Tom DeLay or Newt Gingrich, he certainly equals them in hypocrisy, dishonesty, and lack of concern for the well-being of our country.

A HYPOCRITE'S HYPOCRITE

As this is written Sen. Frist is appalled, truly appalled, that Senate democrats think the Senate select Committee on Intelligence might be able to extend their investigation of intelligence failures to the White House. *The Washington Post* quotes him as saying—the democrat who wrote a leaked memo on the topic should "identify himself or herself . . . disavow this partisan attack in its entirety" and deliver "a personal apology" to Sen. Pat Roberts (R-Kan.), chairman of the Select Committee on Intelligence.

Only then, according to Frist, "will it be possible for the committee to resume its work in an effective and bipartisan manner—a manner deserving of the confidence of other members of the Senate and the executive branch."

We are left breathless at the senator's exquisite sensitivity to partisanship, the deep psychic pain he must feel in contemplating that political opponents might want to take advantage of epochal incompetence on the part of his party.

But consider the following:

In *Lies and the Lying Liars Who Tell Them,* Al Franken writes that during the 2002 Senatorial campaign Paul Wellstone was running against Norm Coleman. The Republican NRSC ran an ad called 'Pork' that attacked Wellstone

> for voting 'to spend thousands of dollars to control seaweed in Maui,' claiming that he prioritized seaweed control over national defense. In fact, Wellstone did vote for S.1216, as did Strom Thurmond, Trent Lott and 84 other senators. That bill did appropriate the seaweed control spending—but it also provided $21 billion for veterans' health care, $27 billion for veterans' compensation and pensions, and block grants to assist New York City's recovery from 9/11. The NRSC was chaired that year by Bill Frist, who later replaced Lott as Senate majority leader. Before the memorial, Frist spoke with the Wellstones' older son, David, who later recounted the conversation to me.
>
> "I'm sorry about your parents and your sister," Frist told David.
>
> "Did you authorize the seaweed ad against my dad?" David asked.
>
> "Yes," said Frist.
>
> "And did you vote for the seaweed bill?"
>
> There was a pause. They both knew that the answer was yes. Finally, Frist said, "It wasn't personal." (pp. 179-180)

Frist lies about Iraq

Frist is equally without integrity involving the Iraq War.

On June 26, 2003, on the "Today Show," Frist told the American people regarding the issue of Iraq and weapons of mass destruction: "I'm not sure that's the major reason we went to war."

BUT consider his earlier words to us, before the falsehoods of the WMD claims became obvious to all reasonable intelligent people: [1]

"We simply cannot live in fear of a ruthless dictator, aggressor and terrorist such as Saddam Hussein, who possesses the world's most deadly weapons." (March 31, 2003)

"Let there be no mistake about our Nation's purpose in confronting Iraq—Saddam Hussein's regime poses a clear threat to the people of United States, its friends and its allies, and it is a threat that we must address now." (March 7, 2003)

"Getting rid of Saddam Hussein's regime is our best inoculation. Destroying once and for all his weapons of disease and death is a vaccination for the world." (March 16, 2003)

"The United States . . . is now at war so we will not ever see" what terrorists could do "if supplied with weapons of mass destruction by Saddam Hussein." (March 20, 2003)

THE MAN WITHOUT QUALITIES

It takes a special kind of person to lie to animal shelters—to tell them he will adopt cats as pets, and then take the animals to his labs and operate on them. (The cats all died.) [2]

Bill Frist's ethics haven't improved since his days in the laboratory. He uses his background as a physician to urge people to trust him, while even lying about his medical experience. [3]

1. See: http://billmon.org/archives/000281.html
2. See: http://www.ftcr.org/healthcare/nw/nw002986.php3
3. See: http://slate.msn.com/id/2077484/

But this time he is using his dishonesty and hypocrisy not to feather his nest as a well-paid doctor of dubious morality, not to further his political career as a sleazy manipulator, but to put our national security at risk by placing partisanship ahead of truth, prohibiting important investigations to protect his allies in the White House—and then accusing others of being partisan.

Bill Frist gives partisanship a whole new meaning.

Dennis Hastert

from deal-with-it.org

Gus DiZerega

In March, just prior to the Iraq war, House Speaker Dennis Hastert, R-Ill., said remarks in a speech made by the Senate minority leader "may not give comfort to our adversaries, but they come mighty close." What passes for near-treason in Hastert's mind? The following:

In a March 17 speech, Senator Tom Daschle had said he was "saddened that this president failed so miserably at diplomacy that we're now forced to war."

And Hastert calls himself an American patriot? Now we all know that George Bush *intended* to fail at diplomacy. He planned war all along, despite his pious pronouncements of preferring peace, that his mind was not yet made up, and blah, blah, blah. It was a show of lies and deception, put on for domestic consumption only. Daschle was wrong only in his thought that perhaps Bush had tried diplomacy, albeit incompetently. His only error in hindsight was thinking George Bush was an honorable man.

But Hastert is far less than simply a disgrace to the Bill of Rights and those who have given their lives fighting for it. He also has no sympathies with government existing to serve its citizens. Instead, it exists to serve the wealthy, and so do the rest of us in his mind. Harsh words? Consider the following:

One relatively painless means for helping our poorest citizens is the earned income child tax credit. It gives a tax credit to lower income families with children.

Sen. Blanche Lambert Lincoln (D-Ark.) sought to ensure that taxpayers earning above $10,500 a year still qualified for a refund under the child tax credit, even if they owed no income tax. Bush did not include it in his original $725-billion tax cut proposal in January 2003, nor was it in the $550-billion cut initially approved by the Republican-led House. But Lambert's provision did pass the Republican controlled Senate. It would have cost $3.5 billion, 1% of the final tax cut that passed into law.

On May 30, 2003, Nick Anderson and Justin Gest of the *Los Angeles Times* wrote, "Had the proposal been in the final legislation, some tax analysts calculate, nearly 12 million children in families with lower incomes—from $10,500 to $26,625—would have received some benefit. Without it, experts say the expanded tax credit, which rises this year to $1,000 a child from $600, will mainly help families with incomes above $30,000 a year."

Even those who make so little they pay no income tax do not go tax free. Sales taxes in particular fall disproportionately on the poor, who must of necessity spend a larger portion of their income on basics. And the children of the poor are in no way responsible for their situation. But for Dennis Hastert and Tom DeLay, such a tax credit was a luxury the country could not afford, not if it meant cutting 1% from a tax curt that went mostly to the wealthy.

The bill won final approval May 23; the Senate vote was 51 to 50, with Vice President Dick Cheney breaking a tie. [1]

David Brooks is a conservative commentator who occasionally gives signs he argues his principles for reasons of belief rather than income augmentation. On October 28, 2003, he attacked Hastert for his central role in ramming through the now-discredited tanker lease scheme where Boeing would be paid an extra $5.6 billion over the cost of simply buying the planes. (Compare that to the $3.5 billion tax credit for the poor that Hastert helped torpedo.)

Brooks details some of the shadiest elements of this scandal, a scandal that leaves Hastert still in the driver's seat as Speaker because, well, because he pays off the rich who pay him off in return. Citizens be damned.

Finally, as our Blog also reports, Dennis Hastert is upset about how Canada treats Americans seeking to buy prescription medications there. He wants "U.S. action to bring about changes in Canada's prescription drug price control policies," which he claims are unfair to U.S. residents. [2]

All Canada does is allow American citizens to buy drugs there more cheaply than they are allowed to here in the

1. See: http://www.truthout.org/docs_03/053103H.shtml
2. See: http://seattletimes.nwsource.com/html/nationworld/2001813114_drugs12.html

U.S., at least so long as they do not thereby use up Canada's supply of medicine. Hastert finds this unfair to us.

But what is not unfair are attempts by American drug companies to exert control far beyond simply selling their products to willing buyers, which I always thought the market was about. Tamsin Carlisle of the *Wall Street Journal* reported that "Drug maker Pfizer Inc., New York, earlier this month demanded in a letter to Canadian drug wholesalers that the wholesalers limit their dealings to retail pharmacies preapproved by Pfizer."

This exercise in something rather less than free trade was not all Pfizer wanted. "As a condition of doing business, the company also directed Canadian wholesalers to implement 'customer flagging, order screening and related procedures' and to report back to Pfizer on customer orders. Several other big pharmaceutical companies, including GlaxoSmithKline PLC and Eli Lilly & Co., have said they will limit sales of patent-protected medicines to Canada over concerns that the drugs are being re-exported to the U.S." [3]

Hastert is not an advocate of free enterprise or small government. He serves big money—period.

3. See: http://www.siliconinvestor.com/stocktalk/msg.gsp?msgid=19629456

ASSORTED EVIL-DOERS AND INCOMPETENTS

with quotes by Scott McClellan;
and quizzes by Paul Slansky

The Bush Administration has a genius for recruiting soul-less (and sometimes brainless) people to labor in the trenches of bad government. Bear in mind as you read about these orclike beings—the likes of Elliott Abrams and John Poindexter—that in many cases you help pay their salaries.

John Dingell is a Congressman from Michigan's Fifteenth District—and a bit of a wise guy.

Letter to Gregory Mankiw

Rep. John Dingell

February 20, 2004

Dr. Gregory Mankiw
Chairman, Council of Economic Advisers
Executive Office of the President
Washington, DC 20502

Dear Dr. Mankiw:

I noticed in the recently released Economic Report of the President that there was some consternation in the defining of manufacturing. It could be inferred from your report that the administration is willing to recognize drink mixing, hamburger garnishing, French/freedom fry cooking, and milk shake mixing to be vital components of our manufacturing sector.

I am sure the 163,000 factory workers who have lost their jobs in Michigan will find it heartening to know that a world of opportunity awaits them in high growth manufacturing careers like spatula operator, napkin restocking, and lunch tray removal. I do have some questions of this new policy and I hope you will help me provide answers for my constituents:

- Will federal student loans and Trade Adjustment Assistance grants be applied to tuition costs at Burger College?
- Will the administration commit to allowing the Manufacturing Extension Partnership (MEP) to fund cutting edge burger research such as new nugget ingredients or keeping the hot and cold sides of burgers separate until consumption?
- Will special sauce now be counted as a durable good?
- Do you want fries with that?

Finally, at a speech he gave in Michigan this past September, Secretary Evans announced the creation of a new Assistant Secretary for Manufacturing. While I understand that it takes a while to find the right candidate to fill these positions, I am concerned that five months after the announcement no Assistant Secretary has yet been named. I do, however, know of a public official who would be perfect for the job. He has over thirty years of administrative and media experience, has a remarkable record of working with diverse constituencies, and is extraordinarily well qualified to understand this emerging manufacturing sector: the Hon. Mayor McCheese.

With every good wish,
John D. Dingell

He Said It . . .

"This is about imminent threat."

—White House spokesman Scott McClellan, 2/10/03

"I think some in the media have chosen to use the word 'imminent.' Those were not words we used."

—White House spokesman Scott McClellan, 1/27/04

The Bush administration often uses government posts to reward unbearably creepy Republican functionaries, including deranged, murderous people who have proved willing to lie—and worse—for their party.

Public Serpent: Iran-contra Villain Elliott Abrams is Back in Action

from *In These Times* (8/01)

Terry J. Allen

A nursing home aide earning minimum wage caring for Alzheimer's patients is an unskilled laborer. A grade school teacher pulling down $25,000 a year in a crumbling inner-city school is barely a professional. But a politician reaping power, pay, perks and retirement packages is a public servant.

Calling George W. Bush and Jesse Helms "public servants" is like calling Iran-contra criminal Elliott Abrams an "outstanding diplomat"—which is precisely what White House Press Secretary Ari Fleischer did when he announced Abrams' appointment as senior director of the National Security Council's Office for Democracy, Human Rights and International Operations. Fleischer conveyed Bush's faith-based assertion that Abrams is "the best person to do the job," which, happily for the appointee, does not require Senate confirmation.

For those who don't remember, Abrams was one of the most odious participants in a particularly shameful chapter of U.S. history. In the '80s, he was Ronald Reagan's assistant secretary of state for human rights and humanitarian affairs and later the assistant secretary of state for inter-American affairs. In that post, Abrams, in his own words, "supervised U.S. policy in Latin America and the Caribbean."

That policy included backing the contras—a surrogate army dedicated to overthrowing the democratically elected Sandinista government of Nicaragua. It also involved funding the military thugocracy of El Salvador and supervising its war against a popular leftist rebellion. In his role as public servant, Abrams found time to cover up the genocidal policies of the Guatemalan government and embrace the government of Honduras while it perpetrated serial human rights abuses through Battalion 3-16, a U.S.-trained "intelligence unit" turned death squad.

Thick as thieves with Oliver North, Abrams helped evade congressional restrictions on aid to the contras. When Congress—spurred on by protests and embarrassing press disclosures—grew wary of the Central American wars, the Reaganites sought other avenues for funding them. Ever eager to serve, Abrams flew to London under the alias "Mr. Kenilworth" to solicit a $10 million contribution from the Sultan of Brunei.

In the congressional investigations that followed disclosure of the Iran-contra conspiracies, Abrams was never held accountable for the human rights violations backed, hidden and funded by the Reagan administration. Instead Abrams was accused of withholding information from Congress, a Washington euphemism for bald-face lying. In 1991, he copped to two counts of withholding information from Congress (and was granted a Christmas Eve pardon a year later by President George Bush).

Abrams was none too pleased, even with this slap on the wrist. According to a May 30, 1994 article in *Legal*

Times, he called his prosecutors "filthy bastards," the proceedings against him "Kafkaesque," and members of the Senate Intelligence Committee "pious clowns" whose raison d'etre was to ask him "abysmally stupid" questions. (In the spirit of full disclosure: Abrams once called me a "rotten bitch" after I tactlessly noted that much of the world considers him a war criminal.)

Abrams' own "full biography," posted on the Web site of the Ethics and Public Policy Center—an oxymoronic think tank where he wiled away much of the Democratic interregnum awaiting the collective amnesia of the American public—omits his unpleasantness with Congress. In any case, as Fleischer said of Abrams' transgressions, "the president thinks that's a matter of the past and was dealt with at the time."

Loved ones of the thousand unarmed Salvadoran peasants, including 139 children, killed by U.S.-trained contra troops in the 1981 El Mozote massacre may be less inclined to let bygones be bygones. Abrams has been a consistent massacre denier, even calling Washington's policy in El Salvador a "fabulous achievement." He told Congress that the reports carried in the *New York Times* and *Washington Post* a month after El Mozote were Communist propaganda.

In 1993, members of a Salvadoran Truth commission testified about the massacre in a congressional hearing of the House Western Hemisphere subcommittee. Chairman Robert G. Torricelli (D-New Jersey) vowed to review for possible perjury "every word uttered by every Reagan administration official" in congressional testimony on El Salvador. Abrams denounced Torricelli's words as "McCarthyite crap."

Eventually documentation emerged proving that the Reagan administration had known about El Mozote and other human rights violations all along. Abrams, however, carefully denied knowledge of the assassination of Salvadoran Archbishop Oscar Romero, committed shortly after the cleric denounced government terror. "Anybody who thinks you're going to find a cable that says that Roberto d'Aubuisson murdered the archbishop is a fool," Abrams was quoted in a March 21, 1993 article in the *Washington Post.*

In fact, the *Post* notes, the U.S. embassy in San Salvador sent at least two such cables to Washington nailing d'Aubuisson, the right-wing politician who was the chief architect of the plot against Romero. The December 21, 1981 cable notes: "A meeting, chaired by Maj. Roberto d'Aubuisson, during which the murder of Archbishop Romero was planned. During the meeting, some of the participants drew lots for the privilege of killing the archbishop."

Now Bush II has given Abrams a post that rewards his special experience. In the proud ranks of America's public servants, he will join other Iran-contra vets: Secretary of State Colin Powell; Deputy Secretary of State Richard Armitage; Otto Reich, assistant secretary of state for inter-American affairs; and presumably John Negroponte, awaiting confirmation as U.N. ambassador.

And who says you can't get help like you used to?

Quiz

Paul Slansky

Which headline did *not* appear in a daily or weekly U.S. newspaper?

(a) "ADMINISTRATION ESTABLISHES NEW WETLANDS GUIDELINES; 20 MILLION ACRES COULD LOSE PROTECTED STATUS, GROUPS SAY"
(b) "ASHCROFT ORDERS U.S. ATTORNEYS TO SEEK DEATH IN MORE CASES"
(c) "BUSH SEEKS STIFFER PROOF FOR POOR TO OBTAIN AID"
(d) "BUSH PLANS TO LET RELIGIOUS GROUPS TO GET BUILDING AID; WORSHIP SITES INVOLVED"
(e) "BUSH ORDERS A 3-YEAR DELAY IN OPENING SECRET DOCUMENTS"
(f) "BUSH PUSHES PLAN TO CURB APPEALS IN MEDICARE CASES; BENEFIT DENIALS AT ISSUE"
(g) "BUSH DECLARES WAR, WARNS NATION MANY SACRIFICES WILL BE NECESSARY"
(h) "PENTAGON SEEKING TO DEPLOY MISSILES BEFORE FULL TESTING"
(i) "EPA TO ALLOW POLLUTERS TO BUY CLEAN WATER CREDITS"

Answer: (g)

John Poindexter

from deal-with-it.org

Gus DiZerega

The United States has close to 300 million people. Its military is over a million strong. Thousands of soldiers are officers. Many are honest, competent, and devoted to their job. But when the time came for George W. Bush to pick the man who would oversee the greatest government investigative agency in our history, an agency dedicated to acquiring the most private information on the buying, travel, and reading habits of every American, none of these people were selected for the task.

George Bush chose John Poindexter instead. Poindexter got off of a felony rap due to a technicality—he had previously testified to Congress. But the facts remained: that he had lied under oath and in uniform. Thus does George Bush bring honor to the White House. What an inspiring message to send honest servants of their country.

Judgement equal to Bush's

John Poindexter has a reputation as an out-of-the-box thinker. This can be very good. But "out-of-the-box" shouldn't mean out of your mind. Poindexter's activities led him to lie under oath, deceive taxpayers and elected representatives alike, and practice a kind of tunnel vision that befits fanatics who see only their own narrow view of reality as truly important.

As Ronald Reagan's National Security Advisor, John Poindexter was up to his neck in the Iran-Contra scandal, sending weapons to our enemies in order to pursue foreign policy goals prohibited by Congress. Secret sales of arms to Iran were used to finance rebels fighting in Nicaragua at a time when such assistance was banned by Congress.

Poindexter got caught. In 1990 he was convicted on five felony counts, including lying to Congress, destroying documents and obstructing congressional inquiries into the affair. Although his conviction was overturned in 1991—on grounds that Poindexter had been granted immunity from prosecution as a result of his testimony before Congress, there was no question that he was guilty of lying under oath and deceiving elected officials

Poindexter retired to a richly deserved life outside public service. Then George Bush moved to the White House. Bush promised "I'll bring in a group of men and women who are focused on what's best for America, honest men and women, decent men and women, women who will see service to our country as a great privilege and who will not stain the house." (1/15/00) Poindexter's appointment demonstrates how seriously Bush meant it.

Under Bush's sponsorship, Poindexter came up with his idea for the now-defunct TIA (Terrorism Information Awareness) program, where the government would collect all our financial records, health, library visits, so as to try and determine "patterns" of suspicious behavior.

When public outcry led to the demise of that idea, Poindexter developed his now infamous idea for a market in terrorism futures. Poindexter's scheme was based on one true insight and lots of bad thinking. The true insight is that the market often beats experts in predicting future developments and the same kind of dispersed network might be useful in anticipating attacks. But the bad idea is that markets can be manipulated in the short run—as the country just discovered in the case of Enron. There is nothing some people won't do to make a buck. Beating the market on terrorism futures suggests some truly evil methods of self-enrichment. Anyone thinking such methods wouldn't be attempted has been living on the moon. [1]

Poindexter blamed the bad publicity on an unauthorized decision by an outside contractor—Net Exchange—to post "some extremely bad examples" on the program's Web site, giving skeptics ammunition to attack the idea. The "bad examples" included betting on Yasser Arafat's assassination or the overthrow of Jordan's monarchy. Interestingly, Poindexter did not say these "bad examples" were false examples. What made them bad was their capacity to discredit a foolish idea.

In a letter of resignation ending his 20-month stint in the Pentagon, Poindexter continued to argue for using new technologies to discover terrorists' plans by analyzing patterns in credit card purchases, travel reservations and e-mail. Interestingly, information that could have prevented 9-11 was gathered by old-fashioned methods. Those methods fit within our Bill of Rights and did not threaten our privacy. [2]

1. See: http://www.workingforchange.com/article.cfm?itemid=15435
2. See: http://www.truthout.org/docs_03/081403E.shtml

Cheney and the rest of the warmongers in the Bush cabal have to get their so-called "ideas" somewhere. They turn to pseudo-intellectuals such as William Kristol, who have devoted their lives to the task of preserving and misdirecting American power.

All in the Neocon Family

from AlterNet (3/27/03)

Jim Lobe

What do William Kristol, Norman Podhoretz, Elliot Abrams, and Robert Kagan have in common? Yes, they are all die-hard hawks who have gained control of U.S. foreign policy since the 9/11 attacks. But they are also part of one big neoconservative family—an extended clan of spouses, children, and friends who have known each other for generations.

Neoconservatives are former liberals (which explains the "neo" prefix) who advocate an aggressive unilateralist vision of U.S. global supremacy, which includes a close strategic alliance with Israel. Let's start with one of the founding fathers of the extended neocon clan: Irving Kristol. His extensive resume includes waging culture wars for the CIA against the Soviet Union in the early years of the Cold War and calling for an American "imperial" role during the Vietnam War. Papa Kristol, who has been credited with defining the major themes of neoconservative thought, is married to Gertrude Himmelfarb, a neoconservative powerhouse on her own. Her studies of the Victorian era in Britain helped inspire the men who sold Bush on the idea of "compassionate conservatism."

The son of this proud couple is none other than

William Kristol, the crown prince of the neoconservative clique and editor of the Rupert Murdoch-owned *Weekly Standard*. In 1997, he founded the Project for the New American Century (PNAC), a front group which cemented the powerful alliance between right-wing Republicans like Dick Cheney and Don Rumsfeld, Christian and Catholic Right leaders like Gary Bauer and William Bennett, and the neocons behind a platform of global U.S. military dominance.

Irving Kristol's most prominent disciple is Richard Perle, who was until Thursday the Defense Policy Board chairman, and is also a "resident scholar" at the American Enterprise Institute, which is housed in the same building as PNAC. Perle himself married into neocon royalty when he wed the daughter of his professor at the University of Chicago, the late Alfred Wohlstetter—the man who helped both his son-in-law and his fellow student Paul Wolfowitz get their start in Washington more than 30 years ago.

Perle's own protege is Douglas Feith, who is now Wolfowitz's deputy for policy and is widely known for his right-wing Likud position. And why not? His father, Philadelphia businessman and philanthropist Dalck Feith, was once a follower of the great revisionist Zionist leader, Vladimir Jabotinsky, in his native Poland back in the 1930s. The two Feiths were honored together in 1997 by the right-wing Zionist Organization of America (ZOA).

The AEI has long been a major nexus for such interfamilial relationships. A long-time collaborator with Perle, Michael Ledeen is married to Barbara Ledeen, a founder and director of the anti-feminist Independent Women's Forum (IWF), who is currently a major player in the Republican leadership on Capitol Hill. Richard Perle,

Douglas Feith, and another neo-con power couple—David and Meyrav Wurmser—co-authored a 1996 memorandum for Likud leader Binyamin Netanyahu outlining how to break the Oslo peace process and invade Iraq as the first step to transforming the Middle East.

Though she doesn't focus much on foreign-policy issues, Lynne Cheney also hangs her hat at AEI. Her husband Dick Cheney recently chose Victoria Nuland to become his next deputy national security adviser. Nuland, as it turns out, is married to Robert Kagan, Bill Kristol's main comrade-in-arms and the co-founder of PNAC.

Bob's father, Donald Kagan, is a Yale historian who converted from a liberal Democrat to a staunch neocon in the 1970s. On the eve of the 2000 presidential elections, Donald and his other son, Frederick, published "While America Sleeps," a clarion call to increase defense spending. Since then, the three Kagan men have written reams of columns warning that the currently ballooning Pentagon budget is simply not enough to fund the much-desired vision of U.S. global supremacy.

And which infamous ex-Reaganite do the Kagans and another leading neocon family have in common? None other than Iran-contra veteran Elliott Abrams.

Now the director of Near Eastern Affairs in Bush's National Security Council, Abrams worked closely with Bob Kagan back in the Reagan era. He is also the son-in-law of Norman Podhoretz, long-time editor of the influential conservative Jewish publication *Commentary*, and his wife, Midge Decter, is a fearsome polemicist in her own right.

Podhoretz, like Kristol Sr., helped invent neo-conservatism in the late 1960s. He and Decter created a formidable political team as leaders of the Committee on the Present

Danger in 1980, when they worked with Donald Rumsfeld to pound the last nail into the coffin of detente and promote the rise of Ronald Reagan. In addition to being Abrams' father-in-law, Norman Podhoretz is also the father of John Podhoretz, a columnist for the Murdoch-owned *New York Post* and frequent guest on the Murdoch-owned Fox News channel.

As editor of *Commentary*, Norman offered writing space to rising stars of the neocon movement for more than 30 years. His proteges include former U.N. ambassador Jeane Kirkpatrick and Richard Pipes, who was Ronald Reagan's top advisor on the "Evil Empire," as the president liked to call the Soviet Union. His son, Daniel Pipes, has also made a career out of battling "evil," which in his case is Islam. And to tie it all up neatly, in 2002, Podhoretz received the highest honor bestowed by the AEI: the Irving Kristol award.

This list of intricate, overlapping connections is hardly exhaustive or perhaps even surprising. But it helps reveal an important fact. Contrary to appearances, the neocons do not constitute a powerful mass political movement. They are instead a small, tighly-knit clan whose incestuous familial and personal connections, both within and outside the Bush administration, have allowed them to grab control of the future of American foreign policy.

Congressman John Dingell—Democrat from Michigan—received this letter in early 2004. His reply begins on page 348.

BUSH CHENEY '04

WWW.GEORGEWBUSH.COM

Marc Racicot
Chairman

January 9, 2004

John
Dear ~~Mr. Dingell~~,

Will you become one of the first to join the Bush-Cheney '04 Team as a Charter Member in Virginia? I would be thrilled to tell the President you are with us.

As a small token of appreciation and to welcome you to our team, I am proud to present you with the enclosed photo of the President and Laura Bush—complete with a special, personal inscription to you.

Your photo is a symbol of the commitment we share—the commitment between you, the Bush-Cheney '04 campaign and President Bush. I hope you are as proud of this commitment as we are, Mr. Dingell, and I also hope your photo will serve as a reminder of the importance of Charter Members of the Bush-Cheney '04 Team: to provide continuing grassroots support for President Bush and Vice President Cheney as we work to get the campaign up and running.

(Over, please)

Post Office Box 10729 • Arlington, VA 22210 • 800-531-6789 • www.GeorgeWBush.com
Not Printed at Taxpayers' Expense
Paid for by Bush-Cheney '04, Inc.

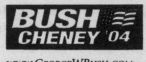

We believe this election will be very close. We believe it will be difficult. The Democrats will be relentless in attacking the President, distorting his record and trying to mislead the voters.

We are relying on our Charter Members to be the leaders in their area for President Bush and the Bush-Cheney '04 campaign.

And there are two things you can do today to help:

1) Send back the enclosed Receipt Confirmation Form to let me know that your photograph arrived in good condition and is suitable for framing and display. This may seem like a little thing, but it is very important to me personally to know that your support has been properly acknowledged.

2) When you send back your Receipt Confirmation, please include a contribution of $100, $50, $25 or whatever you can afford to help the Bush-Cheney '04 campaign Team to help reach out to other grass-roots leaders like you.

Mr. Dingell, your support is critical. The 2000 and 2002 elections revealed that our national political contests are extremely competitive but, if we work together, we can prevail.

It is essential we fully fund our voter outreach program—this special program will make the difference between winning and losing in 2004. Our goal is to reach out to register 3 million voters who support President Bush's bold vision for America.

It has become clear that the Democrats have lost the battle of ideas based on their stall and delay tactics in the U.S. Senate.

Some left wing activists are even using outrageous charges and outright distortions in attacking and vilifying President Bush and Vice President Cheney.

President Bush is relying on you and other friends to help turn back these Democrat assaults and elevate the political debate for his positive, optimistic agenda for America:

- an agenda that continues the War on Terrorism and protects the homeland,
- an agenda that strengthens the economy and creates new jobs,
- an agenda that makes it possible for every American to own a home, health and retirement plan and, if they want, their own business, and
- an agenda that focuses on results in schools so every child learns to read and no child is left behind.

But the liberal national media won't deliver this message to the American people. They have their own agenda. It is up to supporters like you to help us get the message directly to the voters.

Thanks to the generous support of Bush-Cheney Charter Members we are on our way to meeting our budget goal, but we still have a way to go.

<u>So please return your signed Receipt Confirmation Form today along with a contribution of $100, $50, or $25 to help us meet our goal and keep our voter contact programs moving forward.</u>

I hope you will display your photo of the President and Laura Bush proudly—not only as a token of appreciation for your contribution to join as a Charter Member of the Bush-Cheney '04 campaign—but also as a reminder of why we cannot afford to fall short now.

Mr. Dingell, on behalf of President Bush and Vice President Cheney, thank you for your support.

Sincerely,

Marc Racicot
Chairman

P.S. Your early support of President Bush and his campaign will mark you as a grassroots leader in Virginia. Only with your help as a Charter Member can the Bush-Cheney '04 campaign create a viable grassroots organization. Please join the Bush-Cheney '04 Team as a Charter Member with your contribution of $100, $50 or even $25 to help us lay the groundwork to win in 2004.

Dingell's reply . . .

JOHN D. DINGELL
FIFTEENTH DISTRICT
MICHIGAN

January 30, 2004

Marc
Dear ~~Mr. Racicot~~,

I am truly flattered to have received your invitation to join the Bush-Cheney '04 Team as a Charter Member. I have been waiting for nearly four years for a senior Republican to take me up on my numerous offers to work together across the aisle—though I have to admit, this isn't exactly what I was expecting.

In fact, I was very surprised to learn that the RNC is so desperate for money that it is now soliciting sitting Democratic Congressmen for donations. With all the special interest giveaways to contractors like Halliburton, energy companies like Enron, or the pharmaceutical industry, I would think the Bush-Cheney re-election fund would be flush with contributions. I really didn't realize times were so tough at GOP HQ. This makes me very sad.

I was even more surprised to learn that you, President Bush and I share a commitment with regard to the President's re-election. I was worried that you wanted to keep the Bush-Cheney team around for four more years of historic job loss and unemployment, record-setting deficits and continued attacks on Medicare, Social Security, veteran's benefits, and working families.

I can't tell you how overjoyed I am that you share my goal of seeing the Bush-Cheney team have another second place finish in 2004.

This is nothing personal. I have always thought that President Bush would make a fine partner for hunting, fishing, or watching TV, but when it comes to the serious issues facing this country—including jobs, healthcare, the war on terror—he's had three years to show what he could do to improve matters. However, I feel America is worse off now than it was four years ago.

You are right to think this election will be difficult for the President, but you won't have to worry about Democrats "distorting his record and trying to mislead the voters." We know we can win just by laying out the President's record including being the first President to actually lose jobs since Herbert Hoover—another fine Republican—led us into the Great Depression.

Oh, by the way, if it's accuracy and credibility you're concerned about, you should worry more about Republicans "misleading the voters." Remember, it was your candidate who said his tax cuts for the rich wouldn't bust the budget, claimed to barely know his largest campaign contributor, Enron' s "Kenny-Boy" Lay, and came up with "weapons of mass destruction" as a way to get our country into Iraq. Or was all that just made up by the "liberal national media" that you describe in your letter as having its "own agenda"?

Mr. Racicot, if MY support is critical to President Bush's efforts to pass his "leave no millionaire behind" tax schemes or divert attention from our growing manufacturing crisis, he's in even bigger trouble than previously thought.

You might not have seen my comments in the newspapers or on television, but I would think someone in your campaign knew of my positions. The person responsible for your letter could be a wonderful candidate for your new job re-training programs mentioned in the State of the Union. I hope you search for the campaign staffer who sent this letter with the same vigor that you have shown in the search for the White House employee responsible for leaking the name of a U.S. operative.

In closing, I wanted to thank you for the lovely picture of President and Mrs. Bush complete with its personal inscription to me. I liked it so much that I'm sharing it with all my friends. As a token of my appreciation, I am enclosing one of my own for you and your friends, in which I got to wear a flight suit—something that both top Democrats and top Republicans like to do.

With every good wish,

Sincerely,

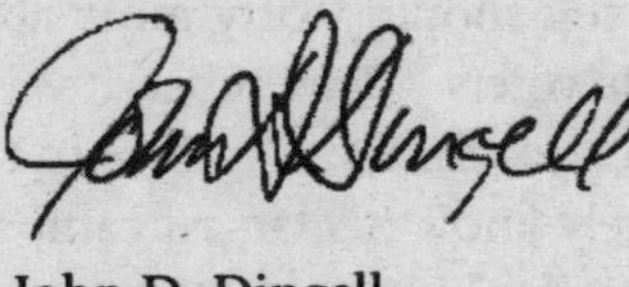

John D. Dingell

P.S.—I appreciate knowing that a senior Republican like yourself is willing to correspond with me. Do you think you could get President Bush or Vice President Cheney to respond to some of my letters on saving our manufacturing jobs, no-bid Halliburton contracts, or the records of Mr. Cheney's Energy Task Force? Thanks!

NOT PRINTED AT GOVERNMENT EXPENSE

A No-Compassion Conservative?

from *The Nation* (11/19/03)

David Corn

Every once in a while a reporter snags what I call a Naked Lunch moment. *Naked Lunch* is, of course, the title of the crazed and surreal novel by William Burroughs, the Beat-friendly author. Supposedly Burroughs' pal Jack Kerouac conjured up the name for Burroughs' disjointed manuscript, explaining that the title referred to the instant when a person can see exactly what is on the tip of his or her fork—that is, what is truly going on. (Remember, Kerouac was a be-bopping poet.)

Such a moment came when veteran Australian journalist John Pilger interviewed John Bolton, the under secretary of state for arms control, for a documentary on the Iraq war that aired in England a few weeks ago.

Sitting with Bolton in a media room at Foggy Bottom, Pilger asked Bolton about civilian casualties in Iraq. Bolton replied, "I think Americans like most people are mostly concerned about their own country. I don't know how many Iraqi civilians were killed. But I can assure you that the number is the absolute minimum that is possible in modern warfare. . . .One of the stunning things about the quick coalition victory was . . . how low Iraqi casualties were."

This was not a surprising response, nor was it the revelatory moment. Bolton is a hawk's hawk in the Bush administration. He is the *agent conservateur* in Colin Powell's State Department. He has led the administration's effort against the International Criminal Court. Last year, he single-handedly tried to revise U.S. nuclear policy by asserting that Washington no longer felt bound to state that it would not use nuclear weapons against nations that do not possess nuclear weapons. (A State Department spokesman quickly claimed that Bolton had not said what he had indeed said.) Bolton also claimed that Cuba was developing biological weapons—a charge that was not substantiated by any evidence and that was challenged by experts. In July, he was about to allege in congressional testimony that Syria posed a weapons-of-mass-destruction threat before the CIA and other agencies, who considered his threat assessment to be exaggerated, objected to his statement. When England, France and Germany recently tried to develop a carrot-and-stick approach in negotiating an end to Iran's suspected nuclear weapons program, Bolton huffed, "I don't do carrots."

His remarks to Pilger, then, were hardly surprising. He is a no-apologies ideologue. Pilger asked if 10,000 civilian casualties in Iraq would be a "quite high" amount. Bolton answered, "I think it is quite low if you look at the size of the military operation that was undertaken."

Then when the interview ended, Bolton, as he stood up and removed the microphone, asked Pilger, "Are you a Labour Party member?" As if that explained Pilger's questions about dead and injured civilians in Iraq. Clearly, Bolton had not been briefed. Pilger is an investigative reporter specializing in national security matters who has long been seen as a left-of-center crusader. A critic of his recently dubbed Pilger "the Eeyore of the left." One wonders who at the State Department let Pilger get this close to Bolton? (By the way, when Pilger interviewed Douglas Feith, the undersecretary of defense for policy, a Pentagon media official ordered Pilger to shut off his camera once Pilger began questioning Feith about civilian casualties.)

Replying to Bolton's jab, Pilger explained to him the current politics of Britain: "Well, Labour Party—they're the conservatives." Pilger meant "conservative" as in supporting Prime Minister Tony Blair's embrace of the war in Iraq.

By now Bolton was walking away from Pilger, looking like he much desired a fast separation. With a mischievous (or, some might say, wicked) smile on his face, Bolton shot back, "You're a Communist Party member?"

That was the Kodak moment, and it was captured by Pilger's camera operator. On Planet Bolton, if you inquire too forcefully about civilian casualties, you must be a commie. The Cold War might be over. But at least one senior Bush aide is keeping its spirit alive.

Pilger's documentary, as far as I can tell, has not aired in the United States. I've only seen the scenes involving Bolton and Feith. So I cannot vouch for the entire film. But in a flash, Pilger captured on tape a brief but telling exchange. Call it Bolton unplugged, and it's mean and ugly.

Quiz

Paul Slansky

Which headline did *not* appear in a daily American newspaper during the early days of the George W. Bush presidency?

(a) "FDA TO SUSPEND A RULE ON CHILD DRUG TESTING"
(b) "EPA IS SET TO EASE RULES ON POLLUTING POWER PLANTS"
(c) "U.S. JOBLESS RATE INCREASES TO 6%, HIGHEST IN 8 YEARS"
(d) "EPA PROPOSES TO LET MINES DUMP WASTE IN WATERWAYS"
(e) "WHITE HOUSE CUT 93% OF FUNDS SOUGHT TO GUARD ATOMIC ARMS"
(f) "IN SHIFT, JUSTICE DEPT. PUSHES TO WIDEN RIGHTS TO OWN GUNS"
(g) "CHENEY RETURNS TO U.S. WITH FULL HEAD OF THICK, WAVY HAIR"

Answer: (g)

ANONYMOUS PHONE CALLS

NIGERGATE THUGGERY
DAVID CORN–357

WHOPPER OF THE WEEK:
KARL ROVE, ARI FLEISCHER, AND DICK CHENEY
TIMOTHY NOAH–361

with a cartoon by Ruben Bolling

Bush apologists often say outrageous things in public—at times, they seem to have no shame at all. So you know they're really up to something filthy when they resort to anonymous leaks or blame their behavior on information that can't be traced.

Nigergate Thuggery

from *The Nation* (8/4/03)

David Corn

Did senior Bush officials blow the cover of a US intelligence officer working covertly in a field of vital importance to national security—and break the law—in order to strike at a Bush Administration critic and intimidate others? It sure looks that way, if conservative journalist Robert Novak can be trusted. In a recent column on Nigergate, Novak examined the role of former Ambassador Joseph Wilson IV in the affair. On July 6 Wilson went public, writing in the *New York Times* about the trip he took to Niger in February 2002—at the request of the CIA—to check out allegations that Saddam Hussein had tried to purchase uranium from Niger for a nuclear weapons program. Wilson came home and told the CIA that it was "highly doubtful" Saddam had been able to buy uranium from Niger. (His findings were later confirmed by the International Atomic Energy Agency.) Reports, including Wilson's own, of his trip revved up the controversy over Bush's claim—which he made in his State of the Union address—that Iraq had attempted to obtain uranium in Africa for a nuclear weapons program. News of Wilson's mission provided more reason to suspect the Administration of misrepresenting intelligence in making its case for war on Iraq.

Soon after Wilson disclosed his trip in the media, the payback came. Novak's July 14 column contained the following sentences: "Wilson never worked for the CIA, but his wife, Valerie Plame, is an Agency operative on weapons of mass destruction. Two senior administration officials told me Wilson's wife suggested sending him to Niger to investigate."

Wilson caused problems for the White House, and his wife was outed. "I will not answer questions about my wife," he says. "This is about me and less so about my wife. It has always been about the facts underpinning the President's statement in the State of the Union speech." He will neither confirm nor deny that his wife works for the CIA. But assuming she does, that would seem to mean that the Bush Administration has screwed one of its own top-secret operatives—and compromised national security—in order to punish Wilson or to send a message to others who might dare challenge it.

The sources for Novak's assertion about Wilson's wife appear to be "two senior administration officials." That is, a pair of top Bush officials told a reporter the name of a deep-cover CIA officer who has had the dicey and difficult mission of tracking parties trying to buy or sell weapons of mass destruction or WMD material. If that's true, her career has been destroyed. Without acknowledging whether she is a CIA employee, Wilson says, "Naming her this way would have compromised every operation, every relationship, every network with which she had been associated in her entire career." If she is not a CIA employee and Novak is reporting accurately, then the White House has wrongly branded a woman known to friends as an energy analyst for a private firm as a CIA officer.

This is not only a possible breach of national security; it is a potential violation of law. Under the Intelligence Identities Protection Act of 1982, it is a crime for anyone with access to classified information to intentionally disclose a covert agent. The punishment is a fine of up to $50,000 and/or up to ten years in prison. Journalists are mostly protected from prosecution. Thus, Novak need not worry.

Novak tells me he was indeed tipped off by government officials and had no reluctance about naming her. "I figured if they gave it to me," he says, "they'd give it to others." Was Wilson's wife involved in sending him off to Niger? Wilson will say only, "I was invited out to meet with a group of people at the CIA who were interested in this subject. None I knew more than casually."

So where's the investigation? Remember Filegate—and the Republican charge that the Clinton White House used privileged information against its foes? In this instance, it appears that Bush Administration officials gathered information on Wilson and his family, and then revealed classified material to lash out at him. "Stories like this," Wilson says, "are not intended to intimidate me, since I've already told my story. But it's pretty clear it is intended to intimidate others who might come forward."

Since Bush Administration officials are so devoted to protecting government secrets—such as the identity of the energy lobbyists with whom the Vice President meets—one might (theoretically) expect them to be appalled by the possibility that classified information was disclosed and national security harmed for a political hit job. Yet after the Novak column appeared, there was no immediate comment from the White House—or any other public reverberation. The Wilson smear was a thuggish act, a sign that with this gang politics trumps national security.

Should pseudo-journalist Robert Novak reveal the names of Bush administration sources who told Novak that Valerie Plame was a CIA operative? Cartoonist Ruben Bolling offers his take . . .

Whopper of the Week: Karl Rove, Ari Fleischer, and Dick Cheney

from Slate.com (9/28/01)

Timothy Noah

"They also made it clear they wanted to get us up quickly, and they wanted to get us to a high altitude, because there had been a specific threat made to Air Force One [on September 11]. . . . A declaration that Air Force One was a target, and said in a way that they called it credible. . . . So they wanted to get us up quickly. They also wanted to get us up with fighter air cover."

—White House senior counselor Karl Rove, quoted by Nicholas Lemann in the Sept. 28 New Yorker.

"We have specific and credible information that the White House and Air Force One were also intended targets of these attacks."

—White House spokesman Ari Fleischer, Sept. 12 briefing.

Q: It was] yesterday reported that some of the people in the Pentagon were a little bit skeptical about your comments yesterday that the White House and Air Force One were attacked—were targets of attack, given that the plane had come from the south. What do you—

FLEISCHER: Who are these people?

Q: Well, I don't know. They weren't my sources, so—
(Cross talk.)

FLEISCHER: No. There's—I wouldn't have said it if it wasn't true.

Q: Can you confirm the substance of that threat that was telephoned in . . . that Air Force One is next and using code words?

FLEISCHER: Yes, I can. That's correct."

—*White House "press gaggle" with Ari Fleischer, Sept. 13.*

VICE PRESIDENT CHENEY: The president was on Air Force One. We received a threat to Air Force One—came through the Secret Service . . .

TIM RUSSERT: A credible threat to Air Force One. You're convinced of that.

VICE PRESIDENT CHENEY: I'm convinced of that. Now, you know, it may have been phoned in by a crank, but in the midst of what was going on, there was no way to know that. I think it was a credible threat, enough for the Secret Service to bring it to me.

—*NBC's* Meet the Press, *Sept. 16.*

"Finally, there is this postscript to the puzzle of how someone presumed to be a terrorist was able to call in a threat against Air Force One using a secret code name for the president's plane. Well, as it turns out, that simply never happened. Sources say White House staffers apparently misunderstood comments made by their security detail."

—*CBS News reporter Jim Stewart on the Sept. 25* CBS Evening News.

"[Administration officials have] been unsuccessful in trying to track down whether there was such a call, though officials still maintain they were told of a telephone threat Sept. 11 and kept Bush away from Washington for hours because of it."

—Sept. 25 AP report, quoted in the Sept. 27 Washington Post.

KARL ROVE

with a quote by Karl Rove;
and cartoons by Gary Trudeau and Tom Toles

Karl Rove has been back-stabbing political opponents and allies since high school. He's the lonely freshman with the black shoes and briefcase . . . the geeky Young Republican with the Nixon's the One *button . . . the basement vivisectionist who lusts for power over other living creatures . . . He's the guy who, lacking a soul, grew up to be George W. Bush's brain.*

Why Are These Men Laughing?

from *Esquire* (1/1/03)

Ron Suskind

On a cool Saturday a few days before Christmas last year, Karl Rove showed up in a festive mood at David Dreyer's house in suburban Washington, D. C., to trim the tree and have a cup of eggnog. Dreyer is a liberal Democrat, formerly the deputy communications director in the Clinton White House and also a senior adviser to Treasury secretary Robert Rubin. He now runs a small public-relations firm. His daughter and Karl's son were in the same seventh-grade class. After a few brief, friendly encounters at school functions, Dreyer invited Karl and his boy over for a tree-trimming party with the class, about fifteen kids and eight or nine parents in all. It was one of those enchanting days that you remember for a long time. Rove was the ringmaster of fun, brimming with good cheer, Mr. Silly, without a care in the world. All in attendance were warmed by his presence, and you never would have known that his job carried such awesome responsibility. Rove was far too busy decorating cookies and stringing popcorn to betray anything close to that. "Karl completely took charge, absolutely in the most endearing way possible. He had a vision of what each kid could contribute. What they could make or hang, based on how tall they were, or what they could do . . . what ornament, what Christmas ball. Need more lights? "Hey, kids, let's get in the car and go get some more lights!" Dreyer, a sober man, is trying not to go overboard about how all this affected him. "You expect a partisan who's onstage all the time, and it doesn't function that way in real life. You get a father and husband." He pauses. "I think it's sad." What's sad? I ask. "That we so often have such an extraordinarily one-dimensional view of people, of our fellow human beings." Not that Dreyer, having glimpsed Karl in repose, far from his natural habitat, sees him as anything less than extraordinary. "He was magnetic," Dreyer says dreamily. "He picked up my four-year-old son, Sam, so he could place the star atop the tree. It was lovely. Just lovely."

When I heard this story, it made me like Karl Rove. It made him sound like a hero to children, and in my view, there's no better person. But I've never heard another story like this one, because people in Washington, especially Rove's friends, are utterly petrified to talk about him.

They heard that I was writing about Karl Rove, seeking to contextualize his role as a senior adviser in the Bush White House, and they began calling, some anonymously, some not, saying that they wanted to help and leaving phone numbers. The calls from members of the White House staff were solemn, serious. Their concern was not only about politics, they said, not simply about Karl pulling the president further to the right. It went deeper; it was about this administration's ability to focus on the substance of governing—issues like the economy and social security and education and health care—as opposed to its clear political acumen, its ability to win and enhance power. And so it seemed that each time I made an inquiry about Karl Rove, I received in return a top-to-bottom critique of the White House's basic functions, so profound is Rove's influence.

I made these inquiries in part because last spring, when I spoke to White House chief of staff Andrew Card, he sounded an alarm about the unfettered rise of Rove in the wake of senior adviser Karen Hughes's resignation: "I'll need designees, people trusted by the president that I can elevate for various needs to balance against Karl. . . . They are going to have to really step up, but it won't be easy. Karl is a formidable adversary."

One senior White House official told me that he'd be summarily fired if it were known we were talking. "But many of us feel it's our duty—our obligation as Americans—to get the word out that, certainly in domestic policy, there has been almost no meaningful consideration of any real issues. It's just kids on Big Wheels who talk politics and know nothing. It's depressing. Domestic Policy Council meetings are a farce. This leaves shoot-from-the-hip political calculations—mostly from Karl's shop—to triumph by default. No one balances Karl. Forget it. That was Andy's cry for help."

But now the stunning midterm ascendancy of the Republicans boosts Rove into a new category; a major political realignment may hereby be ascribed to his mastery, his grand plan.

At the moment when one-party rule returns to Washington—a state that existed, in fact, in the first five months of the Bush presidency, before Senator Jeffords switched parties—we are offered a rare view of the way this White House works. The issue of how the administration decides what to do with its mandate—and where political calculation figures in that mix—has never been so important to consider. This White House will now be able to do precisely what it wants. To understand the implications of this, you must understand Karl Rove.

"It's an amazing moment," said one senior White

House official early on the morning after. "Karl just went from prime minister to king. Amazing . . . and a little scary. Now no one will speak candidly about him or take him on or contradict him. Pure power, no real accountability. It's just 'listen to Karl and everything will work out' . . . That may go for the president, too."

Over time, I came to know these sources to be serious people with credible information. And, of course, their fear of discovery is warranted, for this White House has defined itself as a disciplined command center that enforces a unanimity of purpose and has a well-known prohibition of leaks, a well-known distaste for openness. But still, the fact that they must veil themselves leaves them open to the charge of being disgruntled employees. I can only attest to the fact that they certainly do not seem to be that. There is, however, one man who, at some personal and professional risk, has now decided to speak openly about the inner workings of the White House.

President George W. Bush called John DiIulio "one of the most influential social entrepreneurs in America" when he appointed the University of Pennsylvania professor, author, historian, and domestic-affairs expert to head the White House Office of Faith-Based and Community Initiatives. He was the Bush administration's big brain, controversial but deeply respected by Republicans and Democrats, academicians and policy players. The appointment was rightfully hailed: DiIulio provided gravity to national policy debates and launched the most innovative of President Bush's campaign ideas—the faith-based initiative, which he managed until this past February, the last four months from Philadelphia.

"There is no precedent in any modern White House for

what is going on in this one: a complete lack of a policy apparatus," says DiIulio. "What you've got is everything—and I mean everything—being run by the political arm. It's the reign of the Mayberry Machiavellis."

In a seven-page letter sent a few weeks after our first conversation, DiIulio, who still considers himself a passionate supporter of the president, offers a detailed account and critique of the time he spent in the Bush White House.

"I heard many, many staff discussions but not three meaningful, substantive policy discussions," he writes. "There were no actual policy white papers on domestic issues. There were, truth be told, only a couple of people in the West Wing who worried at all about policy substance and analysis, and they were even more overworked than the stereotypical nonstop, twenty-hour-a-day White House staff. Every modern presidency moves on the fly, but on social policy and related issues, the lack of even basic policy knowledge, and the only casual interest in knowing more, was somewhat breathtaking: discussions by fairly senior people who meant Medicaid but were talking Medicare; near-instant shifts from discussing any actual policy pros and cons to discussing political communications, media strategy, et cetera. Even quite junior staff would sometimes hear quite senior staff pooh-pooh any need to dig deeper for pertinent information on a given issue."

Like David Stockman, the whip-smart budget director to Ronald Reagan who twenty years ago revealed that Reagan's budget numbers didn't add up, DiIulio is this administration's first credible, independent witness—a sovereign who supports his president but must, nonetheless, speak his mind.

Sources in the West Wing, echoing DiIulio's comments, say that even cursory discussion of domestic policy became much less frequent after September 11, 2001, with the exception of Homeland Security. Meanwhile, the department of "Strategery," or the "Strategery Group," depending on the source, has steadily grown. The term, coined in 2000 by Saturday Night Live's Will Ferrell, started as a joke at the White House, too, but has actually become a term of art meaning the oversight of any activity—from substantive policy to ideological stance to public event—by the president's political thinkers.

"It's a revealing shorthand," says one White House staff member. "Yes, the president sometimes trips, rhetorically, but it doesn't matter as long as we keep our eye on the ball politically."

This approach to policy-making is a fairly radical departure from the customary relationship between White House political directors and policy professionals. Each has always influenced the other, of course, but the political office has rarely been so central to guiding policy in virtually every area, deciding what is promoted and what is tabled.

"Besides the tax cut, which was cut-and-dried during the campaign," DiIulio writes, "and the education bill, which was really a Ted Kennedy bill, the administration has not done much, either in absolute terms or in comparison with previous administrations at this stage, on domestic policy. There is a virtual absence as yet of any policy accomplishments that might, to a fair-minded nonpartisan, count as the flesh on the bones of so-called compassionate conservatism. There is still two years, maybe six, for them to do more and better on domestic policy and, specifically, on the compassion agenda. And, needless to say, 9/11, and now the global war on terror and the new homeland- and national-security plans, must be weighed in the balance. But, as I think Andy Card himself told you in so many words, even allowing for those huge contextual realities, they could stand to find ways of inserting more serious policy fiber into the West Wing diet and engage much less in on-the-fly policy-making by speechmaking."

DiIulio calls the president "a highly admirable person of enormous personal decency . . . [who is] much, much smarter than some people—including some of his own supporters and advisers—seem to suppose." So what, then, is John DiIulio's motivation for now offering his pointed critique? There is, as he says, "two years, maybe six." He has a vision for who George W. Bush might yet become.

If you buy Isaiah Berlin's famous dictum about history being a struggle between foxes and hedgehogs, Karl Rove has, like the hedgehog, stayed focused on a single ideal and pushed it forward relentlessly. A bookish kid born in Denver on Christmas Day 1950, Rove has known George W. Bush for thirty years. He started bobbing up on senior staffs of Texas campaigns in his late twenties, with the unshakable goal of making the Republicans the permanent majority party. He's up early and works late, with an assured disdain for Marquis of Queensberry rules of political engagement. In conversation with scores of people who know him, the assessment ultimately is the same: For Karl Rove, it's all and only about winning. The rest —vision, ideology, good government, ideas to bind a nation, reasonable dissent, collegiality, mutual respect—is for later.

And Rove is disciplined in maintaining his mystery. In visiting the White House frequently from February to April of this past year, I interviewed much of the senior staff, as well as the First Lady. No one would utter so much as a word about Rove. They'd talk about one another, assessing the strengths, weaknesses, and specific roles of Hughes, Card, deputy chief of staff Josh Bolten, media adviser Mark McKinnon, communications chief Dan Bartlett, Cheney aide Mary Matalin, national-security adviser Condoleezza Rice, the vice-president, and, of course, the president himself. When I'd mention Rove, the reaction was always the same: "I can't really talk about Karl." It was odd; it was extraordinary.

Eventually, I met with Rove. I arrived at his office a few minutes early, just in time to witness the Rove Treatment, which, like LBJ's famous browbeating style, is becoming legend but is seldom reported. Rove's assistant, Susan Ralston, said he'd be just a minute. She's very nice, witty and polite. Over her shoulder was a small back room where a few young men were toiling away. I squeezed into a chair near the open door to Rove's modest chamber, my back against his doorframe.

Inside, Rove was talking to an aide about some political stratagem in some state that had gone awry and a political operative who had displeased him. I paid it no mind and reviewed a jotted list of questions I hoped to ask. But after a moment, it was like ignoring a tornado flinging parked cars. "We will fuck him. Do you hear me? We will fuck him. We will ruin him. Like no one has ever fucked him!" As a reporter, you get around—curse words, anger, passionate intensity are not notable events—but the ferocity, the bellicosity, the violent imputations were, well, shocking. This went on without a break for a minute or two. Then the aide slipped out looking a bit ashen, and Rove, his face ruddy from the exertions of the past few moments, looked at me and smiled a gentle, Clarence-the-Angel smile. "Come on in." And I did. And we had the most amiable chat for a half hour. I asked a variety of questions about his relationship with Karen Hughes. Were there ever tensions between him and Karen? Nope. "Oh, we're both strong-willed people, but we work well together." I mentioned a few disputes others had told me of. He dismissed them all. Didn't they sort of bury the hatchet after September 11? Nope—no hatchet to bury. As the president's two most powerful aides, did they ever disagree? "Not often." Any examples? Nope. He couldn't be nicer, mind you. Finally, I asked if one of his role models was Mark Hanna, the visionary political guru to President William McKinley who helped reshape Republicans into the party of inclusion and ushered in decades of electoral victory at the turn of the twentieth century. Rove's a student of McKinley and Hanna. He has talked extensively in the past about lessons he's learned from this duo's response to challenges of their era. "No, this era is nothing like McKinley's. I'm not at all like Hanna. Never wanted to be."

Since then, I've talked to old colleagues, dating back twenty-five years, one of whom said, "Some kids want to grow up to be president. Karl wanted to grow up to be Mark Hanna. We'd talk about it all the time. We'd say, 'Jesus, Karl, what kind of kid wants to grow up to be Mark Hanna?' " In any event, it's clear, when I think of my encounter with Rove, why this particular old friend of his, and scores of others—many of whom spoke of the essential good nature of this man who was a teammate on some campaign or other—don't want their names mentioned, ever. Just like Rove's mates on the current team—the one running the free world—who go numb at the thought of talking frankly, for attribution, about him. These are powerful people, confident and consequential, who suffer gaze aversion when I mention his name. No doubt they've had extended exposure to the two Karls I saw that day last spring.

William Kristol, among the most respected of the conservative commentators—a man embraced by the Right but still on dinner-party guest lists for the center and Left—is untouchable. He is willing to speak.

"Karl and I aren't really friends. I have sort of a vague and indirect relationship with him. But we talk pretty regularly. He has always been fair and straight and honest with me, despite the stories that others have about him." He pauses, as though encountering one of those beware falling rocks signs. "I believe Karl is Bush. They're not separate, each of them freestanding, with distinct agendas, as some people say. Karl thinks X. Bush thinks X. Clearly, it's a very complicated relationship." He goes on to say that he thinks Bush is a "canny manager" who creates competing teams and plays them against one another. As for those who sometimes disagree with that point, he says, "There is criticism of Karl from the friends of the former President Bush who don't approve of the way the current President Bush is doing his job in every case." Kristol notes that "the kid is what he is, and he's different from the father, some differences that I feel good about," but that gray men around "41" who don't approve of "43" have trouble criticizing the son to the father "and ascribe everything to Karl's malign influence." In that, Rove is at the center of the most portentous father-son conversation of modern times. Sources close to the former president say Rove was fired from the 1992 Bush presidential campaign after he planted a negative story with columnist Robert Novak about dissatisfaction with campaign fundraising chief and Bush loyalist Robert Mosbacher, Jr. It was smoked out, and he was summarily ousted.

Mark McKinnon, who would not speak of Rove in my earlier interviews with him for another story on the Bush White House, is now effusive. "Karl's sheer bandwidth is greater than anyone I've ever met. . . . Lots of people have planetary systems, covering history or policy or politics, but Karl covers the whole universe." He goes on: "James [Carville] and Dick [Morris]"—both advisers to Clinton whom McKinnon knows from his days, up until the mid-1990s, as a Democratic consultant—"can drive the car and drive it very well. Karl can take out the engine and put it back together. He's the best ever. And his love for policy is as great or greater than his love of politics." This is the Rove defense. He's really a policy guy, a seeker of best remedies, a nonpolitical.

Senator John McCain knows something of Karl Rove, though he'd rather not think about all that tonight, as a crowd gathers to celebrate the release of the senator's new book. In fact, lots of folks here know Rove well. "Sure, I know Karl," says one man who has worked on several campaigns with him. "At the end of long days, we'd always meet at one bar or another, everybody but Karl. Where's Karl? we'd wonder. The line was always 'Oh, he's out ruining careers.' "

These are virtually all Republicans, gathered in an elegant room off the wide atrium of Union Station. It's a good night for McCain. He and the intellectually lithe Mark

Salter, his longtime aide, have produced their second book in just three years. The first, *Faith of My Fathers*, documented McCain's early life as the rebel son and grandson of legendary admirals who was shot down in Vietnam and held prisoner for five and a half years. This second book, which picks up after Vietnam, is more reflective, angry, and lyrical, as McCain bares his breast and beats it a little. At sixty-six and in middling health, he's settling, it seems, on the idea that he won't get a chance to be president. It's the kind of thing that has liberated his already libertine spirit, though it stands as tragic injustice to everyone else in the room. And people in various corners of the wide room are retelling the story again—they'll tell it forever—the moment when McCain surged in the New Hampshire primary, when he caught, and won the state in a walk. The Bush juggernaut had stalled. McCain, embraced by the media, to whom he gave extraordinary access—"just hang with me, boys, all day, everything on the record"—was seizing the high middle ground, where you win presidential elections. And someone points to a guy in the room—yeah, him over there near the curtains, tall, friendly-looking guy named John Weaver. He was the other genius wunderkind in Texas in the 1980s, along with Rove. They won campaigns left and right, those two. Rove was mostly a direct-mail fundraiser back then, Weaver more a strategist-manager type. Something happened that neither will talk about, and they stopped working together in 1988. Many of the people in this room followed Weaver, who was McCain's political director in his bid for the 2000 Republican presidential nomination, to this side of the Republican party. Since their estrangement, Weaver's relationship with Rove has gotten somewhat odd.

On the night of the vote in New Hampshire, the senator's senior staff was all gathered at the Crowne Plaza in Nashua. A call came in to the penthouse suite moments after McCain's big victory was declared by the networks. It was Rove. A junior staffer cupped his hand over the receiver and told Weaver: "Rove says he's calling to concede."

Weaver was stunned. "Karl's conceding?" He shook off disbelief, gathered himself, and said, "Tell Karl that he can't concede. He's not the candidate. The governor has to bring himself to actually call the senator." Weaver gave Karl a cell-phone number where McCain could be reached, and a few minutes later, the candidates had a brief chat. Then it was off to the showdown in South Carolina, which changed everything . . .

I suddenly hear McCain laugh through the din. He laughs like a pirate. There's a cluster, bent in tight, as he whispers something hysterical. Heads go back. Man can tell a story. Tonight he is ebullient. On Sunday, *The Washington Post* gushed over his book, leading with what it called the strange occurrence that the president is the third-most-popular politician in America, behind Al Gore, who got more votes, and, of course, John McCain.

He loved that, God knows, and tonight he's among his lovers, his troops, cutting between them, slapping and clasping, a man of modest height and fiercely angled, always leaning a few degrees forward, a bit pinched, in his blue suit. He breaks from the cluster; I meet him in the clearing. We huddle for a moment, make small talk about this and that. I ask if historians will consider South Carolina a crossroads moment for the Republican party. "Well, it was unprecedented, South Carolina," he says softly. "But you have to put it past you and move on." He points over to the corner where his top aide, Salter, is now standing next to Weaver and a few others. "Those guys can tell you all about what happened. As for history," he says, offering a pained smile, "I think it will little note nor long remember and all that." I go over. Weaver gets asked about Rove quite often; people know about their history. He always demurs. "Not worth getting into," he says. People around him, though, will talk. "John will never work in the Republican party again, thanks to Karl," says Salter. Weaver now works for the Democratic Congressional Campaign Committee. It's commonly held that Rove ran him out of the party. The word went out: Any Republican who hired Weaver would be held in disfavor by the president. "What can I say?" Weaver says quietly. "Like me, all the moderate Republicans have been run out of the party by the Right. I'm doing what I've always done politically; these guys just call themselves Democrats now."

As for the Waterloo of South Carolina, most of the facts are well-known, and among this group of Republicans, what happened has taken on the air of an unsolved crime, a cold case, with Karl Rove being the prime suspect. Bush loyalists, maybe working for the campaign, maybe just representing its interests, claimed in parking-lot handouts and telephone "push polls" and whisper campaigns that McCain's wife, Cindy, was a drug addict, that McCain might be mentally unstable from his captivity in Vietnam, and that the senator had fathered a black child with a prostitute. Callers push-polled members of a South Carolina right-to-life organization and other groups, asking if the black baby might influence their vote. Now here's the twist, the part that drives McCain admirers insane to this very day: That last rumor took seed because the McCains had done an especially admirable thing. Years back they'd adopted a baby from a Mother Teresa orphanage in Bangladesh. Bridget, now eleven years old, waved along with the rest of the McCain brood from stages across the state, a dark-skinned child inadvertently providing a photo op for slander. The attacks were of a level and vitriol that even McCain, who was regularly beaten in captivity, could not ignore. He began to answer the slights, strayed off message about how he would lead the nation if he got the chance, and lost the war for South Carolina. Bush emerged from the showdown upright and victorious . . . and onward he marched.

Eight months after the South Carolina primary, McCain and Weaver were on a plane campaigning with the nominee. This was the kind of barnstorming finale—closing in on the last week of the campaign—that Rove normally wouldn't miss. But Weaver was with McCain on the plane, and if Weaver is present, Rove will not show. The governor was, nonetheless, ecstatic. With McCain at his side for the better part of two weeks, he'd been on fire. After a stop in Fresno, California, for a joint speech, Weaver slipped out of the hall and Bush slipped out after him. McCain, who was still inside working the crowd, was due to leave now, his promised time with Bush completed. McCain had told Representative Tom Davis, a Virginia congressman heading up the Republican congressional effort, that he'd spend the last week whistle-stopping House and Senate races.

Governor Bush approached Weaver, who was huddling with the McCain staff. They'd known each other for fifteen years. "Johnny, I want you and John to be with me until the end."

"Can't do it, George," Weaver said. "I just talked to

Tom Davis, and he's really counting on us. We've made a commitment."

Bush grew agitated. "You don't seem to understand. I want you with us!" It was already clear that the race was very close. Bush was looking for every advantage. He said, "Look, I'm better when John's with me."

Bush said, "Hold on a minute," stepped away, placed a call on his cell phone, and walked back, looking relieved. "Look, I just talked to Karl, and he says don't worry about the congressional races. It's okay for you to come with me."

Weaver said, "Thanks anyway, but Karl's not in charge of us." McCain walked up. "Weav says you can't stay with me for the last week. Is that right, John?" Bush was simmering. McCain was uncertain what to do. After an awkward moment, Weaver said, "I'm sorry, we've really got to go," and hustled McCain into a waiting limo. The senator slumped into the seat, exhaled, and then, with a smile of relief, turned to Weaver and said, "Thank you."

I've come to meet John DiIulio.

It has been three weeks since our first interview, when he spoke with surprising frankness about the style and substance of the White House. Other White House officials had discussed and corroborated the range of Rove's influence, how all major decisions were passing first through his political-strategic directorate. But I was still regarding this White House in terms of the long-standing model, in which the art of political strategy is carefully balanced against serious policy discussion, in which church-state separations of these two distinct functions are respected, even championed.

It seemed that in the person of Karl Rove such distinctions had been blurred. And I hoped that DiIulio, a true believer in problem solving through sober policy analysis, could clarify how this had happened. He, after all, was present when the architecture of this White House—and the key relationships in it—was established.

But even more striking, he is the most credible independent witness to exit the administration so far.

I race into the Sofitel Hotel in downtown Washington a little late for a cocktail party held by the Nelson A. Rockefeller Institute of Government, a nonpartisan think tank based in Albany, New York, that has brought luminaries together to kick off its three-day conference on religion and social-welfare policy. The French-owned hotel has little bustle in its portico—all cool marble and polished mahogany and whispery potted hydrangeas—and I wander, searching for life, until I see an enormous man near the elevator banks. He's stuffing his hand into a shoulder-slung briefcase, looking for his glasses. He doesn't seem to fit here, or in his blue suit, pulled taut as a windbreak across a frame a few inches shy of six feet that has to be supporting three hundred pounds. He looks up and squints at me, his glasses now slightly askew on a gentle, soft-edged mug, like Big Pussy in The Sopranos.

His story is as unlikely as it is inspiring: a working-class kid from a tough Italian-Catholic neighborhood, the son of a sheriff's deputy and a department-store clerk, who stumbled forward from a local parish school to Philadelphia's exclusive Haverford School—there through a program for lower-income kids—then to the University of Pennsylvania and Harvard for graduate school, picking up speed with each stride. By the time he got his Ph.D. in political science from Harvard—one of the best students his mentor James

Q. Wilson had ever seen—his mass times velocity was bending laws of physics. At Princeton, he was made a full professor after just five years. He was thirty-two.

We talk briefly about our conversation of a few weeks ago; DiIulio knows he has collapsed a wall by offering his frank assessment. "I'm on the record," he says. And then, lightly, "It's not a problem, really not."

His appearance in Washington qualifies as a special event, a top ticket for the guests tinkling glasses inside, where John stops at the reception table.

"Hey, big man!" He turns. It's the Reverend Eugene Rivers, the former gang member who tamed urban violence in Boston, and a DiIulio buddy. They hug as the hive notices DiIulio and surrounds him. They are fans, admirers, but also part of an ideal, that there's nothing odd about Democrats and Republicans dining together and agreeing on a few things, even in regard to fault-line issues like religion and social policy and the bracing possibility of connecting the two.

And disagreeing constructively. Rabbi David Saperstein, director of the Religious Action Center of Reform Judaism and a liberal opponent of federal funding for faith-based institutions, makes small talk with Rivers—a conservative black supporter of such funding—while nearby is Harris Wofford, the former Democratic senator from Pennsylvania, right beside Michelle Engler, wife of Michigan's Republican governor, John Engler. This kind of ecumenical promise, political as well as religious, is what helped get George W. Bush elected—the ideal, at its heart, of "compassionate conservatism" and the pledge of returning a more civil tone to Washington.

"There he is, the face of compassionate conservatism,"

says Richard Roper, who was DiIulio's colleague at Princeton. "Whatever that means." DiIulio has often found himself an enemy of the Left. During the Clinton impeachment drama, he beat the drum for Clinton's removal from office and decried the failure to do so as a signal of the "paganization" of American political culture. And before that, research he conducted in the early 1990s identified the growth of what he called "superpredators" in urban America: youths who seemed to carry a virulent strain of unchecked violence. The research, born of DiIulio's focus on urban America and prison cultures, formed an intellectual framework for mandatory-sentencing statutes that swept the country. DiIulio coauthored Body Count with conservative thinker William Bennett and built a thinking-writing-speaking franchise as the conservatives' favorite intellectual. Then he did something that almost no academician, especially one atop his own mountain, seems ever to do: He said, Hold on a minute. Data he'd started collecting in the mid-1990s seemed to contradict the "superpredator" theory. What this latest evolution of his research showed was that prevention, especially targeted at "at risk" urban environments, really does work.

And that brought him to church. Churches—along with mosques and, in some cases, synagogues—have long stood as a bulwark against chaos in many blighted urban cores, as true sanctuary and often an engine of homegrown social services. Urban analysts know this in a general way; DiIulio wanted to know, as a serious researcher, the whys and hows, variables, structures, etiology, and outcomes. This turned out to be a very bright idea; he swiftly captured an enormous swath of unmapped territory. The early trend line of DiIulio's research evolved into his work for the president.

DiIulio and Bush bonded. At a Philadelphia stop early in the campaign, the two spoke for nearly two hours about the possibilities of federal support for faith-based programs, a nuanced discussion that left DiIulio duly impressed. "The president is up to the task. We had an extraordinary exchange. He had significant knowledge and real sensitivity to the challenges that such an effort would face. It's not as though he's not capable."

Bush started talking about his friend "Big John," and a year later DiIulio was an anchor tenant in the new administration. He would attend the 7:30 a.m. senior-staff meeting every day and offer insights on a broad array of domestic policies while launching programs that, in some fashion, used federal financial support to enhance the efforts of faith-based institutions.

Meanwhile, the White House's political arm was asserting itself in the new Office of Strategic Initiatives, which Rove created. In this period before September 11, 2001, domestic affairs accounted for most of what the White House did every day. So John DiIulio and Karl Rove started to regularly encounter each other, forming one of the most interesting couples in the executive branch.

Each, after all, is among the most accomplished in his field. Rove, the consummate political strategist, having trained at the knee of the master, Lee Atwater, who guided Republicans, including George H. W. Bush, to electoral victory; and DiIulio, the public intellectual and academic heavyweight, the only one to join this administration. In almost every realm of public policy, there are always a few people who lead the intellectual parade, advancing the research and ideas that form the agenda for discussion in that field. It's a ferocious meritocracy, played out in symposia and academic journals, on peer-review committees and editorial pages. Generally, administrations tap several of these leaders to join them. Republicans and Democrats both have their share. In economics, for instance, think Milton Friedman or Herbert Stein; they can sometimes be young up-and-comers, like Pat Moynihan in the Nixon administration. In the Clinton White House, they were numerous, including Robert Reich at Labor and Lawrence Summers, Clinton's Treasury secretary and now the president of Harvard.

It's clear, standing in this room with DiIulio, why such men can be so valuable to a president: In the White House, where political calculation is like respiration, they can make confident, fact-based assessments of which important ideas are worth executing. Ideas, ultimately, that a presidency will be remembered for.

The cocktail party is moving toward dinner. Doors are opened to a baronial chamber that cossets a stunning forty-foot-long table. Almost time for DiIulio's speech. He doesn't seem to notice. His wide back is to the door and he's digging deep, trying as he will to make sense of his strange journey.

He says he loves Bush. He loves him as a man, as a friend. He loves his decency, his compassion, which, he says, is "not a 'feel your pain' thing like Clinton. With Bush it's more grounded, more real."

But mention of Clinton turns him inward, tapping repressed memory. He says he visited the White House five times during the Clinton presidency—Al Gore called upon DiIulio in the mid-1990s to assist with his reinventing-government initiative.

Clinton, DiIulio says, was a wonk-in-chief. "For all his flaws, he had that monster to feed. Bush is just too 'normal,'" DiIulio says, curling his thick fingers into quotation marks around the word normal, this huge man with profound hungers. "Great guy. But he doesn't have a beast to feed, that got-to-know-the-answer beast. It's a problem being president at this time, without that, without that hunger."

Then he pauses, and we're both thinking the same thing. Karl. DiIulio smiles his cockeyed smile. "Yeah, he's got a beast. One problem: He's not the president."

Two days later, I get a very long letter from John DiIulio.

It is a manifesto, really, the work of a scholar, reasoned and sober. It is designed to be constructive criticism of the White House that, in large measure, Karl Rove has created, and to give context to his remarks of a few weeks before. Early on, in its opening section, DiIulio, thinking like a historian, offers a stream of qualifiers. "I'm no 'representative sample,' as it were, but I do have some things that are maybe worth saying now on the record."

In the letter, DiIulio is charitable toward his former colleague. "Some are inclined to blame the high political-to-policy ratios of this administration on Karl Rove," DiIulio writes. "Some in the press view Karl as some sort of prince of darkness; actually, he is basically a nice and good-humored man. And some staff members, senior and junior, are awed and cowed by Karl's real or perceived powers. They self-censor lots for fear of upsetting him, and in turn, few of the president's top people routinely tell the president what they really think if they think that Karl will be brought up short in the bargain. Karl is enormously powerful, maybe the single most powerful person in the modern, post-Hoover era ever to occupy a political-adviser post near the Oval Office. The Republican base constituencies, including Beltway libertarian policy elites and religious-Right leaders, trust him to keep Bush 43 from behaving like Bush 41 and moving too far to the center or inching at all center-left. Their shared fiction, supported by zero empirical electoral studies, is that 41 lost in '92 because he lost these right-wing fans. There are not ten House districts in America where either the libertarian litany or the right-wing-religious policy creed would draw majority popular approval, and most studies suggest Bush 43 could have done better versus Gore had he stayed more centrist, but, anyway, the fiction is enshrined as fact. Little happens on any issue without Karl's okay, and often he supplies such policy substance as the administration puts out. Fortunately, he is not just a largely self-taught, hyperpolitical guy but also a very well informed guy when it comes to certain domestic issues."

According to various sources close to Rove, he and DiIulio had a wary but respectful relationship. DiIulio, like any heavyweight with his own constituency, didn't seem to fear Rove. Rove, who never graduated from college but has a deep love of academic inquiry, seemed to enjoy having DiIulio to fence with. Periodically, he would ask John to advance the administration's political agenda, and John would do what almost no one does currently at the White House now that Karen Hughes has left: tell Karl to take a hike.

For instance, there was Karl's desire to have John cozy up to the conservative evangelicals, with whom DiIulio was having problems. DiIulio recalls Karl telling him to bury the hatchet "and start fighting the guys who are against us." DiIulio says he responded: "I'm not taking any shit off of Jerry Falwell. The souls of my dead Italian grandparents are crying out to me, 'That guy's not on the side of the angels.' " Rove backed off, DiIulio recalls, and said, "Look, those guys don't really matter to this president."

"Sure, Karl," DiIulio responded. "They don't matter, but they're in here all the time."

On his primary mission—push forward ideas and policies to partner government with faith-based institutions—DiIulio says that he saw the beginning of what was to become a pattern: The White House "winked at the most far-right House Republicans, who, in turn, drafted a so-called faith bill that (or so they thought) satisfied certain fundamentalist leaders and Beltway libertarians but bore few marks of compassionate conservatism and was, as anybody could tell, an absolute political nonstarter. It could pass the House only on a virtual party-line vote, and it could never pass the Senate, even before Jeffords switched.

"Not only that, but it reflected neither the president's own previous rhetoric on the idea nor any of the actual empirical evidence. . . . I said so, wrote memos, and so on. . . . As one senior staff member chided me at a meeting at which many junior staff were present and all ears, 'John, get a faith bill, any faith bill.' Like college students who fall for the colorful, opinionated, but intellectually third-rate professor, you could see these twenty- and thirty-something junior White House staff falling for the Mayberry Machiavellis."

DiIulio defines the Mayberry Machiavellis as political

staff, Karl Rove and his people, "who consistently talked and acted as if the height of political sophistication consisted in reducing every issue to its simplest black-and-white terms for public consumption, then steering legislative initiatives or policy proposals as far right as possible. These folks have their predecessors in previous administrations (left and right, Democrat and Republican), but in the Bush administration, they were particularly unfettered."

"Remember 'No child left behind'? That was a Bush campaign slogan. I believe it was his heart, too. But translating good impulses into good policy proposals requires more than whatever somebody thinks up in the eleventh hour before a speech is to be delivered."

Weekly meetings of the Domestic Policy Council "were breathtaking," DiIulio told me. As for the head of the DPC, Margaret La Montagne, a longtime friend of Karl Rove who guided education policy in Texas, DiIulio is blunt: "What she knows about domestic policy could fit in a thimble."

When DiIulio would raise objections to killing programs—like the Earned Income Tax Credit, a tax credit for the poorest Americans, hailed by policy analysts on both sides of the aisle, that contributed to the success of welfare reform—he found he was often arguing with libertarians who didn't know the basic functions of major federal programs. As a senior White House adviser and admirer of DiIulio's recently said to me, "You have to understand, this administration is further to the right than much of the public understands. The view of many people [in the White House] is that the best government can do is simply do no harm, that it never is an agent for positive change. If that's your position, why bother to understand what programs actually do?"

It was encounters with the president—displays of his personal qualities—that time and again restored DiIulio's commitment. From the way he "let detainees come home from China and did not jump all over them for media purposes" to a time, DiIulio writes, when he and Bush were in Philadelphia at a "three-hour block party on July 4, 2001, following hours among the children, youth, and families of prisoners . . . running late for the next event. He stopped, however, to take a picture with a couple of men who were cooking ribs all day. 'C'mon,' he said, 'those guys have been doing hard work all day there.' It's my favorite and, in some ways, my most telling picture of who he is as a man and a leader who pays attention to the little things that convey respect and decency toward others."

Five days later, on July 9, at the administration's six-month senior-staff retreat, DiIulio writes that "an explicit discussion ensued concerning how to emulate more strongly the Clinton White House's press, communications, and rapid-response media relations—how better to wage, if you will, the permanent campaign that so defines the modern presidency regardless of who or which party occupies the Oval Office. I listened and was amazed. It wasn't more press, communications, media, legislative strategizing, and such that they needed. Maybe the Clinton people did that better, though surely they were less disciplined about it and leaked more to the media and so on. No, what they needed, I thought then and still do now, was more policy-relevant information, discussion, and deliberation."

Part of the problem, DiIulio now understood, was that

the paucity of serious policy discussion combined with a leakproof command-and-control operation was altering traditional laws of White House physics. That is: Know what's political, know what's policy. They are different. That distinction drives the structure of most administrations. The policy experts, on both domestic and foreign policy, order up "white papers" and hash out the most prudent use of executive power. Political advisers, who often deepen their knowledge by listening carefully as these deliberations unfold, are then called in to decide how, when, and with whom support policies should be presented, enacted, and executed.

The dilemma presented by Karl Rove, DiIulio realized, was that in such a policy vacuum, his jack-of-all-trades appreciation of an enormous array of policy debates was being mistaken for genuine expertise. It takes a true policy wonk to recognize the difference, and, beyond the realm of foreign affairs, DiIulio was almost alone in the White House.

"When policy analysis is just backfill to support a political maneuver, you'll get a lot of oops," he says.

DiIulio points to the "remarkably slapdash character of the Office of Homeland Security, with the nine months of arguing that no department was needed, with the sudden, politically timed reversal in June, and with the fact that not even that issue, the most significant reorganization of the federal government since the creation of the Department of Defense, has received more than talking-points-caliber deliberation. This was, in a sense, the administration's problem in miniature: Ridge was the decent fellow at the top, but nobody spent the time to understand that an EOP [Executive Office of the President] entity without budgetary or statutory authority can't coordinate over a hundred separate federal units, no matter how personally close to the president its leader is, no matter how morally right it feels the mission is, and no matter how inconvenient the politics of telling certain House Republican leaders we need a big new federal bureaucracy might be."

One has to consider the possibility that John DiIulio just wasn't cut out for working at the White House. Government, after all, is not a graduate seminar. I need to get a reality-based assessment on what the professor himself is proffering. DiIulio's last day running the faith-based initiative was February 1, 2002. He never intended to stay for long, he says, and the commute from Philadelphia was becoming onerous. And though he remains in regular touch with former colleagues, he is not there now—not in the building. I talk to several sources in the West Wing, and one of them agrees to meet me at a neutral site: a restaurant off Pennsylvania Avenue with a dark back room. It's midafternoon. We order coffee. He is nervous about a face-to-face. "You know, this is risky, just being here."

I tell him we'll try to make this quick, and I describe DiIulio's rendering of the White House, its conduct and character, and Rove's enveloping role. Does this resemble reality, or is DiIulio mistaken or misguided?

He nods. "All of that is realistic, basically correct. It's really been even worse since after 9/11. There has been no domestic policy, really. Not even a pretense of it."

He pauses. "You know, if John had stayed, we might have actually had a domestic policy. He's just that smart, that credible. The reason is that he's rigorous, that he demands the data. He asks, What does the evidence indicate? What is the best path? He truly doesn't care about politics, which is all anyone here seems to care about. He just digs in to actually see what policy would most benefit the most people."

We talk for more than an hour. He's an honored member of the political Right with a flawless conservative pedigree and pure faith in ideas emerging from that flank of the Republican party. But he is as pointed in his critique of the processes of this White House as the more moderate DiIulio. It's clear from every word that this is not about politics or ideology. It's not about who's right or wrong. It's about a kind of regret.

"Don't you understand?" he says, his voice rising. "We got into the White House and forfeited the game. You're supposed to stand for something . . . to generate sound ideas, support them with real evidence, and present them to Congress and the people. We didn't do any of that. We just danced this way and that on minute political calculationsand whatever was needed for a few paragraphs of a speech."

He says that in mid-August, Jay Lefkowitz—a longtime policy manager who was hired in early 2002 to work as Margaret La Montagne's deputy at the Domestic Policy Council—became part of an effort to create some forward motion. He and a small group of senior staffers started to meet each week or so to discuss domestic issues and long-term goals. "They're attempting to at least generate some ideas. It's a small sign of hope . . . but everything will have to go through Karl."

We sit for a while and sip coffee, now cold. He says he's not going to leave—he waited too long to get to the White House—but that increasingly he finds himself thinking in the past tense, of missed opportunities.

"Here's what would have worked," he says a bit later.

"Swap DiIulio in for [deputy chief of staff for policy] Josh Bolten. Bolten's a good guy, a smart guy, but DiIulio knows more about everything, every area of policy, than anyone. He would have helped us have the balance—the considerate, thoughtful approach to everything—that administrations are supposed to have."

Shortly after this conversation came the midterm elections. Early the morning after, my White House sources were on the phone, offering the insider view.

"It's unbelievable," one of them says, awe coming across the phone line. "Could Karl be that smart? Could anyone?"

There's just silence for a bit as he maps the frontiers of possibility.

"Maybe the last two years wasn't just a case of benign neglect," says this source, with whom I spoke extensively throughout October. "Maybe it was brilliant neglect."

He went on to explain: From early on, Rove may have been focused on energizing the core, the far Right, for the midterms. An attempt to push centrist policies through a divided Congress would have done anything but that, and it would have violated the prime strategic directive: don't alienate the right wing like the first President Bush. Karl's remedy: co-opt the policy-creation process; put it in a lockbox until after genuine Republican control is established.

"Now the troops are ready to march," the source says. "The question is, What will we do? Will we finally put together a thoughtful policy team to create a coherent plan for America's future, or just push through one political favor after another dressed up like policy? I guess it's really for Karl, Karl and the president, to decide."

John DiIulio knows that because of what he's done here, he will lose friends. The White House will personally attack him. Some longtime Republican colleagues will suddenly be too busy to return his calls. Others may spread rumors. Karl Rove, who would not comment for this story, might say that DiIulio's manifesto is "duly noted." Rove likes to say that after doling out a condemnation—that someone's actions have been duly noted. It's a very adult version, with teeth, of "This will be put on your permanent record."

But DiIulio and an increasing number of people in the White House seem to have their eye on a somewhat different permanent record.

DOONESBURY
by G.B. Trudeau
HOLY COW...
THEY CAN SAY THAT ABOUT ME?
GOOD MORNING, SIR, I...
INCREDIBLE!
UH-OH...
KARL, DID YOU KNOW...
...WE'VE TOPPED 2300 CASUALTIES IN IRAQ, THE POVERTY LEVEL'S UP FOR THE SECOND YEAR, RUSH LIMBAUGH'S BEEN IN DRUG REHAB...
...AND THAT THE WORLD SERIES IS OVER?
UM... YES, SIR, I DID KNOW.
WELL, I SURE AS HECK DIDN'T!
DAMN... WHO GAVE HIM A NEWS-PAPER?!
I WANT THE DETAILS ON THE SERIES! NOW!
www.doonesbury.com

He Said It . . .

"45 percent of all of the dividend income goes to people with $50,000-or-less incomes, family incomes. Nearly three-quarters of it goes to families with $100,000 or less family income."*

—Karl Rove on Bush's dividend-tax cuts, as quoted in *The Washington Post* (1/28/04).

**Actual numbers:*

- *14.7 % of dividend income goes to people earning $50,000 or less*
- *Less than one third goes to families earning $100,000 or less*

(Source: Slate.com and *The Washington Post*)

IF THERE IS ANYONE HERE WHO OBJECTS TO THE UNION OF THESE TWO MEN, LET HIM RUB HIS HANDS TOGETHER IN GREEDY ANTICIPATION OF EXPLOITING ANOTHER WEDGE ISSUE TO DIVIDE AMERICANS FOR POLITICAL GAIN NOW, OR FOREVER HOLD HIS PEACE.
Mass. Supreme Court
KARL ROVE
TOLES
UNIVERSAL PRESS SYND.
2©2004 THE WASHINGTON POST
EXPECT A SHORT HONEYMOON-

2·8·04

Karl Rove: Counting Votes While the Bombs Drop

from *The Los Angeles Times* (5/7/03)

James C. Moore

Karl Rove led the nation to war to improve the political prospects of George W. Bush. I know how surreal that sounds. But I also know it is true.

As the president's chief political advisor, Rove is involved in every decision coming out of the Oval Office. In fact, he flat out makes some of them. He is co-president of the United States, just as he was co-candidate for that office and co-governor of Texas. His relationship with the president is the most profound and complex of all of the White House advisors. And his role creates questions not addressed by our Constitution.

Rove is probably the most powerful unelected person in American history.

The cause of the war in Iraq was not just about Saddam Hussein or weapons of mass destruction or Al Qaeda links to Iraq. Those may have been the stated causes, but every good lie should have a germ of truth. No, this was mostly a product of Rove's usual prescience. He looked around and saw that the economy was anemic and people were complaining about the president's inability to find Osama bin Laden. In another corner, the neoconservatives in the Cabinet were itching to launch ships and planes to the Mideast and take control of Iraq. Rove converged the dynamics of the times. He convinced the president to connect Hussein to bin Laden, even if the CIA could not.

This misdirection worked. A Pew survey taken during the war showed 61% of Americans believe that Hussein and bin Laden were confederates in the 9/11 attacks.

And now, Rove needs the conflict to continue so his client—the president—can retain wartime stature during next year's election. Listen to the semantics from Bush's recent trip to the aircraft carrier Lincoln. When he referred to the "battle of Iraq," Bush implied that we only won a single fight in a bigger war that was not yet over. I first encountered Rove more than 20 years ago in Texas. I reported on him and the future president as a TV correspondent there, traveling with them extensively during their race to the governor's mansion in Austin. Once there, Rove was involved in every important decision the governor made and, according to Bush staffers, vetted each critical choice for political implications.

Nothing is different today in the White House. The same old reliable sources from his days in Texas are in Washington with him. And they say Rove is intimately involved in the Cabinet and that he sat in on all the big meetings leading up to the Iraq war and signed off on all major decisions.

Rove fancies himself an expert in both policy and politics because he sees no distinction between the two. This matters for a number of reasons. There is always a time during any president's administration when what is best for the future of the country diverges from what best serves that president's political future. If Rove is standing with George W. Bush at that moment, he will push the president in the direction of reelection rather than the country's best interests.

The United States is best served when political calculations are not a part of the White House's most important decisions. Rove's calculus is always a formula for winning the next election. He was less concerned about the bombing of Iraqi civilians or the bullets flying at our own troops, according to people who have worked for him for years, than he was about what these acts would do to the results of the electoral college, or how they influence voters in swing states like Florida.

There needs to be something sacred about our presidents' decisions to send our children into combat. The Karl Roves of the world ought to not even be in the room, much less asked for advice.

Rove has influenced dealings with Iraq and North Korea, according to Bush administration sources. For instance, when the U.S. was notified, through formal diplomatic channels, that North Korea had nuclear technology, Congress was in the midst of discussing the Iraqi war resolution. Rove counseled the president to keep that information from Congress for 12 days, until the debate was finished, so it would not affect the vote. He was also reported to be present at a war strategy meeting concerning whether to attack Syria after Iraq. Rove said the timing was not right. Yet. Having the political advisor involved in that decision is wrong.

War, after all, is not a campaign event.

An I Hate Dick Cheney, John Ashcroft, Donald Rumsfeld, Condi Rice . . . *Timeline:* *1966–2004*

Nate Hardcastle

Congressman Donald Rumsfeld criticizes profiteering by future Halliburton subsidiary Brown & Root.

Donald Rumsfeld presents Saddam Hussein with a pair of golden spurs from Ronald Reagan.

Colin Powell says "I don't recall" or "I can't recall" 56 times during his testimony on the Iran-contra affair.

Paul Wolfowitz gives a speech to Congress praising Indonesian dictator Mohamed Suharto's leadership on human rights. (Suharto was recently named the most corrupt world leader of the last 20 years by corruption watchdog Transparency International.)

The neocon think tank Project for a New American Century (PNAC) is born. Its members include eight future Bush administration officials, including Dick Cheney, Donald Rumsfeld, Paul Wolfowitz, John Bolton, Lewis Libby and Elliott Abrams.

2000

January
Condoleezza Rice writes a 7,000-word article for *Foreign Affairs* magazine explaining Bush's approach to national security. She does not mention Al Qaeda.

July
Cheney claims that as Halliburton's CEO his policy was "we wouldn't do anything in Iraq"—news to Iraqis, who during that time bought $73 million worth of oil-field supplies from Halliburton subsidiaries.

August
Cheney, heading Bush's search for a running mate, chooses . . . himself.

September
The PNAC publishes its manifesto, "Rebuilding America's Defenses." The report calls for invading Iraq and setting up military bases to control the world oil supply—a plan the report notes could take decades without "some catastrophic and catalyzing event—like a new Pearl Harbor."

November
Cheney has a little heart attack.

December
Bush names his attorney general: John Ashcroft, who recently lost his Missouri senate race to a dead man.

2001

January
The Hart-Rudman Commission on National Security, presenting the most comprehensive review of national security since 1947, warns the Bush administration that "America will become increasingly vulnerable to hostile attack on our homeland . . . Americans will likely die on American soil, possibly in large numbers."

January
Terrorism czar Richard Clarke asks Condoleezza Rice for an urgent cabinet-level meeting to deal with the threat of Al Qaeda attack. She does not act on his request for eight months.

January
The administration downgrades the position of national coordinator for counterterrorism—Richard Clarke's job—from cabinet- to staff-level.

February
Ashcroft sworn in. Supreme Court Justice Clarence Thomas anoints his head with oil in a private ceremony.

February
Bush names former death-squad organizer John D. Negroponte ambassador to the United Nations.

February
CIA Director George Tenet tells Congress that terrorism is the biggest threat facing the U.S.

April
Richard Clarke meets with cabinet department deputies about the threat from Al Qaeda. Paul Wolfowitz downplays bin Laden's significance and tries to change the focus to Iraq—citing bogus "evidence" produced by Iraq-conspiracy-monger Laurie Mylroie.

April
Dick Cheney meets with Ken Lay to discuss energy policy—one of six meetings Cheney's energy task force holds with Enron executives. The next day Cheney announces that the administration will not consider price caps to solve California's energy crisis (which was caused by Enron price-gouging).

April
Congressmen Henry Waxman (D-CA) and John Dingell (D-MI) first request details about meetings Cheney's energy task force held with energy company representatives. Cheney denies their request.

May
Ashcroft issues a budget memo detailing his seven strategic goals for the Justice Department. Combating terrorism is not among them.

May
Dick Cheney forms a counterterrorism task force. The group never meets.

June
Donald Rumsfeld says the Bush administration would deploy missile-defense technologies whether or not they had been proven to work.

June
Intelligence warnings about potential terrorist attacks surge. George Tenet warns the administration of an imminent Al Qaeda attack.

June
Condoleezza Rice gives a speech to the Council on Foreign Relations about "Foreign Policy Priorities and Challenges of the Administration." She does not mention terrorism.

July
Cheney gets a pacemaker.

2001

July
George Tenet again warns the administration of an imminent Al Qaeda attack

July
The Justice Department scales back monitoring of suspected Al Qaeda operatives in the U.S.

August
George Tenet for the third time in three months warns the administration of an imminent Al Qaeda attack.

September
Condi Rice makes plans to give a speech about national defense on September 11; her speech will focus on missile defense, with barely a mention of terrorism.

September
Richard Clarke finally gets his cabinet-level meeting about Al Qaeda—less than a week before 9/11.

September 11
The PNAC gets its "new Pearl Harbor." Charter member Donald Rumsfeld five hours after the terrorist attacks orders aides to develop plans for striking Iraq.

December
Ashcroft says to civil libertarians: "your tactics only aid terrorists." He goes on to defend potential terrorists' rights to bear arms.

2002

January
John Aschroft and the entire U.S. Attorney's Office in Houston recuse themselves from the Enron investigation because of conflicts of interest.

January
Ashcroft has drapes placed over two partially nude statues in his office.

February
The General Accounting Office sues Cheney to force him to reveal which energy company executives helped him craft his industry-friendly energy plan.

February
The Pentagon pulls intelligence and Special Forces units out of Afghanistan to prepare for invading Iraq.

March
Cheney goes to the Middle East in part to drum up support for a U.S. invasion of Iraq; he fails spectacularly.

June
Rumsfeld reveals that during 2001 he sold somewhere between $20.5 million and $91 million in assets. (Think he's happy about the Bush tax cuts?)

June
Ashcroft announces that the FBI may now spy on domestic political and religious groups, even if there's no reason to suspect criminal conduct.

June
Ashcroft claims that the arrest of Jose Padilla prevented a dirty-bomb attack on Washington D.C. Other officials immediately contradict Ashcroft's statement.

July
Bush undergoes a prostate exam; transfers powers to Cheney.

September
Rumsfeld gives advice to Paul Wolfowitz: "Here's how you deal with the media. Begin with an illogical premise and proceed perfectly logically to an illogical conclusion."

November
The Bush administration finally caves and allows the creation of the Homeland Security Department and a commission to investigate 9/11.

2003

January
Rumsfeld says Germany and France are part of "Old Europe."

February
Secretary of State Colin Powell presents a speech full of errors, distortions and outright lies to the U.N., in an attempt to gather support for an invasion of Iraq. *U.S. News & World Report* reports that prior to the speech Powell threw his briefing materials in the air and yelled "This is bullshit!"

2003

February
Osama bin Laden in a taped message calls for Iraqis to resist the coming U.S. invasion. Powell cites this as proof that Saddam is in league with Al Qaeda, despite the fact that bin Laden on the tape calls Hussein an "apostate".

March
U.S. forces invade Iraq.

April
The Army Corps of Engineers reveals that Halliburton subsidiary Kellogg Brown & Root's contract to fight oil fires in Iraq—awarded without a competitive bidding process—will be worth up to $7 billion.

April
Rumsfeld is asked if Syria is "next"; he replies "It depends on people's behavior."

May
Bush signs a tax cut that will save Cheney $100,000 a year.

June
An Iraqi shepherd sues Rumsfeld for $200 million, citing the deaths of 17 family members and 200 sheep.

June
Rumsfeld claims that he does not "know anybody in any government or any intelligence agency who suggested that the Iraqis had nuclear weapons". Reporters point out that Dick Cheney made precisely that claim in March.

July
An unnamed administration official leaks the identity of undercover CIA agent Valerie Plame—the wife of Bush administration critic Joseph Wilson. Karl Rove denies being the source of the leak, although reports say in 1992 he leaked damaging information about an opponent to the same columnist who published the Plame revelations.

July
Condoleezza Rice says Bush's State of the Union claim that "The British government has learned that Saddam Hussein recently sought significant quantities of uranium from Africa" was technically not a lie, because "The British government did say that."

July
Deputy Defense Secretary Paul Wolfowitz says "I think all foreigners should stop interfering in the internal affairs of Iraq"—presumably meaning all *other* foreigners.

July
Powell calls Saddam "a piece of trash."

September
Powell denies that the U.S. is an occupier in Iraq, saying "we came as liberators."

September
Rumsfeld says tourism will be a major industry in Iraq very soon.

September
Ashcroft orders federal prosecutors not to use plea bargains, but instead to prosecute all defendants for the "most serious, readily provable offense." Prosecutors call the order ridiculous and counterproductive.

October
A leaked memo by Rumsfeld admits that the Bush administration doesn't really have a plan for the war on terrorism.

October
A reporter asks Rumsfeld whether he's lost his mojo.

November
Pentagon advisor and uber-hawk Richard Perle says about invading Iraq, "I think in this case international law stood in the way of doing the right thing."

December
Cheney participates in a "canned hunt," killing more than 70 tame pheasants.

December
Wolfowitz announces that firms from countries that opposed the invasion of Iraq will not be eligible for reconstruction contracts.

2004

January
Cheney cites a thoroughly discredited article as evidence of ties between Iraq and Al Qaeda.

2004

January
Powell admits that he never saw proof that Saddam was in league with Al Qaeda.

January
Cheney gives the Pope a crystal dove, somehow overcoming his urge to blast the bird with a shotgun.

February
Cheney continues his bird massacre, going duck hunting with Supreme Court Justice Antonin Scalia just weeks before Cheney is due to appear as a defendant in front of the high court.

February
Powell says if he had known Iraq had no WMDs he might not have supported the invasion. He quickly retracts the statement.

February
Aschroft subpoenas medical records of women who have had certain abortion procedures.

March
Cheney asks an interviewer "Am I the evil genius in the corner that nobody ever sees come out of his hole?"—then answers his own question: "It's a nice way to operate, actually."

March
CIA Director George Tenet states publicly that he privately has corrected Cheney several times after the vice president misstated intelligence about Iraq.

March
Ashcroft is hospitalized with gallstones.

March
Dick Cheney tells Rush Limbaugh that Richard Clarke "wasn't in the loop," in an attempt to dismiss Clarke's criticism of the administration's counterterrorism policies. Two days later Condoleezza Rice contradicts the vice president: "I would not use the word 'out of the loop.'"

April
The September 11 Commission concludes that the terrorist attacks could have been prevented.

April
More than 100 soldiers die in Iraq—the war's greatest monthly toll so far.

May
Photos show Americans torturing Iraqi prisoners. Cheney calls Rumsfeld the best defense secretary ever.

Acknowledgments

Many people made this anthology.

At Thunder's Mouth Press and Avalon Publishing Group: Thanks to Will Balliett, Maria Fernandez, Nate Knaebel, Linda Kosarin, Dan O'Connor, Michael O'Connor, Paul Paddock, Susan Reich, David Riedy, Mike Walters, and Don Weise for their support, dedication and hard work. I owe particular thanks to Neil Ortenberg for his support and inspiration during the past seven years.

I am especially grateful to Nate Hardcastle who, with help from Sean Donahue and Carol Pickering, did most of the research for this book. Nate participated fully in all editorial decisions and created the *I Hate Dick Cheney, John Ashcroft, Donald Rumsfeld, Comdi Rice . . . Timeline* that begins on page 405. The indefatigable Taylor Smith chased down rights and sorted out other assorted problems. Any errors or omissions are Taylor's fault.

Thanks also are due to the dozens of people who generously took time to help Taylor find and obtain rights. Special thanks to Amelia Nash at Salon.com, Habiba Alcindor at *The Nation*, Sarah Gurfein at *The American Prospect*, Soyoung Ho at *The Washington Monthly*, Laura Obolensky at *The New Republic* and Eleyna Fugman at AlterNet.

The librarians at the Portland Public Library in Portland, Maine, helped collect books from around the country.

Finally, I am grateful to the writers and artists whose work appears in this book.

Permissions

We gratefully acknowledge everyone who gave permission for material to appear in this book. We have made every effort to trace and contact copyright holders. If an error or omission is brought to our notice we will be pleased to correct the situation in future editions of this book. For further information, please contact the publisher.

"A Rogue's Gallery of the Radical Right" by Gus DiZerega. Copyright © 2003 by Gus DiZerega. Used by permission of the author. • "Dick Cheney, Commander in Chief" by Jim Lobe. Copyright © 2003 by the Independent Media Institute. Reprinted by permission of AlterNet (www.alternet.org). • "Vice Grip" by Joshua Micah Marshall. Copyright © 2003 by Washington Monthly Publishing, LLC. Reprinted by permission. • "Dick Cheney's Song of America" by David Armstrong. Copyright © 2002 by *Harper's Magazine*. All rights reserved. Reproduced by special permission. • "On Four Members of the War Cabinet" by Calvin Trillin. Copyright © 2003 by *The Nation*. Reprinted by permission. • "Old McCheney Had a Judge" by Robert Scheer. Copyright © 2004 by the Independent Media Institute. Reprinted by permission of AlterNet (www.alternet.org). • "Contract Sport" by Jane Mayer. Copyright © 2002 by Jane Mayer. Used by permission of the author. • "The First Casualty" by John B. Judis and Spencer Ackerman. Copyright © 2003 by *The New Republic*. Reprinted by permission. • "Armchair Provocateur" by Peter Bergen. Copyright © 2003 Washington Monthly Publishing, LLC. Reprinted by permission. • "2003: Imperial Gong Show Year" by Tom Engelhardt. Copyright © 2004 by Tom Engelhardt. Reprinted by permission from TomDispatch (www.tomdispatch.com). • "Making Money on Terrorism" by William D. Hartung. Copyright © 2004 by *The Nation*. Reprinted by permission. • "Rumsfeld's Personal Spy Ring" by Eric Boehlert. Copyright © 2003 by Salon.com.

Reprinted by permission. • "Nigergate Thuggery" by David Corn. Copyright © 2003 by *The Nation*. Reprinted by permission. • "Why are These Men Laughing?" by Ron Suskind. Copyright © 2003 by Ron Suskind. Reprinted by permission of The Wylie Agency, Inc. • "Karl Rove: Counting Votes While the Bombs Drop" by James C. Moore. Copyright © 2003 by James C. Moore. Used by permission of the author.

Quiz questions by Paul Slansky. Copyright © 2000, 2001, 2002, 2003 by Paul Slansky. Used by permission of Elaine Markson Literary Agency, Inc.

All anagrams used by permission of The Anagram Genius Archive, www.anagramgenius.com.

Oliphant © 2001 Universal Press Syndicate. Reprinted with permission. All rights reserved.

Doonesbury © (2003, 2004) G. B. Trudeau. Reprinted with permission of Universal Press Syndicate. All rights reserved.

The Boondocks © (2002, 2003) Aaron McGruder. Dist. by Universal Press Syndicate. Reprinted with permission. All rights reserved.

Carlson © 2002 *Milwaukee Sentinel*. Reprinted with permission of Universal Press Syndicate. All rights reserved.

Toles © (2001, 2004) *The Buffalo News*. Reprinted with permission of Universal Press Syndicate. All rights reserved.

Tom the Dancing Bug cartoons used by permission of Ruben Bolling.

Bibliography

The selections used in this anthology were taken from the sources listed below.

Allen, Terry J. "Public Serpent." Originally appeared in *In These Times,* August 2001.

Alterman, Eric. "Colin Powell and the 'Power of Audacity.'" Originally appeared in *The Nation,* September 22, 2003.

Armstrong, David. "Dick Cheney's Song of America." Originally appeared in *Harper's Magazine,* October 2002.

Bergen, Peter. "Armchair Provocateur." Originally appeared in *The Washington Monthly,* December 2003.

Billmon. "Victory." Originally appeared on www.billmon.org, 2004.

Boehlert, Eric. "Rumsfeld's Personal Spy Ring." This article first appeared in Salon.com (www.salon.com), July 16, 2003. An online version remains in the Salon archives.

Corn, David. "The Fundamental John Ashcroft." Originally appeared in *Mother Jones,* March/April 2002.

Corn, David. "Nigergate Thuggery." Originally appeared in *The Nation,* July 17, 2003.

Corn, David. "A No-Compassion Conservative?" Originally appeared in *The Nation,* November 19, 2003.

Dingell, John. Letter to Gregory Mankiw. http://www.house.gov/dingell/.

Dingell, John. Letter to Marc Racicot. http://www.house.gov/dingell/.

DiZerega, Gus. "A Rogue's Gallery of the Radical Right." Individual essays originally published by Deal-With-It! (www.deal-with-it.org), 2003.

Dreyfuss, Robert. "War's Preachers." Originally appeared on Tom Paine.com (www.tompaine.com), January 13, 2004.

Engelhardt, Tom. "2003: Imperial Gong Show Year." Originally appeared on TomDispatch (www.tomdispatch.com), January 1, 2004.

Hartung, William D. "Making Money on Terrorism." Originally appeared in *The Nation*, February 23, 2004.

Judis, John B. and Spencer Ackerman. "The First Casualty." Originally appeared in *The New Republic*, June 30, 2003.

Kamiya, Gary. "Bush's Frightening Middle East Appointment." This article first appeared in Salon.com (www.salon.com), December 12, 2002. An online version remains in the Salon archives.

Kaplan, Fred. "The Tragedy of Colin Powell." This article first appeared in Salon.com (www.salon.com), February 19, 2004. An online version remains in the Salon archives.

Kennedy, Edward M. "America, Iraq and Presidential Leadership." Transcript of a January 14, 2004 speech delivered by Senator Edward M. Kennedy to the Center for American Progress at the Mayflower Hotel in Washington, D.C.

Lobe, Jim. "All in the Neocon Family." Originally published by AlterNet (www.alternet.org), March 27, 2003.

Lobe, Jim. "Dick Cheney, Commander in Chief." Originally published by AlterNet (www.alternet.org), October 27, 2003.

Marshall, Joshua Micah. "Vice Grip." Originally appeared in *The Washington Monthly*, January/February 2003.

Mayer, Jane. "Contract Sport." Originally appeared in the February 16-23, 2002 issue of *The New Yorker*.

Moore, James C. "Karl Rove: Counting Votes While the Bombs Drop." Originally appeared in the *Los Angeles Times*, May 7, 2003.

Noah, Timothy. "Whopper of the Week: Karl Rove, Ari Fleischer, and Dick Cheney." Originally appeared on Slate.com, September 28, 2001.

Pizzo, Stephen. "Tom DeLay's Axis of Influence." Originally published by AlterNet (www.alternet.org), May 10, 2002.

Racicot, Marc. Letter to John Dingell. http://www.house.gov/dingell/.

Rotten.com. "John Ashcroft." Originally appeared on Rotten.com, 2004.

St. Clair, Jeffrey. "From Senator 'Lunkhead' to Energy Czar: A Year in the Life of Spencer Abraham." Originally published by CounterPunch (www.counterpunch.com), April 17, 2002.

Scheer, Robert. "Old McCheney Had a Judge." Originally published by Salon.com (www.salon.com), February 17, 2004.

Seely, Hart. "The Poetry of D.H. Rumsfeld." Originally published by SLATE (www.slate.com), April 2, 2003.

Shnayerson, Michael. "Sale of the Wild." Originally appeared in *Vanity Fair*, September 2003.

Suskind, Ron. "Why are These Men Laughing?" Originally appeared in *Esquire*, January 2003.

Trillin, Calvin. "On Four Members of the War Cabinet." Originally appeared in *The Nation*, November 17, 2003.

Clint Willis has edited more than thirty anthologies, including *The I Hate George W. Bush Reader* and (with Nathaniel May) *We Are the People: Voices from the Other Side of American History*. He lives with his family in Maine.